PARALEGAL LITIGATION AND PRACTICE TITLES FROM ASPEN LAW & BUSINESS

BANKRUPTCY LAW AND PROCEDURE: A GUIDE FOR PARALEGALS (THIRD EDITION)
Steven N. Berger, J. Daria Westland, and Thomas J. Salerno

CONSTRUCTION LITIGATION FOR PARALEGALS: CLAIMS PREPARATION AND MANAGEMENT
Dianne D. Zalewski and Cheryl D. Evans

DEPOSITION MANUAL FOR PARALEGALS (SECOND EDITION)
Christine Bergren Greene

ESTATE PLANNING AND ADMINISTRATION FOR PARALEGALS
Charles P. Nemeth

EVIDENCE HANDBOOK FOR PARALEGALS
Charles P. Nemeth

LITIGATION GUIDE FOR PARALEGALS: RESEARCH AND DRAFTING (SECOND EDITION)
Cynthia Monteiro Osborne

LITIGATION ORGANIZATION AND MANAGEMENT FOR PARALEGALS
Lynn M. Randall

LITIGATION PARALEGAL (SECOND EDITION)
Phillip J. Signey

MEDICAL RECORDS REVIEW (SECOND EDITION)
Kristyn S. Appleby and Joanne Tarver

PARALEGAL CAREER GUIDE
Chere B. Estrin

PARALEGAL DISCOVERY: ORGANIZATION AND MANAGEMENT
Joyce Samson and Dianne Zalewski

PARALEGAL DISCOVERY: PROCEDURES AND FORMS (SECOND EDITION)
Pat Medina

PARALEGAL DRAFTING GUIDE
Dorien S. McClellan

PARALEGAL GUIDE TO INTELLECTUAL PROPERTY
Valerie J. Atkinson

PARALEGAL LITIGATION: FORMS AND PROCEDURE
Marcy Davis Fawcett

PARALEGAL LITIGATION: FORMS AND PROCEDURE (DISK EDITION)
Marcy Davis Fawcett

PARALEGAL MANAGEMENT HANDBOOK
Maureen Brophy and Patsy Pressley

PARALEGAL TRIAL HANDBOOK
Beverly K. Hutson

PERSONAL INJURY PARALEGAL (SECOND EDITION)
Sharon Atwood

PERSONAL INJURY PARALEGAL: FORMS AND PROCEDURES
Joyce Walden

PERSONAL INJURY PARALEGAL: FORMS AND PROCEDURES (DISK EDITION)
Joyce Walden

PRACTICAL APPROACHES TO ADMINISTRATIVE LAW: A GUIDE FOR PARALEGALS
Wendy Van Duyne

REAL ESTATE FORECLOSURE: PARALEGAL PRACTICE AND PROCEDURE
Charles P. Nemeth and Grayson P. Van Horn

STARTING AND MANAGING YOUR OWN BUSINESS: A FREELANCING GUIDE FOR PARALEGALS
Dorothy Secol

ESTRIN SERIES

COMPUTERIZED LITIGATION SUPPORT
Despina C. Kartson and Norman F. Strizek

HOW TO SURVIVE IN A LAW FIRM: CLIENT RELATIONS
Dana Graves, Jill Levin, and Nancy Pulsifer

MEDICAL MALPRACTICE GUIDE FOR PARALEGALS
Stephanie A. Danelson

THE PARALEGAL'S ROLE AT TRIAL
Kerri W. Feeney

SMART LITIGATING WITH COMPUTERS
Patricia S. Eyres

STARTING AND MANAGING YOUR OWN BUSINESS

A FREELANCING GUIDE
FOR PARALEGALS

SUBSCRIPTION NOTICE

This Aspen Law & Business product is updated on a periodic basis with supplements to reflect important changes in the subject matter. If you purchased this product directly from Aspen Law & Business, we have already recorded your subscription for the update service.

If, however, you purchased this product from a bookstore and wish to receive future updates and revised or related volumes billed separately with a 30-day examination review, please contact our Customer Service Department at 1-800-234-1660, or send your name, company name (if applicable), address, and the title of the product to:

ASPEN LAW & BUSINESS
A Division of Aspen Publishers, Inc.
7201 McKinney Circle
Frederick, MD 21701

STARTING AND MANAGING YOUR OWN BUSINESS
A FREELANCING GUIDE FOR PARALEGALS

DOROTHY SECOL, CLA

ASPEN LAW & BUSINESS

Published by Aspen Law & Business
Formerly published by John Wiley & Sons, Inc.

Library of Congress Cataloging-in-Publication Data

Secol, Dorothy
    Starting and managing your own business : a freelancing guide for
paralegals / Dorothy Secol.
        p.   cm.
    "Paralegal law library."
    Includes bibliographical references.
    ISBN 0-7355-0659-0 (cloth : acid-free paper).

    1. Legal assistants—United States.   2. New business enterprises
—United States.
I. Title
KF320.L4S43   1994
346.73'065—dc20
[347.30665]   94-31541
                                         CIP

Printed in the United States of America

10 9 8 7 6 5

To my husband Steve, who has supported me in every
endeavor I have undertaken, who has always had an
unshakable faith in me, and who has been patient
beyond belief.

PREFACE

I established my freelance business in 1982 and since then I have been asked many times, "What do you do? How did you get started? How did you sign up your clients? Do you advertise? How do you market yourself?" and so on.

The past 12 years have been ones of great change and great challenge for me; I have grown in many ways. In 1982 the utilization of legal assistants was not a popular practice in my geographic area. I practiced in a small suburban area where attorneys viewed legal assistants as competition. The majority of the attorneys with whom I spoke predicted that my business would fail. They felt that attorneys weren't sure how to utilize legal assistants, let alone a freelance legal assistant. I was determined to succeed and the experience has been one of growth and maturity in a multi-faceted endeavor.

The operation of my business depends on my skills both as a legal assistant and as a business person. Its success hinges on my ability to communicate with attorneys, accountants, bankers, court personnel, corporate officers, and vendors whose cooperation is integral to the everyday operation of my business. Over the years, through trial and error, failure and success, I have been able to make the financial, managerial, and ethical decisions needed to succeed in fulfilling my goals.

I have also participated in the growth of the paralegal profession, in turn that participation has been educational as well as extremely satisfying to me. I have shared in the responsibility of improving the paralegal education and in the creation and implementation of an ethical standard for all legal assistants.

What does it take to be a freelance legal assistant? On the following pages is my answer to you. The book is divided into nine chapters, each chapter addressing the important subjects basic to the success of the freelance legal assistant. The topics covered in the pages of this book include:

- The evolution and growth of the paralegal profession, highlighting changes.
- Ethical responsibilities of legal assistants. Freelance legal assistants must be especially mindful of these ethical obligations.
- The decisions to freelance. How do you make the decision to go into business? Do you want to go into business? What type of person do you have to be? Where do you start? The answers to these questions will help you find out if you have what it takes.

- Office logistics. Where should you set up your office? How do you organize your business? Analyze different areas of law in which a paralegal can practice. Interviews with freelance legal assistants who practice in different parts of the country will give you insight into the daily life of the freelance legal assistant.

- Marketing and advertising. Discover different ways to market your services. You will be operating a service-oriented business with specific marketing requirements. Only sound marketing techniques that are professional as well as ethical may be utilized.

- Implementing Systems. The heart of this book is the information contained in setting up your office, negotiating a lease, leasing or buying equipment, start-up costs, substantive systems, billing and collection, and finances and insurance. What kinds of computer software will be beneficial? The growth and expansion of your business will depend on the proper organization of this information and the implementation of the systems.

- Organizations and opportunities. Learn about the national and local paralegal organizations and the importance of continuing legal education. Membership in these organizations as well as your state bar associations is important to your personal growth and the growth of the profession.

- Case law. The issue of regulation is being studied throughout the country. Be informed and know the issues. Become familiar with case law involving legal assistants.

It is my hope that the contents of this book will guide you in the formation, implementation, management and ultimately, the success of your business. This book is addressed to the experienced legal assistant. Freelancing is not for the paralegal student or those with limited experience. To those in these categories, I hope the book gives you insight into the demands of and the skills needed to operate and sustain a freelance business. When you have gained the experience you need, and feel confident, go for it!

To those seasoned legal assistants who are considering freelancing, I hope you find this book to be informative and helpful as each of you make the decisions necessary to enter the business world.

Good luck!

Allenhurst, New Jersey   Dorothy Secol
July 1994

ACKNOWLEDGMENTS

I would like to acknowledge those who have been extremely helpful to me in the successful completion of this book:

my husband, Steve, for the portable computer

my friend, Barbara Simon, for editing the manuscript

my son, Geoffrey Secol, for helping me with computerized research

my business partner, Peggy Stalford, for listening, and for her suggestions and encouragement

the National Association of Legal Assistants for once again being there for me, to provide information and guidance—special thanks to Marge Dover

I would also like to thank the following for permission to reprint copyrighted material:

Model Code of Professional Responsibility, American Bar Association, ©1982, reprinted with permission.

Model Guidelines for the Utilization of Legal Assistant Services, American Bar Association, ©1991, reprinted with permission.

Model Standards and Guidelines for Utilization of Legal Assistants Annotated, National Association of Legal Assistants ©1984, revised 1991, and Code of Ethics and Professional Responsibility, ©1979, reprinted with permission, together with the Certified Legal Assistant (CLA) Program.

Model Code of Ethics and Professional Responsibility and National Federation of Paralegal Associations, Inc., ©copyright 1993, Mission Statement, March 1987, ©1993, reprinted with permission.

Model Rules of Professional Conduct, American Bar Association, ©1993, reprinted with permission.

ABOUT THE AUTHOR

Dorothy Secol, CLA, has worked in the legal profession for over 30 years and has been a freelance legal assistant since 1982. She maintains an office in Allenhurst, New Jersey. Dorothy is a graduate of Monmouth College, West Long Branch, New Jersey.

Ms. Secol is a member of the National Association of Legal Assistants (NALA) and received her CLA status in 1978. In addition to NALA, she is a trustee of the Central Jersey Paralegal Association and a former vice president and trustee of Legal Assistants Association of New Jersey. She also serves on the Paralegal Committee of the New Jersey State Bar Association and is on the Advisory Board of Brookdale College, Lincroft, New Jersey. She also serves on the Board of Trustees of Temple Beth El, and has recently been appointed to the newly-formed Dispute Resolution Committee in Ocean Township, mediating matters for the Ocean Township Municipal Court.

Ms. Secol has also given seminars on real estate sponsored by title insurance companies as well as independent seminars for paralegals and legal secretaries. In addition, she was a petitioner in the case of *In re Opinion 24 of the Committee on the Unauthorized Practice of Law,* 128 N.J. 114 (1992). The case validated the fact that "there is no distinguishable difference between an in-house and freelance paralegal working under the direct supervision of an attorney."

SUMMARY CONTENTS

DETAILED CONTENTS

CHAPTER 1

INTRODUCTION

§ 1.1   Evolution of the Paralegal Profession

Paralegal, legal assistant, lay assistant, and legal advocate are all names that have been used at one time or another to describe one who is not an attorney but who works under the supervision of an attorney, and performs a number of important legal tasks.

The term "paralegal" is defined by Black's Law Dictionary as follows:

> A person with legal skills, but who is not an attorney, and who works under the supervision of a lawyer . . . or who is otherwise authorized by law to use those legal skills. . . .[1]

Thus the term paralegal would indicate someone who works near or with an attorney, one who works beside an attorney or subordinate to an attorney. The paralegal is an individual who is part of a group critical to the future delivery of legal services in this country—a group that represents, in the words of one legal scholar, "an idea whose time has come."[2]

The legal assistant evolved from the role of the legal secretary. In earlier years, before photocopiers, fax machines, and computers, legal secretaries used their skills in typing and sometimes in longhand, to produce the dictated material required.

When I first started working as a legal secretary in 1957, there wasn't a copy machine in the office. Photocopiers were practically nonexistent; they were just becoming available. If I needed a copy of a document, I typed it! For example, if I were preparing documents for a real estate closing, and needed extra copies of the title binder, I actually had to type them! Easements,

---

[1] Black's Law Dictionary 712 (6th ed. 1990).

[2] Thomas E. Eimermann, Fundamentals of Paralegalism 34 (1980).

restrictions, abstracts, and so forth had to be retyped. I took out carbon paper and typed. That was the only way to secure an extra copy. In 1958 our office purchased the first photocopy machine in our county and it certainly made work easier. We couldn't have imagined a future filled with fax machines.

With the advent of the photocopier, the secretary had more time to pursue other duties. As the legal secretary became more proficient in rendering services, prescient attorneys recognized that certain services, routinely performed by them, could be performed by properly trained laypersons. In training secretaries to do legal research, draft pleadings, and interview witnesses and clients, those attorneys unknowingly formed the concept of the legal assistant profession as it is defined today.

In the early 1960s I worked as a legal secretary for a sole practitioner. I was the only employee. As the practice grew, a part-time file clerk was eventually hired. That allowed me to spend more time learning procedures in order to expand my capabilities. For example, if we needed to institute a quiet title procedure, or institute foreclosure proceedings, or draft certain pleadings, I would consult the appropriate Practice Series, read the section on the specific procedure, outline it, and help draft the pleadings. My employer, Donald J. Pappa, always had faith in my ability to master a procedure, complete it, and learn it for future use. Because of the manner in which I was trained, and the faith that my employer had in my abilities, it was possible for me to eventually proceed on my own, with a firm grasp of the areas of substantive law that I chose as my specialties.

As legal secretaries incurred more complex legal responsibilities, they sought out seminars given for attorneys to increase their knowledge or expertise in specific areas of law. Prior to the 1970s, there was no formal training for paralegals; consequently they attended the seminars given by the bar associations, by the Institute for Continuing Education, by the Practicing Law Institute, and so forth. Although these courses were given for attorneys, paralegals were allowed to attend. Colleges and proprietary schools eventually formulated programs in which paralegals could intensify their training and education.

In the 1950s and 1960s several major professional groups began to make extensive use of paraprofessionals. This movement was led by medical doctors who had begun to utilize nurses as paraprofessionals. The doctors had discovered that by delegating such tasks as taking temperatures and giving injections, they had more time to devote to what they considered to be more challenging and rewarding aspects of their profession. Today the field is populated by such positions as registered nurses, licensed practical nurses, nurses's aides, physical therapists, inhalation therapists, radiologic technologists, laboratory technicians, operating room technicians, and medical records technicians. Other professionals who have made use of paraprofessionals include dentists, teachers, architects, and law enforcement personnel.[3]

---

[3] *Id.*

§ 1.2 Role of the American Bar Association

In 1967 the American Bar Association (hereafter referred to as ABA) Committee on Professional Ethics issued Formal Opinion 316 that clarified the legitimacy of delegating legal work to nonlawyers:

> A Lawyer can employ lay secretaries, lay investigators, lay detectives, lay researchers, accountants, lay scriveners, nonlawyer draftsmen, or nonlawyer researchers. In fact, he may employ nonlawyers to do any task for him except counsel clients about law matters, engage directly in the practice of law, appear in court, or appear in formal proceedings as part of the judicial process, so long as it is he who takes the work and vouches for it to the client and becomes responsible to the client. In other words, we do not limit the kind of assistance that a lawyer can acquire in any way to persons who are admitted to the Bar, so long as the nonlawyers do not do things that lawyers may not do or do the things that lawyers only may do.[4]

In 1968 the ABA created the Special Committee on Lay Assistants for Lawyers. This committee was charged with developing, encouraging, and increasing the training and utilization of nonlawyer assistants to enable lawyers to better discharge their professional responsibilities. The ABA Code of Professional Responsibility and Canons of Judicial Ethics, revised in 1969, included favorable support for the extensive use of paralegals in Ethical Consideration 3-6 by stating "Such delegation {of specialized tasks delegated by an attorney} is proper if the lawyer maintains a direct relationship with his client, supervises the delegated work, and has complete professional responsibility for the work product."[5]

In August 1968 the ABA's House of Delegates adopted Report Number 3 of the association's Special Committee on Availability of Legal Services and formed the Special Committee on Lay Assistants for Lawyers to carry out recommendation number three. That report contained the following recommendation:

> Recognizing that freeing a lawyer from tedious and routine detail thus conserving his time and energy for truly legal problems will enable him to render his professional services to more people, thereby making legal services more fully available to the public, this Committee recommends:
>
> 1. That the legal profession recognize that there are many tasks in serving a client's needs which can be performed by a trained, nonlawyer assistant working under the direction and supervision of a lawyer;

---

[4] ABA Comm. on Professional Ethics, Formal Op. 316 (1967).

[5] ABA Model Code of Professional Responsibility, 1982, American Bar Ass'n. Reprinted with permission. Copies of this publication are available from Order Fulfillment, American Bar Ass'n, 750 N. Lake Shore Dr., Chicago, IL 60611.

2. That the profession encourage the training and employment of such
    employees; and
3. That there be created a special committee of this Association to consider:
    (a) The kinds of tasks which may be competently performed by a non-
         lawyer working under the direction and supervision of a lawyer,
    (b) The nature of the training which may be required is provided to
         develop competence and proficiency in the performance of such
         tasks;
    (c) The role, if any, to be played by the legal profession and the bar in
         providing such training;
    (d) The desirability of recognizing competence and proficiency in such
         assistants as by academic recognition or other suitable means; and
    (e) All appropriate methods for developing, encouraging, and increasing
         the training and utilization of nonlawyer assistants to better enable
         lawyers to discharge their professional responsibilities.[6]

In 1971 this special committee was renamed the Special Committee on
Legal Assistants and conducted studies of the duties performed by legal
assistants in large and small law firms throughout the country. The committee undertook a pilot project for the on-the-job training of legal assistants and
completed a study of the use of legal assistants in other professions. It began
development of a curriculum for the training of legal assistants by educational institutions. The committee released preliminary drafts of reports on
results of research done on paralegal usage, suggested guidelines for the
training of paralegals, and reviewed reports of paraprofessional usage in
other professions.

In 1972 the House of Delegates asked the committee to develop standards
for accreditation of formal educational programs directed to the training of
legal paraprofessionals, and standards for assessment of the proficiency of
legal paraprofessionals. The committee developed tentative guidelines, eval-
uative criteria, and program evaluation procedures.

In 1973 the American Bar Association's Special Committee of Legal
Assistants commissioned Kline Strong of the University of Utah Law
Research Institute to study the economics of utilizing paralegals. Strong
studied 104 law firms of four or fewer partners. He analyzed typical legal
tasks performed by lawyers, tasks performed by paralegals, and tasks performed by secretaries. He then calculated how much money would be saved
by the use of a paralegal as opposed to the lawyer and secretary alone.
Strong used an hourly rate of three dollars per hour (note that this was in
1960) for the secretaries, five dollars per hour for the paralegals and $40 per
hour for the lawyers. Strong concluded that a firm utilizing a paralegal could
form a corporation for $127.50 while it would cost the nonparalegal firm

---

[6] *Id.* at 38.

$253.50 in billable time. If the firm charged a flat fee of $300 for the formation of the corporation, it would increase the profit from $46.50 to $172.50, while leaving the lawyer with 3.5 extra hours to spend on other cases. Strong believed that the key was to have each procedure completed by the least expensive person competent to handle that procedure. If the lawyer were to save just one hour a day through the utilization of paralegal services, the lawyer would be free to earn another $9,600 per year at the billable rate of $40 per hour! Over a 25-year period, that one hour of paralegal assistance could increase a lawyer's income by $240,000.[7]

In May 1973 the Committee sponsored a conference at the University of Denver School of Law for review and refinement of the draft guidelines, after which a final draft was prepared and submitted for House consideration. In August 1973 the House approved the Guidelines for the Approval of Legal Assistant Education Programs and authorized the Legal Assistants Committee to begin implementation of the approval program. The following year a pilot program was undertaken to test the approval procedures.

The committee was granted standing committee status in 1975 and officially approved the first eight schools. As of August 1993, the ABA has given approval to paralegal programs in 177 schools.

In addition to its approval program, the Committee monitors trends in the field. It maintains an information service for those interested in becoming legal assistants.

The primary intention of the Committee is to foster high quality legal assistant education and training through its approval project and the development of standards. The ABA considers these efforts to have had a strong impact on the quality of legal assistant education throughout the United States.

A subcommittee on certification conducted public hearings during 1974–75 and in 1975 concluded that certification was premature.

§ 1.3   ABA Subcommittee on Certification

In December 1985 the Standing Committee on Legal Assistants issued a position paper on Licensure/Certification of Legal Assistants. The position paper was divided into separate sections:

I. Development of the Legal Assistant Profession
from the Perspective of the Standing Committee

The Committee likened today's legal assistant to the British barrister's clerk, defined the services performed by the legal assistant as well as the utilization

---

[7] *Id.*

of those services over the past 20 years. The Committee further commented on the development and growth of paralegal educational programs and generally on the expansion, development, and maturation of the profession.

II. The Definition of a Legal Assistant

The definition of a legal assistant adopted by the Board of Governors of the ABA in 1986 is the definition used by the Committee in this position paper. This definition may be found verbatim in § **1.3.**

III. The Standing Committee's Position
with Respect to Licensure

The Committee defined licensure as "a process by which an agency of state government grants permission to persons meeting predetermined qualifications to engage in a given occupation and/or use a particular title or grants permission to institutions to perform specified functions." It was the conclusion of the Committee that the licensure of legal assistants fulfills no purpose whatsoever in the delivery of legal services. They further stated that it would be unnecessary and cumbersome and that the public is protected by the attorney's license through whom the legal assistant must act.

IV. The Standing Committee's Position
with Respect to Voluntary Certification

The Committee defined certification as "the process by which a nongovernmental agency or a professional association grants recognition to an individual who has met certain predetermined qualifications specified by that agency or association."

At that time the Standing Committee felt it had not discerned that there was a substantial interest in legal assistant voluntary certification among lawyers or among the general public. It did acknowledge the exam given by the National Association of Legal Assistants (NALA), however, the committee felt the exam lacked relevance since it had only been in use for a few years and that it tested for a standard higher than minimum.

The committee further stated that any certification program should be administered by a board including lawyers, legal assistants, educators, and members of the general public and furthermore that any examination given would be time-consuming and costly without like benefit to the legal assistant, lawyer, or general public. The committee did, however, state that it did believe that such a program could ultimately be developed and that it could be a benefit to the legal assistant profession and the general public.

V. Conclusions

1.   Licensure does not afford any benefits to the public, to the legal profession, or to the legal assistant

2.   Certification of minimal legal assistant competence does not yield benefits that would justify the time, expense, and effort of the implementation of an exam

3.   The most favorable method of increasing legal assistant entry quality is through ABA-approved educational programs and through increased legal assistant continuing education

4.   The Committee reaffirmed its position that any voluntary certification of advanced legal assistant proficiency should be under the supervision of a board consisting of lawyers, educators, legal assistants, and members of the general public

5.   The Standing Committee does not consider the ABA to be the appropriate entity to initiate or sponsor such voluntary certification but the ABA would willingly cooperate with other groups in its implementation.[8]

In 1978 the United States Bureau of Labor Statistics predicted that the legal assistant profession would be one of the fastest growing in the 1980s. The Bureau further predicted a growth rate of 132 percent by 1990.

During the 1970s and 1980s the use of paralegals was expanded. Large law firms began using paralegals and became their major employers, in addition to the small law firms and legal aid organizations. In 1972 the National Paralegal Institute was founded under an Office of Economic Opportunity (OEO) grant. This institute was charged with the responsibility of supporting and promoting the use of paralegals in the public sectors of the law and especially in legal services offices. The Institute was designed to assist in the development of training programs and materials as well as to ensure that the certification process would not needlessly cripple paralegal use in the public sector.[9]

In 1975 the federal government recognized the occupation of "legal assistant" and created a new job classification.

In the late 1970s and early 1980s legal assistants began to freelance. These legal assistants would handle specialized matters for attorneys as independent contractors. By offering their services to attorneys, under the attorney's direct supervision, the freelance paralegal could work for several attorneys simultaneously. Many freelance paralegals employed assistants who could provide temporary services to attorneys, substituting for vacationing employees, employees on sick leave, maternity leave, and so forth.

---

[8] Karen Judd, CLA, *The Member Connection,* Facts & Findings, Nat'l Ass'n of Legal Assistants, Inc., Apr. 1986.

[9] Thomas E. Eimermann, Fundamentals of Paralegalism 38 (1980), *citing* Missouri v. Jenkins, 491 U.S. 274, 1095 S. Ct. 2463, 2471–72.

During the last two decades the use of paralegals and legal assistants has grown considerably. Colleges provide education and training for paralegals, bar associations grant associate memberships to paralegals. The use of para- legals has spread to every occupation—from the law office, to the corporate sector, to banks, mortgage companies, insurance companies, colleges and universities, civil service, and the health care profession.

In 1986 the American Bar Association Board of Governors provided a definition for the paralegal/legal assistant as follows:

> A legal assistant is a person, qualified through education, training or work experience, who is employed or retained by a lawyer, law office, governmental agency, or other entity, in a capacity or function which involves the perfor- mance under the ultimate direction and supervision of an attorney, of specifi- cally delegated substantive legal work, which work, for the most part, requires a sufficient knowledge of legal concepts that, absent such assistant, the attor- ney would perform the work.

The American Bar Association has declared that attorneys' fees awarded in litigation should include fees for work performed by paralegals. In August 1993, at the Association's annual meeting, a vote was taken by the ABA's policymaking House of Delegates. The House adopted a resolution that states: "The ABA supports the award of legal assistant/paralegal fees to law firms or attorneys who represent prevailing parties to a lawsuit where statutes or current case law allow for the recovery of attorney fees."

The report to the House of Delegates noted that there are currently five federal statutes that award legal assistant fees to prevailing parties, the Bankruptcy Code, the Employee Retirement Income Security Act, the Sherman Anti-Trust and Clayton Acts, and the Surface Mining Control and Reclamation Act.

According to Committee Chair L. David Shear of Tampa, Florida, there was no opposition to the report in committee and the house approved the measure on a voice vote.[10]

This was one further step in the recognition process of the integral part the paralegal plays in the legal community. Twenty years ago most attorneys did not know what a paralegal was or what services a paralegal performed. Today the paralegal profession is clearly acknowledged by the United States Supreme Court who endorsed the concept that "encouraging the use of lower- cost paralegals rather than attorneys wherever possible" is cost-effective delivery of legal services[11] by the American Bar Association and by bar asso- ciations in a majority of states.

---

[10] Steven Cohn, *News & Trends,* Legal Assistant Today, © 1994. James Publishing, Inc. Jan.–Feb. 1994. Reprinted with permission from Legal Assistant Today. For subscrip- tion information, call (714) 755-5450.

[11] Missouri v. Jenkins, 491 U.S. 274 (1989).

While the majority of paralegals work in-house, the concept of self-employment and freelancing is growing rapidly. In 1987 the National Association of Legal Assistants (hereafter referred to as NALA) determined from their survey on freelance legal assistants that 42 percent resided in the west, 36 percent in the southwest, 13 percent in the east, 6 percent in the midwest and 3 percent in the south.[12]

Law firms, corporations, insurance companies, and banks economize by hiring freelance paralegals.[13] The economy dictates that employers seek legal assistance on a more cost efficient basis. Employers realize that clients need not pay the higher fee of the attorney when the work can be performed at a lower cost by the legal assistant.

When paralegals began to freelance in the 1970s, attorneys were not aware of the skills or qualifications of the paralegals. They were still perceived as highly qualified legal secretaries. With the advent of educational programs for paralegals and the education of the attorneys as to the effective utilization of the paralegal in the 1980s, attorneys began to realize that paralegals—especially freelance paralegals—could be an asset to their firms. When the economy is depressed and firms are downsizing, it is to the freelance paralegal that firms turn. In this way, companies do not have to provide office space or pay a regular salary and benefits to an employee.

With regard to the overall picture of the legal assistant profession, including the freelance sector, according to the 1993 National Utilization and Compensation Survey Report by NALA, recent economic pressures have had an effect on law firms. The survey indicated that many legal assistants changed jobs in recent years but remained in the legal assistant career field[14]:

	Percent Selected		
Type of Employer	1993	1991	1989
Private Law Firms	77%	78%	81%
Bank	1%	1%	1%
Insurance Company	2%	1%	1%
Corporation	8%	9%	9%
Public Sector/Govn.	7%	5%	5%
Self-Employed	2%	4%	4%
Other	2%	3%	1%

---

[12] 1987 Nat'l Ass'n of Legal Assistants, Inc. Reprinted with permission.

[13] Shelley G. Widoff, *On the Docket,* Legal Assistant Today, Sep./Oct. 1993. Reprinted with permission from Legal Assistant Today. For subscription information, call (714) 755-5450.

[14] 1993 Nat'l Utilization & Compensation Survey Report, Nat'l Ass'n of Legal Assistants, Inc. Reprinted with permission.

As evidenced from the statistics, (according to the paralegals who answered the survey) fewer were self-employed in 1993 than four years prior. What does this mean? It could be interpreted several ways. Paralegals responding to the survey may no longer be self-employed, whereas many paralegals who did not answer the survey still are. The recession of 1989–92, including the real estate drought, may have caused many self-employed paralegals to seek fulltime, in-house employment. Those who are no longer in business may have failed to carefully plan for lean times or did not have the business acumen to keep the enterprise profitable.

Paralegals need not become a statistic. It is possible to beat the odds and become a successful entrepreneur. Paralegals should know their capabilities, their limitations, areas wherein they excel, areas needing help. Learn as much as possible, then go do it!

CHAPTER 2

ETHICAL CONSIDERATIONS

§ 2.1   Background

Chapter 1 includes the definition of a legal assistant as adopted by the Board of Governors of the American Bar Association and covers what a legal assistant is and what a legal assistant does. But what are the parameters within which legal assistants can perform these tasks? Specifically, what are the ethical responsibilities of legal assistants?

What is generally referred to as the *ethics* of a profession is merely a consensus of expert opinion as to necessity of professional standards of conduct.[1]

Paralegals are bound by the same ethical considerations as attorneys. At the national level, this refers to guidelines established by the American Bar Association (ABA). In 1908 the ABA adopted the Canon of Ethics at its 31st meeting. There were 47 original Canons. The Canons were then put forth for adoption by the supreme courts of each of the separate states. With the exception of California, all states adopted the Canons. California adopted its own Rules of Professional Conduct at that time and has maintained its own Rules since. The Canons were later updated and on August 12, 1969, the ABA adopted them as the Model Code of Professional Responsibility. The Code was then adopted by virtually all the states and in 1974 the Model Code was updated to its present form. In August 1983, due to the many changes that had taken place since the last amendments to the Code, the ABA adopted the Model Rules of Professional Conduct, which were further amended in 1987, 1989, 1990, and 1991. The Model Rules are much more specific with regard to acceptable conduct and for that reason are less applicable to paralegal activities. By 1992 over half of the states had adopted some

---

[1] Black's Law Dictionary 712 (6th ed. 1990).

11

form of the Model Rules while the remaining states still use the Model Code or have drafted rules of their own.[2]

The Model Code consists of three separate but interrelated parts: nine Canons with Ethical Considerations and Disciplinary Rules specific to each Canon. In the Preliminary Statement of the Model Code, the ABA explains that the Canons, Ethical Considerations, and Disciplinary Rules cannot apply to nonlawyers:

> [H]owever they do define the type of ethical conduct that the public has a right to expect not only of lawyers but also of their non-professional employees and associates in all matters pertaining to professional employment. A lawyer should ultimately be responsible for the conduct of his employees and associates in the course of the professional representation of the client.[3]

The Preamble to the Code together with the Preliminary Statement express the concern that the ABA has for the protection of the public:

> The continued existence of a free and democratic society depends upon recognition of the concept that justice is based upon the rule of law grounded in respect for the dignity of the individual and his capacity through reason for enlightened self-government. . . . Lawyers, as guardians of the law, play a vital role in the preservation of society. . . . But in the last analysis it is the desire for the respect and confidence of the members of his profession and of the society which he serves that should provide to a lawyer the incentive for the highest possible degree of ethical conduct.[4]

The nine Canons express the standard of professional conduct expected of attorneys in the course of their relationships with their clients, with the legal system, and with the legal profession as a whole. The Ethical Considerations represent the objectives toward which all members of the profession should strive. The Disciplinary Rules, unlike the Ethical Considerations, are mandatory in character. They describe the minimum level of conduct which will be tolerated, below which the attorney is subject to disciplinary action. Set forth below are the nine Canons. I have omitted the ethical considerations and disciplinary rules:

---

[2] Deborah K. Orlik, Ethics for the Legal Assistant 2d ed. (1992).

[3] Excerpted from the Preliminary Statement, Model Code of Professional Responsibility, © 1982, American Bar Ass'n. Reprinted with permission. Copies of this publication are available from Order Fulfillment, American Bar Ass'n, 750 North Lake Shore Dr., Chicago, IL 60611.

[4] Excerpted from the Model Code of Professional Responsibility, © 1982, American Bar Ass'n. Reprinted with permission. Copies of this publication are available from Order Fulfillment, American Bar Ass'n, 750 North Lake Shore Dr., Chicago, IL 60611.

Canon 1.

A Lawyer Should Assist in Maintaining the Integrity and Competence of the Legal Profession.

Canon 2.

A Lawyer Should Assist the Legal Profession in Fulfilling Its Duty to Make Legal Counsel Available.

Canon 3.

A Lawyer Should Assist in Preventing the Unauthorized Practice of Law.

Canon 4.

A Lawyer Should Preserve the Confidences and Secrets of a Client.

Canon 5.

A Lawyer Should Exercise Independent Professional Judgment on Behalf of a Client.

Canon 6.

A Lawyer Should Represent a Client Competently.

Canon 7.

A Lawyer Should Represent a Client Zealously Within the Bounds of the Law.

Canon 8.

A Lawyer Should Assist in Improving the Legal System.

Canon 9.

A Lawyer Should Avoid Even the Appearance of Professional Impropriety.[5]

Although the Model Code is directed to attorneys, practicing legal assistants are also bound by these Canons. Be aware of our responsibilities and insure that our behavior does not violate the Canons or cause employers to violate the Canons.

§ 2.2   ABA Model Guidelines

In August 1991 the Standing Committee on Legal Assistants of the American Bar Association adopted the *Model Guidelines for the Utilization of Legal Assistant Services.* It was the view of the Committee that the guidelines would assist many states in adopting their own set of guidelines. See Preamble to the *Model Guidelines* as well as the unabridged version of the *Guidelines,* with comments, as set forth in **Appendix A.**

Judge William Robie, chairperson of the ABA Standing Committee on Legal Assistants, in his report submitting the guidelines to the ABA stated:

---

[5] Excerpted from the Model Code of Professional Responsibility, © 1982, American Bar Ass'n. Reprinted with permission. Copies of this publication are available from Order Fulfillment, American Bar Ass'n, 750 North Lake Shore Dr., Chicago, IL 60611.

The development of the Model Guidelines was undertaken with the view that written guidance for lawyers on the utilization of legal assistants would encourage the use of the legal assistants and ensure that legal assistants and the lawyers who supervise them have a clear statement of the area in which legal assistants can work under the supervision of a lawyer without encountering professional responsibility and unauthorized practice of law problems.[6]

The ABA *Model Guidelines for the Utilization of Legal Assistant Services* are as follows:

1.   A lawyer is responsible for all of the professional actions of a legal assistant performing legal assistant services at the lawyer's direction and should take reasonable measures to ensure that the legal assistant's conduct is consistent with the lawyer's obligations under the ABA Model Rules of Professional Conduct.

2.   Provided the lawyer maintains responsibility for the work product, a lawyer may delegate to a legal assistant any task normally performed by a lawyer except those tasks proscribed to one not licensed as a lawyer by statute, court rules, administrative rule or regulation, controlling authority, the ABA Model Rules of Professional Conduct, or these guidelines.

3.   A lawyer may not delegate to a legal assistant:

   (a) Responsibility for establishing an attorney-client relationship.

   (b) Responsibility for establishing the amount of a fee to be charged for a service.

   (c) Responsibility for a legal opinion rendered to a client.

4.   It is the lawyer's responsibility to take reasonable measure to ensure that clients, courts, and other lawyers are aware that a legal assistant, whose services are utilized by the lawyer in performing legal services, is not licensed to practice law.

5.   A lawyer may identify legal assistants by name and title on the lawyer's letterhead and on business cards identifying the lawyer's firm.

6.   It is the responsibility of a lawyer to take reasonable measures to ensure that all client confidences are preserved by a legal assistant.

7.   A lawyer should take reasonable measures to prevent conflicts of interest resulting from a legal assistant's other employment or interest insofar as such other employment or interests would present a conflict of interest if it were that of the lawyer.

8.   A lawyer may include a charge for the work performed by a legal assistant in setting a charge for legal services.

9.   A lawyer may not split fees with a legal assistant nor pay a legal assistant for the referral of legal business. A lawyer may compensate a legal assistant

---

[6] *ABA Adopts Model Guidelines for Use of Legal Assistants,* Legal Assistant Today Nov.–Dec. 1991. James Publishing, Inc. Reprinted with permission from Legal Assistant Today. For subscription information call (714) 755-5450.

based on the quantity and quality of the legal assistant's work and value of that work to a law practice, but the legal assistant's compensation may not be contingent, by advance agreement, upon the profitability of the lawyer's practice.

10. A lawyer who employs a legal assistant should facilitate the legal assistant's participation in appropriate continuing education and pro bono publico activities.[7]

As in the Model Code, these guidelines are directed to the conduct of the attorney and not directly to the conduct of the legal assistant, however, as paralegals we are responsible for professional behavior.

The ABA also issues Formal and Informal Ethics Opinions. These opinions are in response to inquiries made to the Committee on Ethics and Professional Responsibility. Some of these opinions pertain to legal assistants and they are:

ABA Informal Opinion 66-909 permits persons to use business cards which identify them as employees of the law firm they work for. This opinion was specifically directed to those employees doing investigative work for a law firm as an "investigator."

ABA Informal Opinion 67-316 authorizes the use of nonlawyer assistants so long as it is the lawyer who takes the work and vouches for it to the client and becomes responsible to the client.

ABA Informal Opinion 71-1185 permits paralegals to use business cards identifying them as legal assistants and must clearly show they are not attorneys. This opinion recognized that the term "legal assistant" was coming into common usage, referring to those individuals who were lay assistants to lawyers. The opinion went on to state that since Opinion 909 permitted investigators to carry business cards, it would appear to be proper to designate legal assistants as such on a business card, provided the designation is accurate and the duties involved are properly performed under the direction of an attorney.

ABA Informal Opinion 76-1367 permits paralegals to sign certain correspondence relevant to their responsibilities. This opinion recognized the growth in the use of the legal assistant to perform specialized tasks. In the opinion of the Committee, the legal assistant could properly sign correspondence that was necessary to the proper conduct of his or her duties, providing the legal assistant was properly identified so that the receiver of the correspondence would not be misled.

---

[7] Excerpted from the Model Guidelines for the Utilization of Legal Assistant Services, American Bar Ass'n, © 1991. Reprinted with permission.

ABA Informal Opinion 88-1526 issued on June 22, 1988, permits paralegals formerly employed by a firm with an adversarial matter with another
firm, to become employed by the second firm provided consent is
obtained from the client, the adversary, and a "Chinese wall" created. This
means insuring that the paralegal will have no contact whatsoever with
any cases previously worked on while employed by the first firm.

ABA Informal Opinion 89-1527 permits paralegals to use business cards,
to be included in the advertisement of the law firm, and to also sign certain correspondence on the attorney's letterhead when properly identifying
themselves as a nonlawyer.

ABA Informal Opinion 91-360 prohibits lawyers from forming partnerships with nonlawyers.

Various opinions of the American Bar Association apply universally to all
legal assistants. Each state in which you reside and/or work issues ethical
opinions pertaining to the responsibilities of attorneys and nonattorney personnel; many states have issued ethical opinions with regard to legal assistants. Be familiar with the ethical opinions of the ABA and those of your
state. There are several sources of research available:

ABA/BNA Lawyers Manual on Professional Conduct (Washington, D.C.:
Bureau of National Affairs, 1983, Looseleaf). This multi-volume set contains state ethics opinions from all 50 states as well as the ABA.

Digest of Bar Association Ethics Opinions (Chicago, Illinois: American
Bar Foundation, 1970–80). This multi-volume set contains digests of
ethics opinions from all 50 states issued during the 1970s.

National Reporter on Legal Ethics and Professional Responsibility
(Frederick, Maryland: University Publications of America, 1982–) Contains
current ethics opinions from all 50 states.

In addition, both LEXIS® and WestLaw® have ethics databases available
online.[8]

You may also research your state and local bar association ethics opinions
in the county law library in which you reside or work.

In New Jersey, for example, there have been quite a few opinions with
regard to legal assistants. Some of the most recent from the New Jersey
Supreme Court Advisory Committee on Professional Ethics include:

---

[8] Richard A. Leiter, *Researching Professional Ethics for Lawyers,* Legal Assistant Today,
Mar.–Apr. 1993. James Publishing, Inc. Reprinted with permission from Legal Assistant
Today. For subscription information call (714) 755-5450.

Opinion 665 which modifies Opinion 546. Opinion 546, issued in 1984, prohibited the hiring of a paralegal formerly employed by a firm with whom the prospective employer is presently involved in adversarial matters. Opinion 665, rendered in 1992, recognizes that a conflict may arise, however it permits disclosure and the creation of a "Chinese wall," whereby the paralegal would be shielded from any information or knowledge of any matter in which a conflict may arise.

Opinion 647, issued in 1990, modified all previous Opinions whereby paralegals were not allowed to carry business cards in New Jersey. This opinion, recognizing the importance of the utilization of paralegals, states in part:

> It cannot be gainsaid that the utilization of paralegals has become, over the last 10 years, accepted, acceptable, important and indeed, necessary to the efficient practice of law. . . . They are trained and truly professional. . . . They understand ethical inhibitions and prohibitions. . . .

The Committee therefore modified the previous opinions to allow paralegals in New Jersey to carry business cards clearly designating the fact they are paralegals working under the supervision of an attorney, with the name of the attorney employer on the card.

Opinion 611, issued in 1988, again modified previous opinions in that it allows paralegals to sign correspondence "consisting exclusively of purely routine matters such as a request to a court clerk for a docket sheet or inquiring as to a court calendar or consisting simply of a covering letter forwarding a document originating elsewhere." The committee did stress, however, "that the attorney must sign and thereby retain clear responsibility for even marginally substantive correspondence with his clients, his adversaries and the tribunal before which he is appearing."

And most recently, the New Jersey Supreme Court Committee on Attorney Advertising issued Opinion 16, which supersedes Opinion 296 of the committee that was issued in 1975. Opinion 16 permits the inclusion of paralegals' names on attorney letterhead. "At this time, we limit the scope of this opinion to the inclusion on attorney's letterhead of the names of paralegals as opposed to other support personnel. . . ."[9]

To further supplement the ABA Model Code and Rules of Conduct, paralegals must also be aware of and adhere to the Rules of Professional Conduct (RPCs) of their individual states. Certain RPCs apply to nonlawyer personnel:

RPC 1.6 Confidentiality of Information

Legal assistants are constantly privy to information that, of necessity, must remain in the office as confidential. You are bound to preserve the sanctity of

---

[9] 3 N.J.L.J. 162, Jan. 24, 1994.

the lawyer-client relationship and must insure that you do not become involved in a situation where you inadvertently divulge confidential information.

RPC 1.7 Conflict of Interest

Many paralegals work within a small geographic area and it is very possible to work for an attorney on one case involving several parties, then, sometime later, work for another firm that represents one of the adverse parties in the same case. Previously, under Opinion 546 of the New Jersey Supreme Court, lawyers were prohibited from hiring a paralegal formerly employed by a firm with whom the prospective employer presently was involved in adversarial matters. This opinion was recently modified in Opinion 665, which determined that a firm may hire a paralegal previously employed by a firm with whom the present firm is involved in an adversarial matter, and the hiring attorney must caution the paralegal not to disclose any information relating to the representation of the client of the former employer and ensuring that the paralegal does not perform work on any matter for which the paralegal received compensation from the prior employer. This is what has been called creating a "Chinese wall," guaranteeing that the paralegal is not involved in any aspect of the case.

RPC 3.3 Candor Toward the Tribunal

Very important sounding, isn't it? To what does this refer? For lawyers, it means they did not make any false statements to the court. It also means they must disclose material facts in a timely manner and not submit false evidence, and so forth. What does it mean for a paralegal? It means that if the time comes when you are asked to tell the court that your supervising attorney is ill, therefore you need an adjournment on the case, and in reality that attorney is playing golf or otherwise predisposed, don't do it. Don't do anything that you know to be wrong, including submitting evidence you know to be false, failing to disclose information you know exists, or making false statements to the court or other attorneys.

RPC 4.1 Truthfulness in Statements to Others

This RPC is self-explanatory. Don't make false statements to anyone—to lawyers, to clients, to the court, or to any third persons.

Communication with Person Represented by Counsel

Your first responsibility to your attorney's clients is to inform them that you are a legal assistant. All communication with your attorney's clients must proceed on that basis. There are several Supreme Court Opinions in New Jersey on this subject discussed above.

RPC 5.3 Responsibilities Regarding Nonlawyer Assistants

It is the attorney's responsibility to supervise the nonlawyer, the legal assistant, and remain responsible for that legal assistant's behavior. It is the paralegal's responsibility to adhere to the professional code of ethics as to those responsibilities.

RPC 5.5 Unauthorized Practice of Law

This is probably the most important RPC of all. This is where all paralegals walk the fine line between what they may do and what they may not do. Paralegals may not give advice, share a fee with an attorney, represent a client in court, or sign a legal document or pleading. What can paralegals do? They may draft and prepare pleadings and legal documents, interview clients and witnesses, research and write briefs, prepare real estate closings for review by the attorney, prepare files for trial, assist in deposition preparation, discovery proceedings, assist in all activities related to fact gathering and case preparation under the direct supervision of an attorney. See §§ **2.3** and **4.10.**

While it is the attorney's responsibility to instruct, supervise, and, if necessary, admonish the paralegal, a paralegal must adhere to the Rules, Opinions, and common sense application of professional responsibilities.

1. A paralegal has the responsibility to know his/her limitations.

2. If a question of interpretation or application arises, seek attorney direction.

3. Use common sense when making decisions. Do nothing fraudulent, deceptive, or misleading. If you are unsure about something, don't do it; be guided by your conscience.

4. Follow the *Dondi* Civility Standards adopted by the ABA in 1988, 121 F.R.D. 284. Deal respectively, sensitively, courteously, and carefully with clients, adversaries, judiciary and members of the justice system.

5. Respect the attorney/client and attorney/work product privileges. A paralegal is exposed to client confidences, substantive facts, and strategies which are protected as a matter of law, not just of ethics.

6. Do not use court rules as procedural weapons. See F.R.C.P. 11. There is an ethical and legal way to obtain anything.

7. Maintain your legal education by attending continuing educational seminars. Join your local paralegal association. Cultivate your knowledge of the law for the benefit of the client. Remain aware of changes to court rules and recently enacted legislation, availability of resources, case law and other laws governing your field of law.

8. Pro Bono—RPC 6.1: an attorney has an obligation to assist in the delivery of legal services to those who cannot afford adequate legal assistance. Be mindful of the poor and their right to equal access to justice; be cognizant of contributions which can be made by paralegals devoting professional time and civic influence to the delivery of legal services through bar and paralegal association pro bono programs.[10]

In addition to these opinions and guidelines, the two national paralegal organizations have adopted guidelines with regard to professional responsibility.

In May 1975, NALA adopted the Code of Professional Responsibility that was revised in November 1979 and further revised in September 1988. See **Appendix B.** In 1984 NALA adopted the Model Standards and Guidelines for Utilization of Legal Assistants Annotated, revised 1991. The Model Standards and Guidelines are fully set forth in **Appendix C.**[11]

In 1977 the National Federation of Paralegal Associations (hereafter referred to as NFPA) adopted its Affirmation of Professional Responsibility, which was revised in 1981. In May 1993 NFPA adopted the Model Code of Ethics and Professional Responsibility. This document encompasses and replaces the "Affirmation" previously set forth. See Code in **Appendix D.**[12]

We are also bound by individual state bar association codes and Rules of Professional Conduct.

On January 1, 1980, Kentucky became the first state to adopt a paralegal code, Kentucky Supreme Court Rule 3.700 "Provisions Relating to Paralegals." Since then, three additional states have adopted guidelines by the Supreme Court. They are:

New Mexico Supreme Court, SCRA 1986, Judicial Pamphlet 16, "New Mexico Rules Governing Legal Assistant Services."

Rhode Island Supreme Court Provisional Order No. 18, "Guidelines for Use of Legal Assistants."

South Dakota Supreme Court Rule 92-5, "Guidelines for the Utilization of Legal Assistants."

In 1993 New Jersey became the first state to have the Supreme Court appoint a committee to study the regulation of legal assistants working under the direct supervision of an attorney.

---

[10] Susan D. Kligerman, An Overview of Ethics for Paralegals, 6th ed., © 1993. Reprinted with permission of Susan D. Kligerman.

[11] Model Standards and Guidelines for Utilization of Legal Assistants Annotated, © 1984, revised 1991, National Ass'n of Legal Assistants, Inc. Reprinted with permission.

[12] NFPA Model Code of Ethics and Professional Responsibility, National Federation of Paralegal Ass'ns, Inc., © 1993. Reprinted with permission.

In addition, other states, through their state bar associations, have now enacted guidelines that apply to paralegals. They are as follows: Arizona, California, Colorado, Connecticut, Florida, Georgia, Illinois, Iowa, Kansas, Kentucky, Michigan, Minnesota, Missouri, Nebraska, New Hampshire, New Mexico, New York, North Carolina, Oklahoma, Oregon, Rhode Island, South Carolina, South Dakota, Texas, Washington, and West Virginia.[13]

You have read the Codes of Professional Responsibility of the ABA and of the national paralegal organizations. You understand that you must adhere to the Code of Professional Responsibility in your home states. You realize that you have a duty—an obligation to yourself and to your profession—to support those codes. At times this may seem difficult. For instance—whistle-blowing, that is, the reporting of unethical behavior—may cause loss of job or client. If an attorney asks you to do something you know is unethical (backdate a letter, witness or notarize a signature without actually seeing the person sign the document, double bill a client, manufacture evidence, destroy necessary documents, withhold evidence, any one of a dozen wrongdoings) you have a moral obligation to yourself, your profession, and to the attorney's client to perform within your ethical boundaries. If you do engage in unethical activity, can you become liable criminally or civilly for such activity? According to Robert P. Cummins, senior partner at the Chicago firm of Bickel & Brewer, and a member of the ABA's standing committee on Lawyer's Professional Responsibility, "Whether the individual is an attorney or a paralegal, the criminal liability is the same. We indict judges and we indict lawyers. There is no reason to believe we will not indict paralegals."[14]

§ 2.3   Unauthorized Practice of Law

Restrictions on the practice of law in the United States can be traced back to colonial times. Untrained practitioners caused the local courts to adopt rules requiring the attorneys who appeared before them to have a license granted by the court. Additional rules were adopted limiting the amount of fees that could be charged and dictated that attorneys could not refuse to accept a case. The purpose of the rules was to prevent litigation by unscrupulous and mercenary attorneys and to stop incompetence that harmed not only the clients but also the administration of justice and dignity of the courts, and to prevent excessive fees.

The first unauthorized practice of law statutes were adopted in the 1850s, prohibiting court appearances by anyone not licensed as an attorney. The first

---

[13] NALA NET, June 1993.

[14] Phillip M. Perry, *Should you Rat on Your Boss?*, Legal Assistant Today, Mar.–Apr. 1993.

unauthorized practice of law cases were brought during this period. The definition of the practice of law being formulated in these cases was gradually broadened to cover activities beyond court appearances.

Some legal historians and commentators believe that the height of unauthorized practice of law restrictions came during the Depression when lawyers needed to protect their economic interests from competition. The bar associations became especially powerful trade organizations during this period. At this time, unauthorized practice of law statutes were passed in virtually all states, making it a crime to practice law without a license. The definition of the practice of law was expanded to include "all services customarily rendered by lawyers."

In 1930 the American Bar Association created the Special Committee on the Unauthorized Practice of Law.[15]

Every state has rules governing the unauthorized practice of law. These rules may vary in form and enforcement, but they all restrict the practice of law to those who are properly licensed. Commentators often criticize the strict regulations as an attempt by the bar to insulate the legal profession from outside competition. The bar insists that the rules that regulate the practice of law exist for the protection of the public. Specifically, the American Bar Association reasons that prohibiting nonlawyers from practicing law protects the public from ineffective assistance.[16]

The ABA Code of Professional Responsibility, EC 3-6 states:

> Such delegation (of tasks by an attorney) is proper if the lawyer maintains a direct relationship with his clients, supervises the delegated work, and has complete professional responsibility for the work product . . .

EC 3-5 of the Code states in part:

> It is neither necessary nor desirable to attempt the formulation of a single, specific definition of what constitutes the practice of law. . . and thus the public interest will be better served if only lawyers are permitted to act in matters involving professional judgment . . . . Where this professional judgment is not involved, non-lawyers . . . may engage in occupations that require a special knowledge of law in certain areas.

ABA Model Rules of Professional Conduct, Rule 5.3 provides:

> With respect to a nonlawyer employed or retained by or associated with a lawyer:
>> (a) a partner in a law firm shall make reasonable efforts to ensure that the firm has in effect measures giving reasonable assurance that the person's conduct is compatible with the professional obligations of the lawyer.

---

[15] Theresa A. Cannon, Ethics and Professional Responsibility for Legal Assistants, 1992.
[16] 34 Ariz. L. Rev. 873 (1992).

(b) a lawyer having direct supervisory authority over the nonlawyer shall make reasonable efforts to ensure that the person's conduct is compatible with the professional obligations of the lawyer; and

(c) a lawyer shall be responsible for conduct of such a person that would be a violation of the rules of professional conduct if engaged in by a lawyer; if

(1) the lawyer orders or, with the knowledge of the specific conduct ratifies the conduct involved; or

(2)   the lawyer is a partner in the law firm in which the person is employed, or has direct supervisory authority over the person, and knows of the conduct at a time when its consequences can be avoided or mitigated but fails to take reasonable remedial action.[17]

On November 15, 1990, the Unauthorized Practice of Law Committee of the New Jersey Supreme Court issued Advisory Opinion 24 that freelance legal assistants were engaged in the unauthorized practice of law.[18] This was the first direct challenge to the use of freelance legal assistants.

The committee reported that a number of complaints with respect to paralegals engaged in the independent practice had been held pending the committee's investigation. The committee asked for written comments from interested individuals through a notice published in the *New Jersey Law Journal.* That request resulted in the receipt of information from paralegal groups, associations, state-wide organizations, and so forth. The committee agreed that legal assistants/paralegals were divided into three categories:

1.   The paralegal who works as an employee of an attorney or law firm
2.   The paralegal who offers legal assistance directly to the public
3.   The paralegal who is not employed by an attorney or a law firm but who, as an independent contractor, offers services only to attorneys.

The committee sanctioned the first category, agreed that the paralegal practicing in the second category was engaged in the unauthorized practice of law, but felt that the third category—the independent contractor offering services to attorneys—presented a more difficult problem.

Upon receipt of the written material, the committee decided to hold a hearing. Testimony was invited through a notice in the *New Jersey Law Journal.* The committee considered the hearing well-attended. I participated in the hearing with a number of paralegals, both freelance and in-house, as well as representatives of the paralegal organizations and attorneys.

---

[17] Excerpted from the Model Rules of Professional Conduct © 1993, American Bar Ass'n. Reprinted with permission. Copies of this publication are available from Order Fulfillment, American Bar Ass'n, 750 North Shore Dr., Chicago, IL 60611.

[18] 126 N.J.L.J. 1306, Nov. 15, 1990.

The freelance paralegals testified as to the manner in which they worked—that although they were not physically located in the attorney's office, the attorney still supervised their work, and was directly responsible for their work product.

The committee was concerned with the fact that there was no mechanism in place that would regulate the conduct of the paralegal. The committee was also very concerned with conflict of interest due to the fact that freelance paralegals work for a number of attorneys. All of the freelance paralegals testified as to their methods of conflict control.

Basically it was the committee's opinion that the freelance paralegal was too removed from the attorney both by distance and relationship to be properly supervised. Although paralegals testified that the attorneys checked their work, either by fax, telephone, or in person, that the attorney was ultimately responsible for the work product and that the work was directed by the attorney, the committee ultimately decided that paralegals functioning outside of the supervision of an attorney employer were engaged in the unauthorized practice of law.[19]

Immediately after the opinion was issued, my partner, Peggy E. Stalford, and I contacted as many freelance paralegals as we could find in New Jersey, which at the time was 11. We retained the firm of Ansell Zaro Bennett & Kenney, Esqs., Eatontown, New Jersey, to represent us. We obtained a stay of the Opinion pending our petition to the New Jersey Supreme Court to overturn the Opinion. We began with 11 petitioners, however by the time the matter was heard by the Supreme Court, two years later on February 4, 1992, we included five participating paralegals. The two major paralegal associations, the National Association of Legal Assistants together with their affiliate, Legal Assistants Association of New Jersey, and the National Federation of Paralegal Associations, together with the American Association for Paralegal Education filed amicus briefs in our behalf. On May 14, 1992, the court handed down its decision:

> Neither case law nor statutes distinguish paralegals employed by an attorney or law firm from independent paralegals retained by an attorney or a law firm. Nor do we. Rather, the important inquiry is whether the paralegal, whether employed or retained, is working directly for the attorney, under that attorney's supervision. Safeguards against the unauthorized practice of law exist through that supervision.

The court continued:

> There is no question that paralegals' work constitutes the practice of law. N.J.S.A. 2A:170-78 and 79 deem unauthorized the practice of law by a nonlawyer and

---

[19] *Id.*

make such practice a disorderly-persons offense. However, N.J.S.A. 2A:170-81(f) excepts paralegals from being penalized for engaging in tasks that constitute legal practice if their supervising attorney assumes direct responsibility for the work that the paralegals perform. N.J.S.A. 2A:170-81(f) states:

> Any person or corporation furnishing to any person lawfully engaged in the practice of law such information or such clerical assistance in and about his professional work as, except for the provisions of this article, may be lawful, but the lawyer receiving such information or services shall at all times maintain full professional and direct responsibility to his client for the information and service so rendered.

Consequently, paralegals who are supervised by attorneys do not engage in the unauthorized practice of law.[20]

Opinion 24 was aimed directly at freelance paralegals. There have been, however, many other cases where paralegals have been accused of the unauthorized practice of law. Whether a freelance, or an in-house paralegal, be aware of these cases, and what the improprieties were, so that you are careful to never put yourself in a situation where you might be questioned or accused of a violation of any of the codes of the ABA, the state, or any national or local organization of which you are a member. The freelance paralegal is in a tentative position. Be certain that you are at all times supervised by and are accountable to an attorney who in turn is responsible for your work product.

A few other cases dealing with the unauthorized practice of law of interest are:

In *In re Frosch*[21] an attorney was suspended for not properly supervising the paralegal to whom he had delegated the responsibility of depositing funds in office and personal accounts.

In *Black v. State Bar*[22] the California Supreme Court ruled that although an attorney cannot be held responsible for knowing every single thing that goes on in the office, the attorney must accept responsibility for supervising the work of the staff. In this matter, attorney Black's employees failed to make bank deposits, filled in checks signed by Black for individuals whose deposits were not yet made, and misappropriated approximately $900 in cash. Mr. Black's testimony, although unclear, suggests that the asserted failure and acts of his secretary may have occurred while he was away from the office. The court further stated that even if petititoner's employees were in some manner responsible for insufficient funds to pay the amount due to his client and he did not know at the time that he improperly withdrew her funds, he was misappropriating them. These facts would not exonerate him.

---

[20] *In re* Opinion 24, 607 A.2d 962, 128 N.J. 114, 123–27 (1992).

[21] 602 N.E.2d 131 (Ind. 1992).

[22] 499 P.2d 968, 103 Cal. Rptr. 288 (Cal. 1972).

In re Kirkaldi and Hudson[23] is a case in which two people were cited for "constructive contempt," for the unauthorized practice of law. The judge had been asking people appearing pro se in his courtroom who had helped them with legal papers. He had kept thorough records regarding the people whom these two individuals had helped. The district attorney's office was not interested in pursuing charges against them, however the judge brought them into court under a contempt charge. The court ordered a fine of $500 each plus 90 days in jail. The 90 days was suspended on the condition that they cease and desist from the unauthorized practice of law.[24]

Considering *In re Harris,*[25] the defendant was found to be practicing law wherein it offered a typing service to enter information provided by clients on bankruptcy petitions. In its discussion of what constitutes the practice of law, the court noted that "the focus when determining whether a given action constitutes practicing law is upon whether its performance requires 'the exercise of legal judgment.' If it does, one is practicing law. (cite omitted) One is practicing law when performing the action involves legal knowledge, training, skill and ability beyond what the average lay person possesses" (cite omitted).[26]

The court further noted that "a typing service may not, however, make inquiries nor answer questions pertaining to completion of bankruptcy forms and schedules and may not give advice to clients as to how they would be filled out. Moreover the solicitation and preparation of the forms and schedules by a typing service constitutes practicing law."[27]

In *In re Calzadilla,*[28] Daniel Schramek, Sal Davide, and L.A.W. Clinic were enjoined from unauthorized practice of law. Their only activities may be that of a "typing service." They may not engage in personal legal assistance in conjunction with the typing service business activities that included correcting what they believed to be errors or omissions, advising clients on the bankruptcy system, completion of bankruptcy schedules, and answering questions with regard to bankruptcy forms. Schramek, Davide, and the Clinic were ordered to return to the debtor a sum representing excessive charges.[29]

In *People v. Felker,*[30] an attorney was disbarred for inter alia, permitting a nonlawyer employee to render legal advice to a client.

---

[23] 26th Judicial Dist. Court, Bossier Parish, La. (July 1993).

[24] Volume XX Issue 5 Facts & Findings, National Ass'n of Legal Assistants, Inc. Feb. 1994.

[25] 152 B.R. 440 (Bankr. W.D. Pa. 1993).

[26] *Id.*

[27] *Id.*

[28] 151 B.R. 622 (Bankr. S.D. Fla. 1993).

[29] *Case Law Updates,* Membership Newsletter, National Ass'n of Legal Assistants, Inc., July 1993.

[30] 770 P.2d 402 (Colo. 1989).

In *Louisiana State Bar v. Edwins*,[31] an attorney was disbarred for aiding in the unauthorized practice of law by delegating the exercise of professional judgment to a paralegal and allowing that paralegal to handle and disburse the client's money without close supervision. The court specifically held that a lawyer may delegate many tasks to paralegals, but those tasks may not include the lawyer's role in appearing in court on behalf of a client nor the giving of legal advice to a client. The court strongly stressed the need for close supervision of the person to whom the work is delegated.

In *De Vaux v. American Home Assurance Co.*[32] the plaintiff sustained a personal injury as the result of a fall in a store in 1971. The plaintiff called the defendant attorney's office seeking legal advice and was advised by a secretary in the attorney's office to write a letter to the store where plaintiff had fallen to advise them of the injury. The secretary proceeded to set up a medical examination of the plaintiff with the store's insurance company and also advised the plaintiff to write a letter to the defendant attorney requesting legal assistance.

The plaintiff followed these instructions, delivered the letter to the defendant attorney's office, and gave it to the secretary. The secretary misfiled the letter; it was not discovered until three years later in 1974, after the statute of limitations on plaintiff's tort claim had expired. From the time of delivery of the letter, the plaintiff called the attorney's office a number of times but never spoke to the attorney. The plaintiff was told the attorney would return the calls, but the attorney never did.

In 1978 the plaintiff filed a complaint in Superior Court alleging that the plaintiff had retained the attorney to represent her with regard to the fall. The defendant attorney answered by stating he was never retained by the plaintiff. The plaintiff argued that there was an attorney-client relationship established because the secretary's knowledge was imputed to the attorney. The plaintiff further argued that the attorney placed the secretary in a position where prospective clients might reasonably believe that the secretary had authority to act. The court found support for both theories and quoted Ethical Consideration 3-6 of the American Bar Association, Code of Professional Responsibility and Canons of Judicial Ethics (1970):

> A lawyer often delegates tasks to clerks, secretaries, and other lay persons. Such delegation is proper if the lawyer maintains a direct relationship with his client, supervises the delegated work, and has complete professional responsibility for the work product. This delegation enables a lawyer to render legal services more economically and efficiently.

The court stated that the supervised use of laypersons in a legal office is intended to permit their involvement in most matters, but not in the direct

---

[31] 540 So. 2d 294 (La. 1989).

[32] 444 N.E.2d 355 (Mass. 1983).

practice of law. The case was thereafter remanded to the Superior Court for trial on the issues.

In *In re Martin*[33] the supervising attorney was sanctioned for allowing the nonattorney employee to sign the attorney's name to a bankruptcy petition. The attorney did not participate in the filing of the petition. The court found that the attorney "improperly authorized a layman to engage in the unauthorized practice of law in violations of the Rules of Court." The Court drew attention to ABA Opinion 316 (1967) which authorizes the use of nonlawyer assistants "so long as it is the lawyer who takes responsibility for the work product."

In *Spindell v. State Bar of California*[34] the matter involved a proceeding to review a recommendation of the disciplinary board of the state bar that petitioner Frederick A. Spindell be suspended from the practice of law for a period of one month.

The petitioner was retained by Mrs. Amey to represent her in a domestic relations proceeding. Petitioner accepted employment and received compensation as requested. Mrs. Amey tried to contact the petitioner from January 1966 until the fall of 1969, but Mr. Spindell did not communicate in any way. On one occasion, upon calling the petitioner's office, the petititoner's secretary advised Mrs. Amey at that time that she could remarry. Relying on that information, Mrs. Amey did remarry in January 1967. In fact, no final decree of divorce had been entered, as the complaint was not filed until June 1968.

Mrs. Amey contacted the state bar concerning the petitioner's failure to communicate. The petitioner, after several inquiries from the state bar, finally contacted Mrs. Amey to advise that he could not make personal service upon her husband and finally had effected service by publication. This representation as to service by publication was untrue.

The petitioner argued that his conduct was not wilful as he had no knowledge of the facts making the actions wrongful. He claimed that his secretary failed to give him a substantial number of Mrs. Amey's telephone messages and on some occasions her correspondence. The secretary confirmed some of the petitioner's testimony in part. The secretary did admit to withholding as many as three or four out of ten messages. Petitioner terminated the secretary's employment and hired a new secretary. Although petitioner admitted that he thought Mr. Amey had been served, the secretary advised that service was not made due to defects in the application.

The local committee and the board found that petitioner failed to adequately supervise office personnel. In addition, petitioner's failure to communicate with his client, and his delay in obtaining a dissolution of marriage demonstrated extreme neglect. The one-month suspension was found to be fully justified.

---

[33] 97 B.R. 1013, 1021 (N.D. Ga. 1989).

[34] 530 P.2d 168, 118 Cal. Rptr. 480 (1975).

In re Easler set the following standard for permissible paralegal activities:

Paralegals are routinely employed by licensed attorneys to assist in the preparation of legal documents such as deeds and mortgages. The activities of a paralegal do not constitute the practice of law so long as they are limited to work of a preparatory nature, such as legal research, investigation, or the composition of legal documents, which enable the licensed attorney-employer to carry a given matter to a conclusion through his own examination, approval, or additional effort.[35]

Clearly the judiciary is concerned with the relationship between the attorney and the client. Although the paralegal may perform many tasks, the attorney-client relationship is sacrosanct. There must be no impropriety shown by the nonlawyer to disturb the appearance of that relationship.

Except as otherwise provided by statute, court rule or decision, administrative rule or regulation, or the attorney's Code of Professional Responsibility, and within the parameters above described, a legal assistant may perform any function delegated by an attorney, including, but not limited to the following:

1. Conduct client interviews and maintain general contact with the client after the establishment of the attorney-client relationship, so long as the client is aware of the status and function of the legal assistant, and the client contact is under the supervision of the attorney.

2. Locate and interview witnesses, so long as the witnesses are aware of the status and function of the legal assistant.

3. Conduct investigations and statistical and documentary research for review by an attorney.

4. Conduct legal research for review by the attorney.

5. Draft legal documents for review by the attorney.

6. Draft correspondence and pleadings for review by and signature of the attorney.

7. Summarize depositions, interrogatories, and testimony for review by the attorney.

8. Attend executions of wills, real estate closings, depositions, court or administrative hearings and trials with the attorney.

9. Author and sign letters provided the legal assistant's status is clearly indicated and the correspondence does not contain independent legal opinions or legal advice.[36]

[35] 272 S.E.2d 32, 32 (S.C. 1980).

[36] Model Standards and Guidelines for Utilization of Legal Assistants Annotated, © 1984, revised 1991, National Ass'n of Legal Assistants, Inc. Reprinted with permission.

§ 2.4   Conflict Control

The freelance legal assistant may work for many different lawyers at any given time. You may work on a negligence file for an attorney, thoroughly reviewing the file, answering interrogatories, propounding interrogatories, compiling witness lists, and so forth. You finish the work, deliver the file to the attorney's office, or if you have worked directly in the office, you finish the assignment. Six months later a different attorney offers you an assignment with regard to a certain negligence file. The attorney would like you to summarize depositions, review interrogatories, and so forth. You discover that this is the same file you worked on six months prior for the other side. Do you take this assignment? Absolutely not! This is a definite conflict of interest.

Suppose you work on the estate file of John Smith for your attorney client, handling the administrative paperwork, opening the estate bank account, drafting the inheritance tax return, helping with the marshalling of all the estate assets, and the income tax returns, and of course, dealing with the executor of the estate, James Smith. The estate is eventually closed. Within the year, you are working for a plaintiff's attorney on a contract dispute when you learn that the landlord of the defendant's business will have to be brought into the case as a defendant. The landlord is the executor of the former John Smith Estate, namely James Smith. Do you draft pleadings naming Mr. Smith as a defendant in this matter that eventually will lead to discovery? Absolutely not!

As a freelance legal assistant you will be working on files in different offices. It is imperative that you have a running list of current files, the files you have worked on, and files you have already closed in order to keep track of conflicts. The list should include the names of the plaintiffs and defendants as well as the attorneys. It is conceivable that in the future you will be asked to work on a file in which you have participated for the other side. By checking your open and closed file lists, it will be easy for you to accept or reject the work.

It is just as unethical for a paralegal who has worked on a file for one side, and who has been privy to strategy as to the issues, to work for the other side, as it would be for an attorney.

One of the major areas of concern to the court in Opinion 24 was conflict of interest.

> Regulation may also solve another ethical problem—conflicts of interest. We agree with the Committee's observation that
>> [t]he appearance of and potential for conflict will increase dramatically when independent paralegals offer their services to multiple law firms to assist them in litigated matters. Although the paralegal may be sensitive to avoid functioning for two adversary attorneys in the same case, the potential for conflict increases in the same magnitude as is represented by the one

paralegal . . . . The problem is exacerbated to a point which may not be controllable when the relationships multiply by virtue of a single, independent paralegal representing multiple law firms.[37]

At that point in the decision, the court noted that the paralegals who testified were aware of potential conflict situations and pointed out that an independent paralegal explained that she keeps accurate records on each attorney's clients:

> MS. SECOL: I have—I have all my files—they're all logged and noted. I have a list of all of the files for each attorney.

*   *   *

Lists of files may be stored on the computer and added to periodically. These lists may be indexed by the client's, (the attorney) name, and cross-indexed by plaintiff or defendant's name, whichever you prefer. The list should include the name of the file, the date it was opened, the type of file, (probate, real estate, and so forth) whether you are working for plaintiff or defendant, the date you close the file, and a number assigned upon closing. This would determine whether your files are kept numerically or alphabetically. You may also keep this list manually in a looseleaf notebook. See **Form 2–1.**

Brenda Lee Eutsler, a freelance paralegal, specializes in probate work. When Ms. Eutsler establishes new files, she not only records the name of the estate and the attorneys involved, but also records the names and addresses of all beneficiaries and heirs in order to have a complete cross-index for the future. She enters the information into the computer, and maintains a ledger sheet for each attorney-client. When a new case comes into the office, Ms. Eutsler retrieves that attorney's ledger sheet, enters the information, and prints it. The ledger is then put into a binder so that, "I can manually look at it as well, so if anybody calls me, I can check it and see. A name jumps into your head immediately."

Patricia G. Elliott, CLAS, also a freelance paralegal, uses computer software to maintain conflict control. The program she uses is ABACAS®. This program will be explained in more detail in § **6.6.**

In addition to the list for your file opening book or computer records, maintain a complete record of the names and addresses of parties involved whether they are plaintiffs, defendants, heirs, beneficiaries, purchasers, sellers, stockholders, and so forth. You can maintain this information manually, or on your computer, or use both methods. The important point is that you maintain complete records.

The freelance paralegal must be conscious at all times of responsibilities to attorney clients and to their clients.

---

[37] 126 N.J.L.J. 114, 130–31 (1992).

ETHICAL CONSIDERATIONS

FORM 2–1
CASE REGISTER

NAME OF CASE	TYPE OF MATTER	DATE OPENED	CLOSED	LAWYER	FILE NO.

When interviewing with attorneys for prospective work, always be sure to mention your conflict control management. It is very important to set their minds at ease with regard to their vulnerability in releasing a file to you; consequently it will boost their view of your professionalism regarding ethical considerations.

CHAPTER 3

MAKING THE DECISION

§ 3.1   Terminology

The legal assistant profession is constantly developing and changing. Much of this development has occurred since 1986. While the majority of legal assistants work in traditional law office settings, the number of paralegals who freelance is increasing.

The term "freelance" paralegal and "independent" paralegal have been used interchangeably for the past 20 years. However, with the advent of the movement in California (and now in many other states) by paralegals who provide legal services directly to the public, the term "independent" has evolved into a different usage. The phrase "legal technician" and/or "independent" has been coined to apply to those paralegals who work directly for the public.

In 1987 the California State Bar Association formed a committee known as the California Public Protection Committee to determine whether the public would benefit by nonlawyers providing law-related services directly to the public. This committee determined that the public would benefit from these services and that there was a need for the public to have access to lower cost services. The term for the nonlawyer providing such services was identified as "legal technician." The California paralegals chose to identify the paralegal contracting services to attorneys as "freelance" paralegals and "independents" as legal technician. The State Bar of California is currently considering a recommendation to license "legal technicians" to handle simple divorces, bankruptcies, and landlord-tenant disputes.[1]

---

[1] A.B.A. J., Oct. 1990, at 40.

Since 1987 several regulatory bills have died in the California legislature. The latest attempt, AB 1287, introduced in March 1993 was a significant departure from the previous California bills. This bill called for only the identification and registration of legal technicians and excluded those paralegals working under the direct supervision of a member of the California State Bar. It was reported in the September 14, 1993 issue of the *Daily Journal* that the bill had been placed on the Assembly floor "inactive file," which will delay the bill until next year.[2]

Almost every state is investigating the nonlawyer practice issue. However, Washington is the only state at this time that regulates and thereby sanctions nonlawyers serving the public. Under its Limited Practice Rule for Closing Officers, passed in 1983, more than 1,003 nonlawyers have been licensed as "limited practice officers" to prepare specific real estate documents.

According to Karen Withem in *Legal Assistant Today,* independent paralegals are defending their right to deliver services directly to the public—in bar association hearings, state legislatures, and even in the courtroom. Those who agree that paralegals should be allowed to practice to the public believe that the consumer would benefit by receiving low cost legal services. Not only attorneys but also local and state bar associations are strongly opposed to paralegals providing legal services directly to the public. The major objection is that there is no system in place to insure the protection of the consumer from unlicensed, unregulated practitioners who lack proper training. William Fry, the executive director of the advocacy group, HALT-Americans for Legal Reform, lobbies for state sanctioning of regulated, trained paralegals. He believes that legal technicians should be able to prepare legal documents without attorney supervision and to advise and represent clients directly in certain situations.[3]

It is only to the freelance paralegal who contracts services directly to attorneys and for whose work product the attorney is ultimately responsible, that this book is directed.

Note that the terms legal assistant and paralegal are used interchangeably, one term implying no more than the other.

§ 3.2   Independent Contractor or Employee?

While deciding whether or not to go into business for yourself, how do you determine whether you will be an independent contractor or an employee of the attorney or attorneys for whom you will be working? How you will be

---

[2] Membership Newsletter (Nat'l Ass'n of Legal Assistants, Boston, Mass.) Oct. 1993.

[3] Karen Withem, *The Independents Movement,* Legal Assistant Today, Nov.–Dec. 1993 at 40. Reprinted with permission from Legal Assistant Today, James Publishing, Inc. For subscription information call (714) 755-5450.

paid will define your designation. If considered an independent contractor, a federal identification number or a social security number will be required, and a 1099 form will be issued at the end of the tax year. If an employee, a W-2 form will be received that must be attached to the income tax return.

Internal Revenue Service Revenue Ruling 87-41 identifies 20 factors to help determine whether an individual is an independent contractor or an employee. The 20 factors are as follows:

_____ 1.   Are you required to comply with company instructions about when, where and how the work is done?

_____ 2.   Are you trained by the company?

_____ 3.   Are you integrated into the company's general business operations?

_____ 4.   Do you have to render the services personally?

_____ 5.   Do you use assistants provided by the company?

_____ 6.   Do you have a continuing relationship with the company?

_____ 7.   Are you required to work a set number of hours?

_____ 8.   Must you devote substantially your full time services to the company?

_____ 9.   Must you work on the company's premises?

_____ 10. Must you perform your work in a preset sequence?

_____ 11. Must you submit regular progress reports?

_____ 12. Are you paid by the hour, week or month?

_____ 13. Are you reimbursed for all business and travel expenses?

_____ 14. Do you use the company's equipment and supplies?

_____ 15. Do you have a significant investment in the facilities that are being used?

_____ 16. Do you have any risk of loss?

_____ 17. Do you work for only one company?

_____ 18. Do you offer your services to other companies?

_____ 19. Can you be discharged by the company?

_____ 20. Can you terminate your relationship without incurring liability?

The test of whether a worker is an employee or independent contractor is generally determined by applying the above list of factors to ascertain whether the employer has sufficient control over the service the worker provides. The test, however, is subjective at best, and often unevenly applied by the IRS. Because the common law test is so uncertain, Congress passed a law in 1978 that prevents the IRS from reclassifying independent contractors as employees if a reasonable basis for classification as an independent contractor exists. There are three principal safe harbors that satisfy the reasonable basis test:

1. Reliance upon a prior judicial or administrative determination
2. Reliance on a prior IRS audit
3. Reliance on industry practice.

To avoid a dispute with the IRS, existing agreements should be restructured and future agreements structured within the safe harbor parameters.[4]

Common law maintains that workers are considered employees if all aspects of their work are directed and controlled by the entity for whom the job is being accomplished. Furthermore, common law details 20 factors that determine the existence of an employer-employee relationship. These factors include instructions, training, integration, services rendered personally, continuing relationship, set hours of work, oral or written reports, furnishing tools and materials, right to discharge, right to terminate, and realization of profit or loss. These factors are used by courts, government agencies, and the Internal Revenue Service in classifying service providers.[5]

In 1989 the Internal Revenue Service started to take repressive measures on firms that it suspected were using independent contractors as a way of avoiding the payment of employment taxes.

While firms pay for one half of the cost of employment taxes, including the Federal Insurance Contributions Act (FICA), which goes towards the payment of Social Security taxes and Medicare taxes, the other half is withheld from the employee's paycheck. If the company uses independent contractors, those contractors must pay all the taxes themselves. Consequently the government may be losing revenue, since not all independent contractors may be paying their full share of taxes. Companies have classified workers as independent contractors who should have been declared employees. Some firms owe the government billions of dollars in back taxes and are subject to fines so substantial that some companies have declared bankruptcy.

When severe economic conditions exist, employers have been known to lay off employees, rehiring them as independent contractors, thereby avoiding the payment of bonuses, vacations, benefits, and taxes. It is in these instances that Internal Revenue perceives a potential problem. Although independent contractors are responsible for the payment of taxes, a number of them apparently don't pay them, or may not pay in full. Therefore, the IRS is scrutinizing employers, and small businesses are examined most closely.[6]

When in business for yourself, and in control of the work schedule, workplace, hours, assistants, and supplies, you are an independent contractor. You are responsible for the payment of taxes. A responsible business person

---

[4] 24 Monmouth Bar Ass'n Tax Bulletin 8, Feb. 1994.

[5] Robert A. Filcher & Sabin Rodriguez, *IC's or Employees: the Common Law Standard,* 24 Compensation & Benefits Review 111, July–Aug. 1992 at 32(2).

[6] Roy Furchgott, *Careers, the Crackdown on Part-Time Workers,* Self Magazine 96, Dec. 1993.

considers all the tax ramifications, obligations, and accountability incurred with the decision.

§ 3.3   Flexibility of Self-Employment

Getting started is the most difficult part. Some individuals feel that they need the flexibility of self-employment to be "masters of their fate." Others need the flexibility of self-employment to provide for families or to supplement income. Being your own boss is appealing, yet no one should ever consider self-employment as an easy way out. It is not. Being self-employed means hard work, commitment, and discipline. It means marketing yourself and your services, learning how to handle business accounts, employees, and payrolls, to buy or lease equipment, manage an office, deal with clients, and pay bills.

Are you an energetic type of person? Do you always do things yourself rather than delegate because it's easier, or because you think no one can do it better? Then becoming your own boss might be for you! Do you prefer to be independent; do you want complete autonomy? Do you want to go out on the high wire without a net? That's what it will feel like when you decide to go out on your own, to start your own business, to be your own boss. It's exciting! But there's much more.

Those who want to start their own businesses, take risks, and go out on limbs have certain characteristics in common. Generally they are hard workers, self-confident, and self-motivated. They hold very high standards for themselves and their work product and are usually intolerant of anything less from others. They strive for perfection and like to be in control of situations at all times. They cannot and will not tolerate failure. They are goal-oriented and usually "workaholics." They are risk takers, have good communications skills, and can get along well with all types of people.

According to a study by Dun & Bradstreet, approximately 90 percent of all small businesses fail! Approximately 20 percent of businesses started this year will be functioning in 10 years. Of course, these statistics refer to businesses generally. The freelance paralegal is in a more unique position. There is a very limited market for these services. You may only advertise to and work under the direct supervision of an attorney. The more attorneys in a geographic area, the more potential a paralegal has for business. You do, however, need all the skills, experience, training, and business acumen necessary to handle any business situation. Do you have what it takes?

1.   You hold high standards. You are committed to be the very best. You are willing to work long hours to achieve goals. You recognize that you may have to change what you did yesterday to meet tomorrow's requirements. You are not afraid of change, of being different, of trying various approaches to problems.

2. You do not tolerate failure. You adapt to situations and modify your approach to certain problems. If you cannot solve a problem one way, you will create a new way to solve it. You work with clients to produce the best results possible.

3. You take risks. You look for opportunities in areas where services are not being met. You create opportunities where none existed. You are creative, inventive, and take advantage of your knowledge, experience, and expertise. You convince your prospective clients that they need you, that you can make life easier for them, lighten their workload, and provide assistance par excellence!

4. You look to the future. What will be the state of the profession in 10 years? Which areas of law will be current? Which areas will be outmoded? Do you have to learn new skills, acquire training for state of the art equipment, or learn new areas of substantive law? Do you have the foresight to grow and change focus with the times?

5. You are enduring. You realize that a business is not likely to prosper immediately. You must be resilient, patient, and steadfast. It takes considerable effort to manage a business and keep it profitable through bad times. When freelancing, you seem to be either very busy or very slow. During the slow times, you must have the resilience to keep in touch with clients, market services, provide new and unique ways to keep your name known in the community. It takes a great deal of time to build a clientele and all your knowledge, expertise, and salesmanship to keep that clientele.

6. You have a positive attitude. You strive for perfection, have a good self-image, a good grasp of the intricacies of your profession, and are ready to deal with whatever happens. You have confidence in your abilities and impart that self-confidence to those with whom you deal on a daily basis.

7. You have the skills that it requires. In order to be successful you must have a firm grasp on your market area, on what is current. You must be up-to-date on rules, regulations, and new laws. Your business skills must be finely tuned and you must have a firm grasp on new ideas and equipment, on what it will take to make your product the best. Your skills in dealing with people, that is, clients, employees, vendors, and suppliers must be developed.

To assess your management skills, complete the following survey, answering the questions honestly in order to insure maximum results. Circle the number that best describes the degree to which you possess the trait:

		To a great extent					Not at all
1.	I am independent	5	4	3	2	1	0
2.	I am self-reliant	5	4	3	2	1	0
3.	I possess high energy	5	4	3	2	1	0
4.	I am flexible	5	4	3	2	1	0
5.	I have a keen sense of humor	5	4	3	2	1	0
6.	I am tenacious	5	4	3	2	1	0
7.	I am optimistic	5	4	3	2	1	0
8.	I need to be in charge	5	4	3	2	1	0
9.	I question the status quo	5	4	3	2	1	0
10.	I am organized	5	4	3	2	1	0
11.	I am persuasive	5	4	3	2	1	0
12.	I am a hard worker	5	4	3	2	1	0
13.	I am creative	5	4	3	2	1	0
14.	I am self-motivated	5	4	3	2	1	0
15.	I am a problem solver	5	4	3	2	1	0
16.	I am people oriented	5	4	3	2	1	0
17.	I have a strong desire to win	5	4	3	2	1	0
18.	I am profit oriented	5	4	3	2	1	0
19.	I am decisive	5	4	3	2	1	0
20.	I am honest	5	4	3	2	1	0
21.	I am persistent	5	4	3	2	1	0
22.	I have high self-esteem	5	4	3	2	1	0
23.	I am goal oriented	5	4	3	2	1	0
24.	I am patient	5	4	3	2	1	0
25.	I am a risk taker	5	4	3	2	1	0
26.	I am inquisitive	5	4	3	2	1	0
27.	I easily accept criticism	5	4	3	2	1	0
28.	I am innovative	5	4	3	2	1	0
29.	I am willing to sacrifice	5	4	3	2	1	0
30.	I am accountable	5	4	3	2	1	0
31.	I have good judgment	5	4	3	2	1	0
32.	I spend time doing things I enjoy most	5	4	3	2	1	0
33.	I am happy	5	4	3	2	1	0
34.	I have a strong marriage	5	4	3	2	1	0
35.	I have family support	5	4	3	2	1	0

If you rate yourself three or lower on any even numbered skill, carefully consider how important these traits are to a new business owner. If your total score is between 140 and 175, you probably will do well as an entrepreneur. If your score is between 115 and 140, you probably will be successful but will need to improve your skills in the weaker areas. If you scored between

90 and 115, you probably should not attempt to start a business of your own. If you score below 90, you should consider working for someone else.[7]

To many, being a freelance paralegal and being your own boss seems exciting—just what you've dreamed of. That dream has a very high price, and being a freelance paralegal isn't for everyone. It is not the answer to job dissatisfaction; it is not the easy way out!

I first considered freelancing in 1981. I read about paralegals in California and in the Southwest who were opening their own offices and working independently for attorneys. I thought this would be a great thing to do—to work for myself instead of for someone else. I contacted the National Association of Legal Assistants, of which I was a member, to verify that this was ethically within the boundaries of working as a legal assistant. NALA replied that as long as I was working under the supervision of an attorney, who was directly responsible for my work, I would not be in violation of my canon of ethics as a legal assistant. I then began to plan my own business. At that time, I had been employed in the legal field for over 20 years. In 1982 I started my business, renting a small (very small) office from an attorney who also provided equipment such as a copy machine, postage meter, and various supplies—all for a fee, of course. Today I share space with another paralegal. We each have assistants and at times employ additional secretarial and/or paralegal help. We have a five-room office suite, a telephone system, copy machine, fax machine, four computers, three laser printers, four typewriters, desks, chairs, a library, dictating equipment, filing cabinets, supplies, postage meter—a complete business. We have a payroll to meet weekly, monthly expenses, and so forth, but I'm getting ahead of myself. I will discuss furniture, equipment, and supplies in **Chapter 6.** Are you interested? Read on!

Being self-employed is hard work. It is also very satisfying. Advantages and disadvantages are set forth in § **3.4.**

§ 3.4   Advantages and Disadvantages

Being your own boss sounds great! No one to answer to, no one to tell you when you must work, when you should work, and for how long. You can take off when you want and work when you want.

That does sound great; unfortunately, it doesn't always work smoothly. Being your own boss means working harder than ever before, putting in longer hours, making crucial decisions with no one to consult. It would seem at times that the disadvantages outweigh the advantages, however, the self-employed are generally committed, resourceful people with a great desire to achieve.

---

[7] This questionnaire was inspired by material appearing in Gene Dailey's Secrets of a Successful Entrepreneur (1993).

There are specific disadvantages of freelancing:

- Consider the financial risk. When you go into business as a freelancer, you must build up a client list. This is a slow process and you will not have a steady income in the beginning. For this reason, many freelancers begin on a part-time basis while still employed to maintain a steady income.

- You are still not your own boss, not in the strictest sense of the word. Your business is your boss. Your clients are your bosses. Your suppliers to whom you pay bills and who furnish your office needs are bosses.

- You will work long and hard hours. The business will only grow and prosper if you are dedicated. This may involve working 10 to 12 hours a day, six or seven days a week.

- You will have to sacrifice family time and social time—especially at the onset. You may have to give up vacations if you cannot safely leave or have no one to cover the business. When you do go on vacation, there is no paid vacation.

- There are no paid benefits of any kind. You do not have paid health benefits or sick leave.

- There will be isolation, especially in the beginning when you are working alone. If you are accustomed to a large office, with many employees and a considerable support staff, you will have to adjust to working alone, without the benefit of feedback from your colleagues.

- You will have to adjust to doing everything yourself. Those tasks that in the past were delegated to other office staff will now be done by you, no matter how many other tasks you have pending. You will have to make photocopies, pack up the mail, attach postage, and so forth. You will have to file and do all the clerical tasks that perhaps someone else has always done.

- There will be times when you are very busy and there will be times when you are not busy at all. You have to allow for these fluctuations and adjust accordingly.

- You must abide by the decisions you make. There is no other boss to assume responsibility for mistakes. The proverbial "buck" stops with you, and you sink or swim with your decision. If a mistake is costly, you must bear the cost.

- You often experience failure before you achieve success. You must be psychologically ready to deal with this.

- Stress as the result of disrupted family plans, overwork, underwork, financial problems, poor business planning.

- You may lose all the money you have saved in order to open a business and possibly the money of others, such as relatives and friends.

You must be wondering what (if any) are the advantages of freelancing? There certainly are advantages to consider.

- Although you are in fact working for your business, you still maintain control. It is still your business! There is great flexibility in self-employment. If you must take time off during the day, there is no one to say you can't work all night. That is your choice. If you want to take Friday off and work Saturday or Sunday, that, too, is your choice.
- There is a tremendous feeling of self accomplishment, of being able to master the business world, of being an independent thinker, planner, and participant, of being able to accomplish a job well.
- Of course, there are monetary rewards once you have built up a business and developed a client list.
- You are creating job security for yourself, for as long as you want it.
- You are doing what makes you happy and what you enjoy.
- You will be dealing with a wider range of tasks and clients who have diverse personalities. There is far less chance of stagnation and a far greater chance for individual growth and expansion of knowledge, ideas, and expertise.
- You won't have to deal with office politics, staff meetings, and so forth, unless your business grows to the point where you have enough employees to warrant staff meetings. Then they will be your meetings.
- You are providing a necessary service; you are dealing directly with clients, with business people.
- You will enjoy financial rewards and secure your future by accruing a retirement fund.
- You will command respect in the community.
- You will have developed into an individual with business acumen and a definite knowledge of how to function in the business world.
- You will have grown both individually and professionally by learning to deal with situations in the business world.

Shelley Widoff of Boston, Massachusetts is a freelance paralegal. She is president of Paralegal Resource Center, Inc., a temporary and permanent placement service. Ms. Widoff also counsels paralegal students and graduates at Boston University, performs administrative work for the University, and teaches a paralegal program. In addition, she writes a column entitled "On the Docket" for *Legal Assistant Today.*

> I very much enjoy the freedom of not having a boss. I did it personally to develop my own lifestyle in that I prefer to start late in the morning and work late at night . . . the fact that you are reaping the financial rewards seems to motivate

me and make it all worthwhile, plus I did feel I had control of my hours and time. Of course you lose that when you start getting busy and you have to put in more and more time and hours. You can't take a vacation and there is no one to help you out at that point. Fortunately, I was capable financially to hire support. . . . The minuses are—I don't find too many minuses, other than I think my vacation breaks which I found for a long time less and less able to take time off and even to this day when I think I'm taking a week's vacation, I'm calling the office every hour and they're leaving a message for me.

"I have the freedom to turn down jobs that I don't want to do—the freedom to work as hard or as little as I wish," says Cheryl Evans of Chandler, Arizona. In December 1992 Ms. Evans quit her job as an in-house paralegal after 20 years, most of which was with a major law firm. Evans could see that her career goals of specializing in computer applications in the legal field were destined to clash with her employer's cost-cutting measures, so she left to open her own business. Now, as the owner of Computer Coach, Evans contracts her skills to firms that require her expertise. Among her clients is the law firm where she formerly worked.[8]

"There are a number of minuses, but those minuses don't seem to weigh as heavily as the pluses," says Patricia G. Elliott, CLAS, a freelance paralegal in Phoenix, Arizona. "I like the ability to come and go as I please, and yet, I am always here. But since it's my choice to be here, it's different. I like the money. If I'm willing to work good, long hours, I can make a lot of money. If I don't want to work long hours, if I want to work shorter hours, I can still make more than I would have in a traditional setting. Now I'm to the point after all these years that I have the ability to take on the projects that interest me, not necessarily ones that I just have to. In the beginning I took anything that came in, but now, you can be a little more selective. I like meeting new people and it seems that you're treated with more respect. Minuses, of course, it would be in the beginning you could never turn anything down and everything was always a rush because by the time they called you in, they had 24 hours to do it. The minuses again are benefits, no benefits . . . and sometimes it felt at the beginning when there was just me or maybe one more person that you weren't part of anything."

Lisa Sprinkle, CLAS, owner of Legal Works, El Paso, Texas finds that one big advantage of freelancing "is the kind of work I get to do, lots of research and brief writing and other things . . . I was never given the opportunity, so the opportunity for a variety of work has been tremendous and the challenge has really been there." Lisa also feels the quality of work that she is doing is higher than that she did when employed by a particular person. "I know that my reputation rests on every document I deliver, and so I put a lot more

---

[8] Rosalie Robles Crowe, *When Is it Time to Leave? Changing Jobs Easy for Some, Hard for Others,* Phoenix Gazette, Mar. 17, 1994, at C1.

effort into the work that I do . . . it affects everything. It's just enhanced because I'm on my own."

Ms. Sprinkle maintains a home office and notes that one of the disadvantages is the fact that she has a more difficult time keeping up with changes in the law. There is no one with whom she can discuss current cases. She also misses having an employer finance her continuing education.

In response to the NALA 1987 Survey on Freelance Legal Assistants, 50 percent of those freelancers answering the survey worked as many hours as they would like, 31 percent worked as many hours as they would like most of the time, and 13 percent rarely worked as much as they would like. Such problems as making time for family commitments, location, and lack of attorney awareness of their own needs were reported.

The most common causes for the failure of small businesses is lack of planning, inexperience, and incompetence. These traits are usually manifested by:

- Failure to seek advice, especially financial
- Failure to keep adequate and accurate financial records
- Inadequate market research at the outset
- Deteriorating cash flow and working capital
- Growing too big too fast
- Poor location
- Inadequate promotion and advertising
- Poor knowledge of competition affecting prices and marketing policies
- Excessive personal draws for private use (vacations, car payments, and so forth)
- Failure to maintain cash reserve for contingencies
- Overextension of credit, excessive overdraft, and loans, causing liquidity problems
- High interest costs
- Financing expansion with interest rates higher than can be earned by the funds borrowed
- Lack of time management
- Failure to insure against possible risks
- Inability to assess a risk and act appropriately
- Inability to motivate employees
- Failure to see macroeconomic, social, and political trends, to understand how these might affect the business, and to be flexible enough to be able to benefit from them.[9]

---

[9] John Day, Small Business in Tough Times (1993).

§ 3.5 Necessary Skills

In accordance with the survey conducted by NALA in 1987 concerning free-lance legal assistants, it was determined that the typical legal assistant is approximately 40 years of age, has a baccalaureate degree, and has six to ten years of paralegal experience. Of course this does not mean you cannot free-lance if you do not fit the pattern. The survey is an average taken from responses given in 1987. Since that time there have been many changes with regard to freelance paralegals. What this does mean, however, is that you must be thoroughly familiar with your specific field of law and have a good working knowledge of general law office management and the judicial system. You are advertising a product, specifically your services, and those services must be exemplary because your reputation and future in the profession depend on it.

If you are considering the freelance profession, it is extremely important to be fully experienced in the field of law you choose for your specialty. In a tradi-tional office setting you can call on any number of people to help with a prob-lem. You cannot ask your boss; you *are* the boss. If the attorney who assigns a file to you for completion must instruct you, that attorney does not need your services. Someone in the attorney's office can be used. The freelance paralegal should "free up" the attorney by handling a file in the area of law for which the paralegal is trained. The freelance paralegal must be able to field all questions, maintain professionalism at all times, and know the field completely.

To be successful in your endeavor, you must have a good command of the English language, considerable communication skills, both oral and written, and the ability to solve problems. Above all, you must be proficient in your chosen field of law and knowledgeable about current court rules and proce-dures. It also helps to have a network of attorneys and/or paralegals upon whom you can call when you encounter a problem. There will be times when you are not completely sure of an assignment. You must have someone to consult. Just as attorneys discuss their strategies with regard to certain cases, you should have someone to talk to about your particular needs and prob-lems. In addition, you must possess a practical working knowledge of how to operate a business. You are, after all, making a decision to go into business. The business happens to be that of a freelance paralegal. Once your primary skills are acquired, be cognizant of the proverbial "bottom line," what it will take to make a profit in your business. What are you going to charge? How much rent should you pay? How much can you afford in monthly expenses"?

Michael Gerber, the best-selling author of *The E-Myth: Why Most Small Businesses Don't Work and What to Do About It*, recently released the top ten list of "Why a Small Business Fails" in the following order:

1 Lack of management systems
2 Lack of vision and purpose by principals
3 Lack of financial planning and review

4   Overdependence on specific individuals in the business
5   Poor market segmentation and/or strategy
6   Failure to establish and/or communicate company goals
7   Competition/lack of market knowledge
8   Inadequate capitalization
9   Absence of a standardized quality program
10 Owners concentrating on the technical, rather than strategic, work at hand.

"It is our hope that small business owners will recognize these fundamental 'warning signs' to avoid the disintegration of their dreams," reports Gerber, who has worked with more than 10,000 businesses. "The real reason we hear these alarming statistics with respect to small business is that people in this country go into business for all the wrong reasons."

Mr. Gerber says the key to small business success is to grow by developing and implementing systems that can be replicated to provide consistent responses to customers, suppliers, lenders, and employees. His studies reveal that business format franchises have had a far higher rate of success than other small businesses, due to the systematic approach of their founders.[10]

In order to be successful in business, you must have good business skills. It is not enough to be an experienced and skilled paralegal. That was enough as long as you were working as an employee and someone else was operating the business. Now you will be managing the business. Do you have what it takes? Do you have the requisite skills or do you need to acquire them prior to considering self-employment?

It is important to consider your goals, invest time in researching and preparing to become a business owner, develop business skills by reading business materials, taking business courses, and if necessary, speaking to other business owners. Do you have business experience? At this point you may be thinking that having worked in an office for many years, you know what supplies and equipment are needed, and a good deal about office systems and setting up an office, so it can't be that difficult. Think again! Have you paid the bills for the supplies and equipment? Have you marketed your services in order to produce income? Have you developed advertising for your services? Have you calculated and paid taxes, both federal and state? Have you dealt with vendors and suppliers? Have you researched insurance programs, dealt with a landlord, encountered competition for your services, supervised employees, decided which bills to pay and which to postpone when income is not sufficient? These are but a few of the situations you must evaluate and be prepared to deal with. You must also consider whether or not

---

[10] First appeared in SUCCESS, Apr. 1994. Written by Ingrid Abramovitch (reprinted with the permission of SUCCESS. © 1994 by Hal Holdings Corp.).

you have the personality to be a business owner. This is a key part of your success.

Qualities you will need in business:

- Do you have the technical expertise to control your business? How good are you at what you do? Is your knowledge of substantive law and the judicial system sufficient enough to function on your own?
- Do you have marketing skills? Do you know how to advertise your services? Do you know what market you wish to reach, and how to price your services in order to make a profit?
- Do you have business acumen? Do you know what it takes to make a profit, to cut corners, and survive lean times?
- Do you have a financial background? While you don't have to be an accountant, there are skills you should have in order to control the business cash flow, to raise money, to borrow money, and get through slow times.

In making a decision whether or not to freelance, there are certain steps to take to help in the decision.

Ask yourself the following questions and pursue with some research in order to effectively answer them:

Question: Is there a market for my services? How do you go about answering this question? Inquire by telephone and in person. Contact law firms in your area with whom you have a relationship. Make an appointment, talk with them about the possibility of opening an office to freelance, get feedback on whether they would be interested in your services. Try to obtain a commitment for your services once you open your business.

Question: Can I work part time while trying to start up my business? This is an excellent way in which to test business skills and the geographic area in which you operate. With this method you will still have an income and be able to determine whether you have a viable idea that will work in your geographic location.

Question: Do I have enough experience in any particular area of law in order to manage on my own? Remember, there will be no backup for you; you will be operating alone. If you are given a task to do, you will be expected to complete it efficiently, smoothly, and expertly. If you do not perform adequately the first time, there may not be a second chance. Consider this question carefully. You must have sufficient expertise in the areas of law you have chosen.

Question: Is there competition for my services? Check with your local and state paralegal organizations to see if you have competition in the area. Know your competition; work with them. Remember that competition is healthy! It keeps you alert.

Question: Do I have sufficient funds to sustain me while I am trying to build my business? You may not have any steady income for at least six to nine months. You must be prepared to cope with this. This question will be entertained in **Chapter 6.**

Question: What are the economic conditions of my geographic area? Are the law firms in my area downsizing or expanding? Will they be able to afford my services? Are there enough firms from which to draw for utilization of my services? What are the economics of the small offices in my area? Can they use my services as opposed to employing full-time workers?

Question: Am I familiar with the ethical considerations necessary to operate as a freelance paralegal? You must have a complete working knowledge of the ethical opinions of your local bar association with regard to legal assistants, of the ethical opinions of the American Bar Association, of the Rules of Professional Conduct of your state bar association with regard to the unauthorized practice of law, and of any state statutes that may apply to you with regard to the unauthorized practice of law.

§ 3.6   Dealing with Stress

Stress is a word with which we are all familiar. Do we have enough time to complete the job? Will we do it well? Can we meet deadlines? Will the attorney call again? How many jobs should we undertake at once? Will we have sufficient funds to pay bills? These are questions we have all asked ourselves.

Burnout is a term with which many legal assistants are familiar. You may decide to freelance due to burnout at your job. It is the inability to manage stress. Burnout is the loss of enthusiasm, energy, idealism, perspective, and purpose and can be viewed as a state of mental, physical, and spiritual exhaustion brought on by continued stress. It occurs when an individual's attitude becomes, "a job is a job is a job; getting to the point of just putting in your time, not making waves and merely getting by or going through the motions."[11]

---

[11] Frank Minirth, Don Hawkins, Paul Meier & Richard Flournoy, How to Beat Burnout, Help for Men and Women (1986).

Job burnout is a psychological condition that affects your whole life. You are less able to perform and you care less about performing. There are three variables that affect burnout:

1. Your personality type—if you are highly motivated and intensely driven to compete

2. Your perspective—if you perceive yourself to be indispensable, the hub around which all revolves

3. Your values and motivation—if you display a strong commitment to the work ethic and exhibit compulsive behavior.

Today's workplace is a much safer physical environment than it was 10 to 20 years ago; machinery and equipment are safer. Stress has now become the most pervasive occupational hazard. Stress can affect health. It has been associated with heart attacks, migraine headaches, peptic ulcers, renal disease, hypertension, asthma, and other physical ailments. Doctors have linked stress to depression, anxiety, alcoholism, drug abuse, and the breakdown of interpersonal relationships.

You must learn to deal with burnout and stress. Learn how it affects you so that you can take charge of your life and career:

*   Diet and exercise—practicing good nutrition, participating in an exercise program to maintain good physical health.

*   Time management—Most people don't think they have enough time to accomplish what needs to be done. You feel the quality of your work is slipping because you lack the time within which to complete your tasks. You're under pressure! Use your prime time to tackle your most important jobs. Do not procrastinate.

*   Programmed relaxation—Many people practice yoga, transcendental meditation, or biofeedback. These are valuable tools designed to enhance relaxation.

Assertive Stress Fighters:

*   Say no immediately when you have to refuse someone. Apply this caveat to invitations and tasks.

*   Allow extra time for everything and arrive early.

*   Write angry letters and destroy them.

*   Don't rely on your memory for appointments, addresses, or telephone numbers.

*   Say "so what" more often than "what if."

- Always carry "waiting work" (or a good book to read) so that lines or travel do not become frustrating.
- Double check meeting places, times, and dates.
- Look for humorous aspects to disasters.
- Keep an extra supply of pens, stamps, pads, and other frequently used items.[12]

Job-related pressures and the resulting stress have been around for as long as the workplace itself. It is only recently that the negative effects of stress (decreased productivity, increased absenteeism and rising insurance claims and premiums) have been acknowledged because of illnesses and workplace accidents.

In the 1980s some employers instituted fitness programs, hoping to relieve job stress for employees, and encouraged their employees to seek counseling. These early methods, however, dealt with stress only after its symptoms appeared. Experts now recommend focusing on the cause of the stress rather than the reactions to stress.

In the late 1980s employers tried new approaches. "When they eliminated some of the layers of communication, when workers had frequent, personal contact with the head person, and when they felt they really made a difference, workplace stress was reduced immediately," reports Dr. Stewart Wolf, a stress researcher.

In addition to having marketing skills, today's successful entrepreneurs must be good facilitators who don't merely issue orders but who motivate people to work together. Small business owners must learn to listen to their employees, to maintain an open-door policy and encourage employees to take advantage of it.

A commitment to making a company a more pleasant and more productive place to work has to come from the top. In almost all companies, particularly small ones, it is the boss who sets the tone.[13]

---

[12] Elaine Zuker, Mastering Assertiveness Skills, Power and Positive Influence at Work (1983).

[13] Armin A. Brott, *New Approaches to Job Stress,* Nation's Business, 82 U.S. Chamber of Commerce, May 1994, at 81.

CHAPTER 4

SETTING UP PRACTICE

§ 4.1   The Decision is Made

You've made the decision! You have decided to meet the challenge of going into business for yourself, to take control of your destiny, to give up steady income and become your own boss. You will now offer your services to a variety of attorneys on a case by case basis. Where do you start? As you have surmised, becoming a freelance paralegal entails more than just providing services to attorneys; it means setting up a business structure, and making many decisions. One of the first decisions you must make is whether you are going to set up an office and if you are, where it will be.

You may decide that you do not want to have the bother and detail of an office. You prefer to contract your services to attorneys for work in their offices on a temporary basis. In this manner, you can operate like a temporary employee, that is, using the office space, equipment, and supplies of whomever contracts your services. You will, of course, still be self-employed, have records to keep, and will have to market your services. The need to maintain an office is eliminated. You will, however, also limit your growth potential with regard to the number of clients you can service, since you can only be in one place at a time. This is still a viable way of freelancing.

In § **4.1** however, comments will be directed to those paralegals who prefer to set up their own offices and operate their businesses in that manner.

At the time I made the decision to freelance, I decided to start on a part-time basis. I was working as a paralegal for a sole practitioner. We talked over my situation and decided that I would reduce my time to three days a week. I was working at that time from 8:00 A.M. to 2:00 P.M. since I still had children in school. In this way I could be in my office two full days a week and could still get to my office by 3:00 P.M. on the other three days to pick up messages, (if there were any) or to do whatever I could in a short time. A lot of my time in the early years was spent calling for appointments, selling my services, and meeting with attorneys. As I began to pick up clients and my business grew, I eventually reduced my hours with the sole practitioner to one day a week. If I had extra work, I would bring it back to my office and complete it there. I continued in this manner for approximately six years, giving me a monetary cushion until my business was able to function on its own.

Working part-time is an excellent way to start a business and maintain an income. At the time she started in business, for example, Shelley Widoff instituted a paralegal program at Northeastern University in Boston, Massachusetts. She hired an attorney to co-teach with her and developed a very successful venture.

Brenda Lee Eutsler was also involved in education as an instructor at the Omega Institute of Legal Studies in Haddonfield, New Jersey. Ultimately she became the coordinator of their legal studies program.

Lisa Sprinkle, CLAS, has been teaching paralegal courses at El Paso Community College in El Paso, Texas since 1985. She teaches Civil Litigation in the spring, Introduction to Paralegalism in the fall, and the Internship Program both semesters.

My partner, Peggy E. Stalford, team teaches with her attorney husband, Mark, at Ocean County College. She alternates between teaching Law Office Management and Litigation I and II.

§ 4.2   Home or Office

After you have made the decision to maintain an office, the next consideration is where. Many paralegals opt for offices in their homes in order to keep the overhead expenses down, especially in the beginning. Still others seek out office space they can share in an attorney's office or on the same floor as an attorney in order to use the facilities and keep costs down. If doing research, you would want to be near a library in order to minimize the time spent traveling back and forth. There are, of course, pros and cons with regard to renting an office versus home space.

§ 4.3   —Pros and Cons

The most obvious benefit of having a home office is the fact that you do not have to pay monthly rent.

If you have small children, a home office insures a flexible schedule so that you may be home in order to tend to your children's needs.

Working at home also minimizes the outlay of money when you are setting up your office with regard to furnishings and equipment.

You need to be very disciplined in order to work at home. It is very easy to put off your responsibilities and even more difficult to separate your home life from your office life.

Having a home office tends to isolate you and can sometimes be very lonely.

An outside office tends to give you the feeling of professionalism and credibility in the business world.

An outside office will give you more flexibility for growth, depending on how large you want your business to become and how many employees you will have.

For clients coming to see you, as well as vendors and suppliers, an outside office conveys a message that you are serious about your profession and intend to be pursuing it for some time.

Many freelance paralegals begin by renting space in attorneys' offices and using their equipment and libraries. In this way, you are also still in the mainstream of what's happening on a daily basis with regard to rule changes, amendments, and so forth. One of the problems of isolating yourself is keeping up with the changing laws and court rules. Until you acquire a library and are on mailing lists, you must use your resources to make sure you are up to date with changes in your areas of law.

If considering a home-based office, check your local zoning laws to ensure that your city does not prohibit business activity from being conducted in a private residence. The main concern with home-based businesses is the need it might create for extra parking and the resulting traffic problems. If you are not going to have your attorney clients, suppliers, and vendors coming to your home, it is probable that no one will even know you are there.

Other factors to consider in choosing an office are:

Where do you want to locate your business?

How much space do you anticipate needing?

How much will it cost?

Is the area safe and secure?

Will you be able to find employees in the area?

Are there zoning restrictions or licensing restrictions on your type of business?

When visiting offices to see what's available to rent, keep in mind that rent for office space in the heart of commercial or professional districts will be higher than office space in less developed areas. In suburban areas, highway office footage is more expensive than the traditional downtown areas or even several blocks off the highway. Depending on your cash flow, you might need to consider opting for a less prestigious area—you can always move.

You will spend a significant amount of time in your office, possibly more time than you spend at home, at least when you are awake. Your office not only should be utilitarian but also should reflect your judgment and personality. We all want our offices to be beautiful, to reflect our tastes; that will come, first things first.

§ 4.4   Business Organization

There are several ways in which to operate your business. In order to determine the structure that will best suit you, answer the following questions:

1. What is the simplest business structure to maintain, the least expensive to establish?
2. Is anyone else going to share in the ownership of this business?
3. Which business structure will require the lowest taxes?
4. Do you want to limit your personal liability?
5. Where do you foresee your business in five years, and in ten years?

You can operate your business as a sole proprietorship, as a partnership, a corporation, or limited liability company. **Section 4.5** covers some guidelines for your decision, however you should discuss options with an accountant or attorney before making a decision.

§ 4.5   Type of Organization

Sole Proprietorship

If you operate your business as a sole proprietor, you and the business are one and the same. There is no separation. Your profits are deemed to be personal income and your personal assets are at risk if your business fails.

Simple to establish

Owner is completely liable

Income is taxed at the individual rate that is lower than the corporate rate

Social security, medicare taxes, and income tax on the business are paid by the sole proprietor

Keogh plan may be established based on profits that may be deducted similar to corporate pension and profit sharing plans

Losses may be deducted in full on an income tax return.

Partnership

In a partnership, as in a sole proprietorship, taxation is at an individual rate and business deduction allowances are similar to those of the sole proprietorship. The important consideration is your choice of a partner. A partnership can be as significant as a marriage. You must consider whether you can work well together, if the prospective partner is enthusiastic, whether you share the same goals, if your prospective partner offers different ideas and concepts, and if the partner brings special talent to the partnership. Your partnership agreement will spell out the terms of the partnership including provisions for disagreement, whether your shares are transferable, and any other provisions you wish to add. The partnership will end, of course, upon the death, bankruptcy, or withdrawal of any partner, unless otherwise stipulated. In a partnership:

There is more than one owner.

A written partnership agreement with any partner will be required.

The losses from the business can be deducted on individual income tax returns in proportion to each partner's investment in the business and amount of liabilities for which each partner is responsible. There are further limitations for real estate losses.

Decisions must be shared by the partners.

Liabilities rest with the partners; if a creditor is unsuccessful in collecting from one partner, the creditor may collect the entire debt due from the other partners regardless of the share of business owned by the remaining partner or partners.

Partnership ends upon death of partner.

Corporation

The corporation is a separate entity and can hire you as the employee. You will pay income tax on the wages earned from the corporation, but not on the profits made by the corporation. The corporation will be run by the board of directors, which may or may not be composed of the stockholders. In a corporation:

It is necessary to draft and file papers with the Secretary of State.

Corporate officers are not liable for corporate indebtedness unless they have personally guaranteed a debt.

Tax rate is higher than individual rate.

Losses cannot be passed through to the individual's income tax return, unless the corporation is a Subchapter S.

Social Security and Medicare taxes are paid at the rate of 50 percent by the corporation and 50 percent by the officer-employee.

Deductions for corporate retirement plans are similar to Keogh plans, however you may borrow from the plan.

Medical reimbursement plan may be classified as a business expense and disability and group life insurance premiums may be deducted.

There is considerable paperwork associated with a corporation.

There are many tax forms to be filed annually, both state and federal.

The corporation has perpetual life.

Subchapter S Corporation

The Subchapter S corporation is an entity between the partnership and the corporation. It offers limited liability to the stockholders but pays no corporate income tax. The profits of the S corporation are passed through to the stockholders who report the profit or loss on individual income tax returns. Election of S corporation status must be made within 30 days after the formation of the corporation and must be signed by all stockholders. Status as an S corporation may be terminated and the corporation may function as a regular C corporation.

Must be a domestic corporation

Must not have more than 35 stockholders

May only have one class of stock

Requires monitoring by a tax professional

Limited Liability Company

Needs more than one member

Is not recognized in every state

Has no individual liability

Requires specific duration

Offers no transferability of shares

Members are taxed as individuals

Pays no corporate tax

There is no set rule on how an individual business should be set up and organized. Many of you will not formalize your practice. You may share office space, work for space, and be involved in other nonpartnership arrangements that are becoming more common. In most cities, management firms offer turn-key space for offices that include secretarial help, equipment, and basic management systems for tenants at a fixed rate.

§ 4.6   Business Name

What will you call your business? Will you use your name or a catchy phrase? You do want people to remember the name of your company, however remember that you are in a professional area of business and want to appear professional at all times. Most attorneys use their own names for their firms. You may use a designation describing your business. My office answers the phone as "Paralegal Services," because there are two of us and we do use our own names. "Paralegal Services" is descriptive, proper, and dignified.

Your name should convey to the public what business you are in, that is, what you do. You also want to convey an image.

> Good name in man and woman, dear
> my lord,
> Is the immediate jewel of their souls:
> Who steals my purse steals trash; 'tis
> something, nothing;
> 'Twas mine, 'tis his, and has been
> slave to thousands;
> But he that filches from me my good
> name
> Robs me of that which not enriches
> him,
> And makes me poor indeed.[1]

If you opt to incorporate your business, all references to your business must indicate the corporate name. Specifically your stationery, bills,

---

[1] W. Shakespeare, Othello, III, iii.

invoices, and checks will all reflect your corporate name so that the public is aware you are doing business as a corporation.

If you are doing business as a sole proprietor, or as a partnership, you may decide that you don't want anyone else in the area to use your specific name, such as "Paralegal Services." You would therefore file a trade name, or business name certificate with the clerk's office in the county in which you are doing business. This certificate would indicate [your name], trading as (t/a) or doing business as (d/b/a) Paralegal Services.

§ 4.7   Business Plan

The major cause of failure in new businesses is lack of proper planning. Planning is an ongoing process. It doesn't stop because you have started your business. You plan to launch your business, to continue your business, and to change strategies according to the market, It is prudent at the onset to draft a business plan stating how you expect to go about forming the business and carry on running the business. Recall the five "W's" used in litigation in drafting interrogatories, or drafting a complaint. You ask, "Who, where, what, why, and when?" You may apply those same questions to your business plan:

WHO?   Who are you? What is the name and location of your business? Who is your competition? Who is your market? Will you specialize in any given area or will you handle all areas of law? Who is going to be your potential client?

WHAT?   What will you do in order to set up your business? What are the advantages of using your services? What will you offer? What do you hope to accomplish? Do you know what is expected from you as a business owner? Do you know your responsibilities? What areas of expertise have you chosen?

WHERE? Where are you going to set up shop? What kind of organization will you have? Where will you market your services? Where will you find clients? Where do you foresee your business in a few years?

WHY?   Why are you doing this? Will your services be necessary in your geographic area? Are there law offices that need your help and your expertise? Will you fill a need in your area?

WHEN?   When will you start? How do you see the growth of your business? Have you made adjustments for lean periods?

SAMPLE BUSINESS PLAN

1. Summary

    a. Name, address
    b. Description of your proposed business
    c. Support with diagrams, charts, illustrations
    d. Market

2. Description of legal form of ownership, organization of business

    a. Describe your qualifications
    b. Describe the special qualities of your services, plans for growth, meeting competition
    c. Describe your objectives, the advantages of the use of your services

3. Management of company

    a. Titles and responsibilities
    b. Plans for staffing of business
    c. Description of initial office facility including equipment, capital improvements
    d. Prospective business at hand—schedule of projected business

4. Marketing techniques

    a. Methods used to promote services
    b. Sample brochure, literature
    c. Profile of target market and geographic area to be served

5. Financial aspects of business plan

    a. Initial capital requirement
    b. Cashflow needed for first year
    c. Sources of debt and financing for start up and growth
    d. Financial projections for several years
    e. Explanation of use of funds
    f. Return for investors

6. Miscellaneous data

    a. Insurance coverage, identification of risks
    b. Tax reporting requirements
    c. Personnel, employees, training.

Your business plan is a guide for running your business. If you need help in formulating this plan, ask for it. Your local bank might be able to help or your accountant might be the logical one to approach. People with experience in the business area provide insight to problem solving or raise questions not considered. If you plan to seek financing from outside sources, it will be necessary to give a business plan to your prospective lender. The more complete your plan, the easier it will be to obtain financing.

§ 4.8   Types of Assignments

What exactly does a freelance paralegal do? How do paralegals work?

As previously indicated, there are many different ways in which freelance paralegals operate. Some work from their homes, some work in their contractor's offices, some work in their own offices, and some travel to county record rooms, to libraries, and to state capitols to do research. Paralegals use modern technology to transmit the work product—computers, modems, and fax machines.

When I am working on a research project for an attorney, I meet with the attorney to go over the facts of the case, plus the issues to be defined and researched. For example, I may be doing research for a summary judgment motion filed by an opposing attorney to dismiss the complaint that the attorney alleges fails to meet the burden of damage due to the verbal threshold. My client and I decide the issues to be addressed in the opposition papers and I either conduct the research in the law library, at the county court house, in the attorney's office, (if there is an extensive library) or in the main branch of our public library where there is a comprehensive legal department. When I have completed the research, I either draft the opposition pleadings for the attorney's review, or I present the attorney with a memorandum with the case law I have found. The attorney-client reviews the draft; we then finalize the pleadings and file them with the court. During the time I am doing the research I may fax the attorney drafts from time to time; I may use a modem to tap into data bases for information not readily available in my area. I am in constant contact with the attorney by telephone, by fax, or in person. My client is always aware of my work progress. In the course of my assignment I will keep track of my conference time with my client, the time spent in research, in writing, in the draft, and in completion of all pleadings. The billing aspect of the business will be discussed in §§ **7.5** and **7.6** in great detail.

Real estate closings are another area of law in which I specialize. I work very closely with my attorney-client from the time that the attorney's clients sign a contract to purchase or sell real estate until the closing date. The attorney informs the clients that the staff paralegal will be contacting them with regard to any information needed for the closing. I may, depending on the attorney's specific requirements, order the inspections in accordance with the contract, monitor the mortgage application, order all title work, and communicate with the seller or buyer attorney with regard to the status of the closing.

Upon receipt of the title binder, and examination of same by the attorney, I will submit the necessary documents to the mortgage company for approval to close, arrange the closing, draw the necessary closing documents (subject to review by the attorney), draw the post-closing letters, the closing statement, and recapitulate all checks necessary to close and deliver the file to the closing attorney. I keep copies of my notes taken throughout the file, telephone numbers, the closing statement, and payoff letters in case there are any questions at the closing or at a later date. At any given time prior to closing, the attorney may request that I send a letter to the client and will advise me as to the contents of same. All correspondence to the attorney's client goes out under the signature of the attorney and must be approved by the attorney before mailing. The only correspondence that a paralegal may sign is correspondence of a ministerial nature, that is, to the county clerk, to a tax assessor or collector, to the mortgage company, and so forth. The correspondence to an attorney or to a client must go out under the attorney's signature. This is in accordance with Opinion 611 of the New Jersey Supreme Court Advisory Committee on Professional Ethics. As set forth in **Chapter 2,** check with your individual state to determine exactly what you may and may not do as a paralegal.

Another area of law in which I am involved is probate work. I handle the administration of the estate for the attorney from the time the will is probated through the final account. Again, the attorney will introduce me to the client as the staff legal assistant. The client is immediately made aware of my identity as a paralegal. I usually attend the initial conference with regard to the assets of the estate and complete all forms necessary for the probate of the will and qualification of the personal representative. I prepare correspondence for the attorney's approval, draft the inheritance tax return, or federal estate tax return, help marshal the assets, attend to the date of death balances, the closing of bank accounts, the liquidation of assets, and the preparation of drafting of the final account, plus any pleadings necessary for the completion of the estate. All work is done under the supervision of the attorney and at the attorney's request and authorization.

There are many areas of law and various ways to work as a freelance paralegal. In this chapter I would like to introduce a broad picture of how various freelance paralegals work and how they differ in their methods.

Shelley G. Widoff is a pioneer in the field of freelancing; she has been freelancing since 1976. Shelly attended the Paralegal Institute in New York upon graduation from Skidmore College. After working as a paralegal for four years, she decided she wanted to do two things, educate paralegals and start her own business. "I guess the entrepreneurial nature came through me because I was a business and psychology major." Shelley felt she wanted to continue to develop based on the experience and background that she had, which was starting a paralegal service or teaching paralegals. Her firm had a client with an estate matter that was being assigned to an attorney out of the office. When Shelley gave notice, her firm suggested to the outside lawyer that her services be retained to help with administering the estate. That was her first client. The client also offered her office space and telephone use. She was in business. The office was in downtown Boston and she could advertise her services with an address. At the same time, Shelley introduced herself to Northeastern University, established a paralegal program, hired an attorney to co-teach, and further developed the paralegal studies program. The program proved to be very successful!

Shelley first started working in the areas of corporate, real estate, and probate law. Today her permanent staff numbers three people including herself, a bookkeeper, and a director of paralegal services. She has since received her Master's Degree in Administrative Science from Boston University, for whom she does paralegal counseling. The counseling involves assisting students with curriculum choices in the paralegal program and exploring career options upon graduation. On occasion she also teaches paralegal courses.

I asked Shelley to describe a typical day.

I do have someone who is my director of paralegal services, so any calls that are urgent or rush I don't deal with directly anymore. Otherwise I would go crazy. We perform services on an hourly basis so if someone needs a docket sheet at the federal court and they need it in ten minutes and they need to have it faxed, we handle that, but I'm not personally put under any pressure to do that, my director of paralegal services is and he handles that really well. A client just called the other day from a bank that needed six temps with corporate experience. Together with my assistant who supports me with the computer printouts on our database of candidates, we pull all those available candidates. I review the resumes, we make calls to see if they are available to start tomorrow; that is like the high pressure, immediate, urgent temping service part. You want to make sure you are sending qualified persons and some might say they were available yesterday and today when you call them, they are not, and sometimes you take it home at night if they don't return your calls. You leave a lot of messages and I get the calls in the evening whether they are available or not—the details. So that is a typical day. When we get orders for permanent placement, the pressure is on there too to send ASAP—recruit available candidates, so once again you go through your database. I usually deal with those things first, then in addition to that, just dealing with the telephone, answering calls. On a typical day I also get calls from Boston University—my students—so I have to deal with those responsibilities which is always a priority as well, counselling or faculty requests, and then I have administrative work—like now it is tax season. I have my pension plan responsibilities, inputting information and giving it to the proper professional to follow through, or administrative matters like being a woman-owned business and filling out those kinds of forms for different kinds of federally funded businesses. Then I follow up with things that my staff leaves on my desk, review bills for services, appropriate changes and at the end of the day, I review matters that are going out in the mail, that are completed, to give a final OK to them, and during the whole day I may have interviews scheduled with candidates to interview them—obviously before we put them in the computer.

Brenda Lee Eutsler, a freelance paralegal in Cherry Hill, New Jersey, was the first freelance paralegal in New Jersey. Brenda went into her business in 1980 after having been Deputy Surrogate in Camden County for four years.

Brenda graduated from the Paralegal Institute in Philadelphia, Pennsylvania, and returned to work as a paralegal in the law firm in which she was a legal secretary prior to attending the Institute. She found she was limited in her duties and thereafter went to work for a large firm in Philadelphia. After approximately two years, her former employer was elected Surrogate of Camden County and appointed Brenda as Deputy Surrogate. Brenda's responsibilities as Deputy Surrogate were to review all documents and pleadings that were filed with the court and to identify the deficiencies in the pleadings, audit the accountings, and communicate back to the attorneys to make the necessary corrections. The longer she worked at this job, the more she was told that she would do well to assist the attorneys, outside of court. That's what gave her the idea that she could freelance, helping the attorneys with accountings, contested estate matters, fact investigation interviews, and assisting with estates from the beginning.

Brenda's initial office situation was working out of her home for three months, during which time she did publicity work, sending out letters, cultivating contacts, letting people know what she was doing, and developing a brochure. When work started coming in, she opened offices in Haddonfield.

> During the time that I was Deputy Surrogate—the last two years—I was an instructor at the Omega Institute of Legal Studies in Haddonfield. This was a paralegal/legal secretary and office administration course and ultimately I became the coordinator of their paralegal studies. When I left the Surrogate's Office I took on those responsibilities almost on a fulltime basis, or I should say, I took on those responsibilities to coordinate paralegal studies more intensively.

Brenda rented her first office from the school. Two years later she moved from Haddonfield to Voorhees. When her son was born, she moved the offices back to the house where she shares an office suite with her husband, Jim, who is an attorney.

Brenda describes a typical day.

> The first thing I do in the morning is to pull out the "to do" list, and see what has to be done and organize the day. I try to book appointments on appointment days. If I have office paper work to do, I don't want to have to run out for an appointment and then come back to what I'm doing. I don't like that skip in the middle there. So I'll schedule a day for appointments. So Monday next week is appointment day and they're all back to back, and then Tuesday and Wednesday are just office days, and Thursday is appointment day. So if I have

appointments it's usually for the entire day. I'll run out and pick up new files, return paper work, go over cases, and so forth, and then a typical in-office day would be preparing the papers and phone calls. I process right into the computer anything I prepare as far as pleadings, documents, or accountings. So I really don't have a need for a separate secretary. I have a couple of paralegals, that when I need assistance, I can call on. But not anyone fulltime in the office.

Patricia G. Elliott, CLAS, is a litigation specialist in Phoenix, Arizona. After graduation from the University of Arizona with a Bachelor of Science Degree in Business Administration, Pat took a job as a legal secretary. She had worked in the summer as a legal secretary during college, and wasn't quite sure what she wanted to do upon graduation. She worked for two different firms at that time and then moved into a legal assistant position, although in the early '70s, "they really didn't call them that. Actually they called me an administrative assistant because they didn't exactly know what to do with me."

Pat continued working as a legal assistant for over ten years before making the decision to freelance. She initially set up an office in her house and hired an assistant after six months. Running out of room in the house, they moved into an executive suite office that accommodated both of them. Pat expanded again, rented a larger office, and hired approximately four paralegals, a secretary, and a part-time secretary. After taking on a partner, further expansion, and leaving the partnership, Pat is now back to working on her own and downsizing in order to do those jobs she enjoys. She works with two major clients, two law firms. One firm is a nine-lawyer firm; one is a two-lawyer firm that is 'of counsel' to the nine-lawyer firm. They have provided her with office space and support staff. The best part is, even though she works for her own clients and bills them, the office space is free.

A typical day for Pat follows.

The first part of my day is spent taking care of business problems, for instance, billing, accounts receivable, accounts payable. From there I move into "real paralegal work." I spend a little while every day doing medical research, on the Med-Line, from the National Library of Medicine. I spend time during the day doing disclosure statements, which are peculiar to Arizona, sort of like a federal 42C. You have to have a pretty complete knowledge of the entire file. I then attend to discovery matters, interrogatories, requests for production, that sort of thing—putting out "fires" from previous days, writing trust account checks for settled cases. I can't see that my typical day is any different than that of an in-house paralegal.

Lisa Sprinkle, CLAS, owner of Legal Works, El Paso, Texas, graduated from the School of the Ozarks in Missouri and received her Paralegal Certificate from El Paso Community College. While attending El Paso Community

College, Lisa worked part-time as a legal secretary. After completion of the course, she worked as a paralegal for approximately eight years before deciding to freelance. Lisa's decision was made because as a litigation paralegal, she felt she was being "pigeon-holed" into doing the same thing all the time, on the same kind of cases. She just didn't feel challenged anymore. She also wanted to keep her own hours. Lisa's husband is a college professor and she wanted to be able to take time off when he was on school vacations.

Lisa made the decision to freelance, filed her business name certificate, gave notice at work, and had a business telephone line installed in her home where she set up an office. In the beginning Lisa started work by word of mouth. Later she placed an advertisement in the *El Paso County Bar Newsletter* and sent out letters to attorneys she had met over the years through her litigation experience. She also had brochures printed, sent them with letters, and left brochures at the county law library.

Lisa's day begins after she sees her daughter off to school at 7:00 A.M. Her phone sometimes starts ringing at 7:30 A.M.

> If I have assignments to work on, I plan the day before. I either go to the library in the morning, do the research that I need, and come back to do a memo on the computer. I try to take care of administrative type work before I leave in the morning, return some phone calls, make phone calls. If I am going to the attorney's office I'm usually there between 9:00, 9:30 A.M.
>
> I am on the NALA Board and I've got to address that at some point and teaching part-time means I have students to deal with, or situations. One of the classes I teach is the internship program, and so I am talking to employers about the intern or talking to the intern about their job; that consumes a lot of time.

I realize that I have not described my typical day. Because I have several specialties, it is difficult to plan my day too far in advance. I will try to capture my typical day.

I usually arrive at the office at 8:00 A.M. at which time it is quiet with few phone calls. I try to accomplish those tasks that either need concentration or are administrative in nature and need to be completed immediately. I normally input my billing from the day before, or two or three days before. At this time I also attend to the payment of the monthly bills due, review administrative mail, and so forth.

I try to have a list in front of me every morning with the priority tasks for the day, that is, those files that need immediate attention, those that need some attention, and a further list of work to be finished by a certain time period, plus the calendar items for the day. I live and die by my lists. Since I handle real estate files, there is always a crisis, always something unanticipated. For instance, in the middle of the day I might receive a copy of a contract and correspondence faxed from one of my attorneys, with the notation, "must close in two weeks," or "must close immediately. Order all title work immediately." Real estate is one area of law that requires many telephone calls. I am on the phone a good part of the day with attorney clients, their clients, mortgage companies, title companies, real estate brokers, other attorneys, and so forth, trying to compile necessary documents for the mortgage company, for the title company, for the seller/purchaser's attorney. I deal with pest inspection companies, home inspection companies, and contingency dates. Considerable time is spent assuring and reassuring everyone that the matter will close, that the mortgage commitment will be issued, and that clients won't be out in the street with no place to live. It's challenging.

Today I have to review research with regard to a summary judgment motion that must be drawn within the next few days. The difficult part is finding the quiet time to review the research. I have to decide whether additional research is necessary and if so, do the research and draft the motion papers and the brief. I also have to confer with my attorney client. In addition to everything else, I also need to submit proposed answers to interrogatories that are overdue.

I will also receive calls from my attorney clients on particular files to discuss certain information, go over certain issues, or to set up appointments to see them. Today I need to drop off a complaint to be signed, (it was reviewed by fax) and pick up some documents needed to complete a foreclosure proceeding. One of my clients represents a bank with regard to foreclosure work, and at certain times the bank will call me to fax a status report on the work in progress, which of course, happened today.

Upon opening the mail, I received two new real estate files that need to be opened, entered, and set up according to my systems, and entered in the computer. Letters have to be sent out to clients and to the title company.

I just received a call from an attorney client to be in the attorney's office in the morning to meet with a client in an estate matter. This means I will be out of the office a good part of the morning.

As you can determine from these interviews, freelance legal assistants basically do the same work as in-house legal assistants. The difference is where they do the work and who they do it for.

One of the major differences in working as a freelance legal assistant as opposed to an in-house legal assistant, is that the pressure to complete all jobs is much greater on the freelancer. As an in-house paralegal assistant, you can complain to your boss by saying, "I can't possibly complete all this by March 25. I just have too much to do; I need help." As a freelance legal assistant, if you tell your attorney you don't have the time within which to complete the work—you're out of work—and probably won't be called again. Regardless of pressures, you get the job done.

§ 4.9   Generalist or Specialist

This section deals with whether or not you intend to specialize. Many free-lance paralegals provide services in all areas of law; others specialize. You may, for example, only provide services with regard to probate law, or bankruptcy law or real estate, or litigation. The choice depends on your background and your experience. If you have had a real estate background you would not provide services in probate, an area with which you are not familiar. Your specialty areas will, of necessity, be those in which you have the most knowledge and experience. According to the survey made by NALA in 1987, the most common area of specialization was litigation, having 41 percent. Probate followed, having 18 percent; real estate, tax, and medical malpractice areas had 5 percent each.

Because of the nature of our legal system, and the changing laws, attorneys specialize. So too, legal assistants have chosen to specialize. These legal assistants can be invaluable to the attorney who does not have sufficient staff to handle the specialty field.

When I opened my office, I originally planned to handle those areas of law with which I was most familiar—real estate, probate, and corporate. However, because I had a varied background and had worked for a general practitioner for over 20 years, I was also well-versed in litigation. In the beginning I handled mostly real estate, probate, and corporate matters but as my clientele list grew, the specialty areas changed. Today I still do what I originally intended, however I do handle more litigation now.

The best specialty you can choose is the one in which you are most experienced. That is where you should start. If, after you have been freelancing for a while, you see other areas opening up, it would behoove you to either learn all you can about those areas or simply decline taking any work that you are not prepared to handle. The other alternative is to find another paralegal with expertise in the areas you lack, and team up, that way, you have all areas covered.

You can, of course, acquire skills in new and different areas. This can be accomplished by either attending seminars on the particular area of substantive law, by completing a course in the paralegal program at a local college, by reading all the material you can on the subject, and by networking with your fellow professionals. Law is change; it never stands still. We all have to anticipate new trends in the law and new areas opening up to us. Years ago environmental law was unknown. Who instituted suits for toxic torts? Today it is a growing field. With the graying of America, elder law has become a viable area. There is always change.

According to Diane Patrick, *What's Hot, Recruiters Report on Hiring Trends,* there will be a continued emphasis on specialization. Important areas will be in litigation, large case management skills, computerized management skills (on data bases); international departments will require legal assistants who are fluent in foreign languages. The important quality is diversity. According to Lori Ginsberg, employers want "real sharp people who can wear lots of hats: who have phenomenal computer skills, are good with clients, can keep the calm, can handle major case management. A well-rounded person."[2]

Ms. Patrick cites examples of hot specialties in the different areas of the country. In the east, she mentions environmental legal assistants, patent and trademark, ERISA, product liability, health care and commercial real estate. In the midwest, litigation, environmental, patent and trademark, music publishing disputes (copyright, publishing) in the entertainment field, and reinsurance are current. In the west, intellectual property, patent and trademark law, bankruptcy, and environmental law take precedence.[3]

In 1994, Ms. Patrick reports the following hiring trends in their geographic order:

Eastern: Civil Litigation, real estate, arbitration and mediation, corporate financing and specialist in fields of trusts and estates, ERISA, foreclosure, trademark.

Central: Medical malpractice/personal injury, product liability, real estate, corporate litigation, intellectual property, alternative dispute resolution.

Western: Freelance paralegals with personal computers in home offices for research-oriented assignments using modems, corporate work, Blue Sky, computer skills, entertainment law, health-care, and intellectual property.[4]

§ 4.10   Sample Specialties—Areas of Law

The following list serves only as a guide for areas of law in which a paralegal may specialize:

Bankruptcy Practice

Criminal Defense

Corporate

Corporate Securities

Elder Law

---

[2] Patrick, Diane, *What's Hot: Recruiter's Report on Hiring Trends,* Legal Assistant Today 51 Mar.–Apr. 1993. Reprinted with permission from Legal Assistant Today, James Publishing.

[3] *Id.*

[4] *Id.*

Entertainment Law

Employee Benefits

Environmental Law

Estate Planning

Estates and Trusts

Family Law

Health Care

Intellectual Property

Mining and Oil and Gas

Municipal Finance

Real Estate

Litigation

Collections

Foreclosures

Worker's Compensation

Public Benefits

Immigration

Tax

Patent and Trademark

Computer Law

Labor Law

These are only some of the areas of law in which you can specialize. What are your responsibilities in these fields? What are the parameters within which you can work? The New Jersey Bar Association published a monograph entitled *The Evolving Role of the Paralegal* in 1983. *The Evolving Role* was updated in 1986 and recently in 1991. This monograph, written by the Law Office Management Committee, Subcommittee on Paralegals, serves to answer these questions. It sets forth those tasks to be performed by a paralegal in certain areas of law. They are as follows:

BANKRUPTCY
- Conduct client interviews to include:
  - Mechanics and procedures
  - Statutory exemption
  - Analysis of debt vs. asset picture

- • Classifications of debts
- • Choices of bankruptcy relief available
- Draft Uniform Commercial Code information and copy requests to appropriate offices; analyze information including preparation of lien priority exhibits to be used in trial.
- Draft judgment searches to appropriate offices.
- Draft, request, and analyze information about real estate owned by debtor; prepare lien priority exhibits for use in trial.
- Assist debtor and maintain calendar on preparation of Chapter 11 cash flow statement.
- Review advance sheets and research on reported bankruptcy cases.
- Review clerk's docket and claims' register.
- Draft appropriate petition, schedules of debts and assets statement of affairs, and additional pleadings as necessary for initial filing.
- Draft reaffirmation agreements and transmittal letters to creditor and client.
- Draft motions and notices re: discharge of non-bankruptcy judgments and lien avoidances.
- Correspond and confer with debtors, creditors, attorneys, and clerks.
- Notify clients of hearing and trial dates and depositions.
- Draft applications, stipulations, proposed orders, notices, and other routine pleadings.

CORPORATE

- Draft and file certificate or articles of incorporation, and subsequent amendments, together with preliminary preparations for incorporation such as name clearance and reservation.
- Drafting by-laws.
- Drafting organizational resolutions or consents, appointing directors and electing officers.
- Preparing stock certificates.
- Preparing and filing various federal and state tax forms.
- Drafting and filing qualification documents in foreign jurisdictions.
- Drafting employment agreements, stock option agreements, shareholder agreements, pension and profit sharing plans.

Ongoing corporate tasks may include:

- Maintaining corporate minute books.
- Preparing and filing annual reports.
- Drafting annual and special meeting resolutions or consents requiring approval of directors and shareholders.
- Preparing meeting notices, agendas, proxies, ballots and waivers.
- Drafting loan documentation such as notes, mortgages, security agreements.
- Checking corporate status.

Partnership tasks may include:

- Drafting partnership agreements.
- Drafting and filing limited partnership certificates and subsequent amendments.
- Drafting and filing fictitious name certificates.

Sales, merger, liquidation, dissolution, or acquisition tasks may include:

- Drafting sale, merger, liquidation, dissolution, or acquisition agreements.
- Drafting resolutions or consents of board of directors approving the contemplated transaction.
- Drafting certifications of corporate officers.
- Drafting and filing Certificate of Merger or Dissolution.
- Conducting appropriate due diligence review and obtaining necessary good standing certificates and certified charter documents.
- Preparing pre-closing and closing activities such as document execution, post-closing filings and transcript preparations, stock cancellations, and reissuances.

Securities practice tasks may include:

- Drafting select portions of offering documents.
- Drafting officer, director, and principal questionnaires.
- Researching blue-sky laws and drafting blue-sky memoranda.
- Filing registration statements, amendments, and post-effective amendments, each with coordination of appropriate exhibits.

LITIGATION

- Initial client interview and follow-up.
- File organization, including analysis, chronologies, and checklists.
- Fact gathering, including investigation, witness interviews, photography, medical reports, and wage analysis.
- Draft pleadings such as complaints, third-party complaints, answers, motions, and discovery requests and responses.
- Assist in arrangements for depositions including the preparation of proposed questions; attend depositions with the attorney; digest/summarize depositions.
- Prepare calculations during attorney settlement negotiations and draft settlement documents.
- Prepare file for trial, schedule witnesses and experts for testifying at trial.
- Organize the trial notebook.
- Attend the trial with the attorney to organize exhibits, retrieve documents, assist with witnesses, note developments in the case, monitor and maintain a list of documents and exhibits used by both sides.
- Assist in the accumulation of expert witness files.
- Maintain a docket, calendar and tickler system.

COMPLEX LITIGATION

- Handle document control; analysis, organization, indexing, and general maintenance.
- Assist in conducting/preparing for the production of documents.
- Examine public records/documents.
- Arrange and attend depositions with the attorney
- Digest and index depositions.
- Research factual and statistical data and prepare analyses.
- Draft pleadings, such as requests and answers to interrogatories, routine notices, motions, petitions, affidavits, and certifications.
- Maintain docket, calendar, and tickler systems.
- Assist in preparation of legal memoranda/briefs: proofreading and cite checking.
- Assist in preparation of trial notebook.
- Organize and prepare exhibits for trial.
- Attend trial with attorney and assist with exhibits.
- Digest and index trial transcripts.

MATRIMONIAL/FAMILY LAW

- Interviewing clients and preparing factual information sheet.
- Drafting complaints and other pleadings.
- Preparing notices of motion, certifications and orders.
- Preparing Case Information Statements.
- Drafting and answering interrogatories.
- Preparing clients for depositions.
- Contacting expert witnesses; arranging for appraisals.
- Drafting subpoenas.
- Preparing documents and exhibits for trial.
- Drafting final judgments of divorce and settlement agreements.

REAL ESTATE

When seller is the attorney's client:

- Preparing a draft of the contract of sale for review by the attorney.
- Obtaining and forwarding to purchaser's attorney for review prior to closing such items as back-title information; water, sewer, oil and tax bills; current mortgage payoff information; and the Certificate of Occupancy for the closing.
- Coordinating date, time, and place of closing with all parties.
- Preparing closing documents: deed, affidavit of title, Real Estate Settlement Procedures (RESPA) and settlement statements, note, and mortgage taken back by seller.
- In commercial transactions, the paralegal may obtain the necessary clearance under the Industrial Site Recovery Act (ISRA) and prepare the forms necessary for that clearance; obtain information with regard to tenants,

leases, adjustments for rent; prepare letters of attornment; prepare documents such as the Security Agreement, UCC-1, Bill of Sale, notes, and mortgages, if required.

- Attend closing.
- Post-closing follow-up.

When purchaser is attorney's client:

- Preparing or reviewing contract.
- Obtaining and reviewing back title information.
- Arranging for survey, termite inspection, structural inspection including radon, if necessary, obtaining flood certification, title insurance binder, mortgage payoff statements, homeowner's insurance policy.
- Coordinating closing with lender; fulfilling all lender's requirements and forwarding all documents for review prior to closing date. This includes preparation of affidavits, releases, notes, mortgages, RESPA statements, and notices of settlement.
- Coordinating closing with all parties.
- Preparing final closing documents, including 1099B and filing same with IRS.
- Attending closing.
- Post-closing follow-up.
  - Forwarding original documentation for recording.
  - Forwarding check for mortgage payoff, pay off all outstanding liens, final letter to title company requesting policy, payment of all taxes and sewer charges.
  - Forwarding canceled mortgage to seller's attorney.
  - Obtaining title policy, then forwarding to client
  - Forwarding deed and all client's papers to client
  - Forwarding mortgage to mortgage company.

Additional responsibilities required for complex transactions may include:

- Foreclosure and recovery work.
- Construction and permanent loan closings.
- Bond closings.

TRADEMARK

- Maintain trademark files.
- Provide attorney and client status reports on new developments in trademark law.
- Maintain firm's docket system for trademark practice. Provide trademark attorney with sufficient notice of pending filings due such as Section 8 and 15 filings, affidavits of use, and other deadlines as appropriate.
- Develop adequate safekeeping procedures for original trademark documents for domestic and international trademarks.
- Conduct trademark searches, including computer-assisted research.

- Draft trademark applications for registration and renewal and Sections 8 and 15 affidavits for the attorney.
- Obtain necessary client records in support of registrations and affidavits.
- Draft response to trademark official actions.
- Draft licensee agreements.
- Draft powers of attorneys.
- Draft correspondence in support of international trademark practice; keep attorney apprised of delays or difficulties.
- Perform trademark watch service on regular basis.
- Draft copyright applications for registration or renewal.
- Assist in trademark infringement proceedings, including file maintenance, factual research, and preparation for trial.
- Arrange exhibits and visual aids for trial use and generally assist in discovery proceedings and trial preparation.

TRUST AND ESTATES

Pre-mortem planning:

- Interviewing clients; gathering information concerning family history, assets, and liabilities
- Preparing preliminary analysis of client's estate in order for the attorney to determine the tax consequences of various estate planning alternatives.
- Drafting of wills, trusts, powers of attorney, and living wills, from preliminary stages to finalization.
- Maintaining bank accounts and assisting with beneficiary notification for the administration of trusts.

Estate Administration:

- Attending initial client conference for discovery of assets, liabilities, and background information required.
- Preparing probate documents.
- Scheduling and attending safe-deposit box inventories.
- Arranging for appraisals of decedent's assets, which may include real estate, jewelry, automobiles, antiques, art collections, personal property, and household furnishings.
- Valuing securities either by in-house means or arranging for valuation by stockbroker assistance. Preparing and filing (if required) an estate inventory.
- Maintaining estate financial accounts and records.
- Correspondence pertaining to all aspects of estate administration.
- Review estate financial records for determination of timely payments of estate expenses and distribution of assets to beneficiaries, to effect tax savings.
- Preparing formal or informal accountings of estate of trust administration from preliminary drafts to finalization.
- Distribution and/or sale of securities by preparing necessary sale or transfer papers and working with brokers or transfer agents.

- Preparing necessary documents for beneficiaries to effect distribution of assets and to release fiduciary's liability.

Tax Preparation:

- Preparing gift, income, federal estate, inheritance, and fiduciary income tax returns as required by:
  - Gathering and reviewing pertinent records.
  - Drafting return for review by attorney.
  - Finalizing return for client signature.
  - Arranging for payment of tax calculated.
  - Filing return with appropriate taxing authority.
  - Determining requirements for filing of any necessary estimated tax payments.[5]

Although only a few of the specific areas of law are listed, it will give you a general idea of the substantive work performed by legal assistants.

---

[5] Excerpted from *The Evolving Role of the Paralegal,* copyright 1991, N.J. State Bar Ass'n. Reprinted with permission.

MARKETING YOUR BUSINESS

§ 5.1   Targeting the Market

Marketing is a total system of interacting business activities designed to plan, price, promote, and distribute want-satisfying products and services to organizational and household users at a profit in a competitive environment.[1]

Is marketing important? You have to let people know you're in business in order for them to contract to use your services. Sounds simple. What is the best way to accomplish this? How do you reach your market, that is, the attorneys in your area? What methods do you employ? Do you hire a professional marketing consultant? Do you try to market on your own?

A service is an intangible product performing tasks that satisfy consumer needs in chosen market segments.[2]

Marketing is a very important part of your business. You are selling yourself and your services. You do not have a product that you can take off a

---

[1] Houston G. Elam & Norton Paley, Marketing for Nonmarketers at 7 (1992).

[2] Arthur H. Kuriloff & John M. Hemphill, Ph.D., Starting and Managing the Small Business (1988).

shelf and sell. Your product is your services, your knowledge, your experience and commitment. You have to convince your market (attorneys) that your assistance will be beneficial to them—that they need your services.

Before you decide on your exact marketing techniques, study your market, that is, the attorneys in your area, or in the area you hope to cover. Determine how many law firms are in the area and the size of those firms. Are they large, medium, or small? In which size firm do you see your services needed the most? In what areas of law do these firms practice? In which areas do you specialize? Are there temporary paralegal agencies in your area? What is your competition? How are you different? What can you offer that is different to make yourself marketable? Other considerations are:

Are your services different from your competition?

Are you flexible if you need to make changes in your services?

What is a realistic profit margin?

Can you employ sufficient help to meet your needs?

What are your plans for expansion?

How will you promote your business?

How broad a geographic base do you plan for your business?

When you make a decision to freelance, one of the first things to do is take stock of the law firms with which you are familiar and who are familiar with you and your abilities. This can be accomplished with the telephone book or the *Lawyers' Diary*. Each *Lawyers' Diary* has a section of attorneys listed by county and municipality. Make a list of the attorneys you know well; make a list of attorneys with whom you have dealt through the course of your employment. Finally, list attorneys in the area whom you think would benefit by your service. Once you have compiled a list of approximately 30 to 35 names, you are ready to start your marketing research. The object is, of course, to approach the attorneys with your concept of opening a freelance business, explain how you plan to operate your service, and let them know how they can benefit from your skills. Based on your experience and expertise, you should be able to convince them that you will make their lives easier and more profitable, always more profitable! At this point, you also need their feedback as to which services they feel they need and how they think you can help them, or in some instances, cannot help them. This will be a learning experience for you and for the attorneys with whom you converse. It will also give you some idea as to the demand for your services, the areas of law in which you would be most needed. Hopefully these areas will fall within your specialties. Remember, if the attorneys you approach do not perceive your concept to be an immediately viable one, this does not necessarily mean that they will not use your services in the future. More often than not, it will take some attorneys a while to get used to the idea of using an independent contractor. Attorneys will be hesitant about letting files out of their offices. They may not readily understand the concept that you can function as an extension of the office. When the attorney is reluctant to use my services, I try to convince that attorney to give me one trial file to work on; that's all I need. Once they feel confident knowing you are in constant touch with them and knowing what you are doing at all times, they are comfortable turning over more files. Keep in mind this initial contact is to get feedback for your ideas, to let the attorneys know that you are planning to have a service that can help their business. The hard sell comes later!

§ 5.2   Marketing Interview

When I called to make my initial appointment with the attorneys, I did not tell them what I wanted to see them about. I made the appointment, and if asked what it was in reference to, I responded that it was in reference to an idea I would like to discuss with the attorney. This way there was no chance of being avoided or discussing the proposal over the telephone. If the attorney is insistent about the reason for the appointment, you can state that you would like to describe a new service you are considering and would like the attorney's input. There are some attorneys who will not be interested in seeing you. You are not going to be able to see everyone on your list.

What do you say to the interviewing attorney? How do you convince attorneys that your services will be profitable and useful?

Before the appointment try to research the firm in order to ascertain the specific areas of law in which they specialize. Do they have a general practice? What kind of staff do they have? Do they employ legal assistants? Do they employ temporary help? What do they do when staff members take vacations or sick time? Are there times when they may have need for your specific services? These are questions you may pose to the attorney during the interview. You will be sure to advise the attorney of your areas of expertise, have samples of your work available for examination, and have references so that the interviewing attorney may check on your credentials.

The most important fact you want to leave with the interviewing attorney is the cost efficiency of utilizing your services. If the attorney wants to develop a real estate practice but does not want to hire a fulltime legal assistant, you could explain how you can handle these files, under the attorney's supervision, without the necessity of hiring fulltime help. In this way you are freeing attorneys so that they can handle additional work, thereby increasing their capacity, but not their workload. This can be done in any area of law.

You can tell them another advantage of using a freelance legal assistant is that you are performing services without involving the firm's support personnel. In this way, the firm does not have to train or retrain its support staff.

Convince them that freelance legal assistants save the firm money. The office does not have to supply benefits of any kind. As independent contractors, paralegals do not receive vacation time, medical benefits, or pension benefits. Freelance paralegals do not take up time and space in their offices, or use their equipment and supplies.

Let them know that you become an extension of the office by contracting your services. You become their legal assistant working on their files. Remind them that the firm is providing a benefit to the public by utilizing services that are cost-effective to clients. Legal assistant services may be billed directly to the attorney's client; naturally they are billed at a much lower rate than the attorney's rate. Many clients are pleased that they are not only billed at a lower rate, but also that they have someone available at all times to give information. The attorney's clients are informed from the start that they will be working with a legal assistant who can help them with ministerial questions. All questions of a legal nature must be directed to the responsible attorney.

The following are considerations for the appointment:

- Look and act professional. Dress for success.
- Bring references from attorneys who have used your services or are familiar with your work product.
- Explain why you feel there is a need for your service.
- Explain how cost-efficient your service is—no insurance benefits, no health benefits to pay, no steady salary, no paid vacation, payment for work upon completion.
- Stress the fact that after you have been instructed by them how to prepare the file, they can go on to other files and therefore increase their productivity while lessening their workload.
- Show them the profitability chart at § **5.4.**

After the appointment, return to your office and write a thank you letter to the attorney for the opportunity to explain your new service and reiterate that you hope to hear from the attorney soon.

The information provided for the marketing interview is also the information you will give to the attorney for whom you wish to provide services. Your first interview will be to introduce the idea of your services and get feedback from the attorneys as to the utilization of your services, marketability of your services, and so forth. The second interview will be to sell your services to the interviewing attorney. At this time, in addtion to providing references, you may be able to provide a client list, and references from your clients, plus furnish the prospective client with a reference list of names and telephone numbers so that the client can call and verify your credentials.

In the early years, when I completed work for my attorney clients, I asked them to write a letter of recommendation addressed to "whom it may concern." I asked them to specifically indicate the services I had performed and their satisfaction; I was able to show these letters to prospective clients.

§ 5.3   Sample Letter

A sample brochure is included in this section at **Form 5–1.** You may use a similar brochure for your interview or you can send one to attorneys on a general mailing list. In the beginning, I sent an introductory letter and brochure together. I felt the brochure might have an impact on an area of law in which the attorney needed paralegal assistance. I also felt the brochure was important for attorneys to have on hand for reference, perhaps at a later time. I had business cards made and enclosed a card with each letter. Freelance legal assistants have a very narrow market. The best way to advertise is by telling attorneys what you can do, what your background and qualifications are, and giving them references to which they can refer. The brochure can provide whatever information you feel is important to you specifically, and it is the marketing tool you need to use often.

You are now ready to draft your first letter introducing yourself and your services. Included in this section are sample letters (**Forms 5–2** and **5–3**) to prospective clients with regard to your services, and a sample list of services at **Form 5–4.** Of course, you will also have to include a résumé/brochure of the services you are offering. This would entail a description of work in your specialty areas, your educational background, and your experience. The letter should be informative enough to pique the curiosity of the reader without disclosing to the attorney how your services will be implemented. As you can see, the letter states that you will call for an appointment to come in and discuss your services. After the letter has been sent, you would diary the various dates on which you send letters and to whom, and follow up with telephone contact. You would then make an appointment with the attorney to meet and discuss your services.

Diary the letter according to the dates you send it to particular attorneys and follow up in two or three weeks with a phone call to inquire whether, after the attorney reviewed your services, you could be of some assistance. You then hope to make an appointment with the attorney to discuss your services and ways in which you can help alleviate the attorney's workload.

FORM 5–1
SAMPLE BROCHURE

Dorothy Secol, CLA
Certified Legal Assistant

Midlantic National Bank Building
Highway 35 and Wyckoff Road
Eatontown, New Jersey 07724

Dear Attorney,

How often have you wished you had a "right arm" '- someone to assist you with your heavy caseload?

Have you ever put off doing that foreclosure that's been sitting on your desk - or the New Jersey Inheritance Tax Return or federal estate tax return or put off answering or propounding interrogatories - or forming or dissolving a corporation.

How often have you sought out ways to increase your productivity without substantially increasing the costs of providing efficient and expedient services to your clients?

No doubt, QUITE OFTEN!

The additional assistance you have been seeking is available though the legal support services described in this brochure. These services are provided on an as-needed basis, thus enabling you to expand your practice in a cost-efficient manner.

To discuss YOUR needs, contact me at (201) 542-0711

Sincerely,

DOROTHY SECOL

Please Keep This Brochure Handy.

Legal Support Services

Independent Paralegal Services
For Attorneys

Dorothy Secol, CLA
Certified Legal Assistant

Midlantic National Bank Building
Highway 35 and Wyckoff Road
Eatontown, New Jersey 07724
(201) 542-0711

Independent Paralegal Services for Attorneys

FORM 5–1 (*continued*)

Services Available

Probate

Complete estate proceeding including drafting New Jersey Inheritance Tax Returns, Federal Estate Tax Returns, drafting wills, guardianship procedures, adoption procedures, incompetency proceedings.

Real Estate

Set up real estate files, handle contracts through closings, draft pleadings for Bills to Quiet Title, Foreclosures, draft Easement Agreements, sales of businesses including security instruments, etc.

Corporate

Set up corporations from Certificate of Incorporation through minutes, corporate agreements, professional corporations - agreements, minutes, drafting stockholders agreements, dissolutions of corporations, Buy-Sell agreements

Litigation

Drafting pleadings including complaints, answers, counter-claims, etc., drawing Interrogatories, trial preparation, interviewing clients, witnesses.

Legal Research

Determine available case law, brief cases, drafting memoranda of law, drafting briefs.

Law Office Management

Consultation services with regard to setting up and organizing law office structure including filing systems, diary systems, check writing systems, time sheets, streamlining office expenditures, allocating work loads, bookkeeeping methods, interviewing prospective employees.

Professional Liability Insurance with National Union Fire Insurance Company, coverage - $1,000,000.00

Experience

Extensive law office experience over a span of 25 years
Lecturer in Field
Member National Association of Legal Assistants
Member Legal Assistants of New Jersey, Inc.
Received certification as Certified Legal Assistant June 12, 1978 from National Association of Legal Assistants, This certification was obtained after passing a two day examination There are 556 CLAs in the United States to date.

Education

Monmouth College, West Long Branch, N.J.
Institute for Continuing Legal Education
   Seminars —
              Probate Reform Act
              Estate Tax Returns
              Condominium Law
              Real Estate
              Econbmic Recovery Tax Act
              Corporations
Fairleigh Dickenson University
   Continuing Education Courses
Rutgers University
   Continuing Education Courses
Practicing Law Institute
   Estate Tax Returns

Excellent References Available
Upon Request

FORM 5–2
SAMPLE LETTER TO PROSPECTIVE CLIENT

Dorothy Secol, CLA
Certified Legal Assistant

100 Main Street
Allenhurst, New Jersey 07711
(908) 517-8555
Fax: (908) 517-8545

Independent Paralegal Services for Attorneys

As a lawyer, you are well aware of the rising costs of maintaining your office, including the cost of the time of attorneys, legal assistants and secretaries. As the cost of supplies, rent and staff increases, your profit margin decreases.

I would like to offer you a cost effective, efficient method of decreasing your work loan and increasing that profit margin.

Enclosed is my resume, indicating the work I can do for you on an hourly basis. By utilizing a freelance legal assistant, you ar free to work on matters which may require your personal attention, and, of course, you can bill your clients for the work I perform for you, in my office (or yours), as your legal assistant.

Your consideration of my proposal would be appreciated, and I will contact you in a week to ten days to make an appointment to come in to discuss any questions you may have.

Very truly yours,

Dorothy Secol

DS:s
enc.

FORM 5–3
SAMPLE LETTER TO PROSPECTIVE CLIENT—ALTERNATE

Dorothy Secol, CLA
Certified Legal Assistant

100 Main Street
Allenhurst, New Jersey 07711
(908) 517-8555
Fax: (908) 517-8545

Independent Paralegal Services for Attorneys

March 9, 1993

John Lawyer, Esq.
100 Anderson Street
Asbury Park, New Jersey 07712

Dear Mr. Lawyer:

As an attorney, you are well aware of the rising costs of maintaining your office, including the cost of the time of attorneys, legal assistants and secretaries. As the cost of supplies, rent and staff increases, your profit margin decreases.

Through the use of our services, you can effectively reduce your costs. We do not take up space in your office for which you must supply furniture, supplies, etc. We are not covered by any medical-health plan; we do not take vacation time. Your only cost is per file for the work we complete.

Real estate closings are handled on a flat fee basis, while all other work is on an hourly basis. If you are inundated with discovery materials, interrogatories, notices to produce; if you need an accounting completed, or an incompetentcy proceeding, day to day hands on administration of an estate, wills, living wills; motions for sumary judgment, foreclosures, partitions, corporate minutes, agreements, etc., call us. A complete list of all services available is enclosed.

> *We conclude that given the appropriate*
> *instructions and supervision, paralegals,*
> *whether as employees or independent*
> *contractors, are valuable and necessary*
> *members of an attorney's team in the*
> *effective and efficient practice of law.*
> *In re Opinion 24 of the Committee on the*
> *Unauthorized Practice of Law* 128 N.J. 114 (1992).

If you have any questions with regard to any of the above, please call.

Very truly yours,

DOROTHY SECOL

DS:s
enc.

FORM 5–4
SAMPLE LIST OF SERVICE

Dorothy Secol, CLA
Certified Legal Assistant

Peggy E. Stalford, LA
Legal Assistant / Bankrupt Trustee

100 Main Street
Allenhurst, New Jersey 07711
(908) 517-8555
Fax: (908) 517-8545

Indepentent Paralegal Services for Attorneys

PARALEGAL SERVICES AVAILABLE

PROBATE

Assistance with complete estate proceedings including drafting New Jersey Inheritance Tax Returns, Federal Estate Tax Returns, drafting wills, guardianship procedures, adoption procedures, incompetency proceedings.

REAL ESTATE

Set up real estate files for closing, including administrative paperwork ordering binder, survey, payoff letters; communicating with mortgage company re requirements, drafting mortgage closing documents including respa, post closing letters; assistance in drafting Bills to Quiet Title, Foreclosures, drafting easement agreements; assistance with drafting documents for sale of businesses including security instruments, etc.

CORPORATE

Assistance in setting up corporations including contract with Secretary of State, drafting Certifications of Incorporation through minutes, assisting in drafting corporate agreements; drafting documents for formation of professional corporations, assistance in drafting stockholders agreements, drafting documents for dissolutions of corporations, mergers of corporations, drafting Buy-Sell Agreements

BANKRUPTCY

Assistance in drafting and preparation of bankruptcy petitions (Ch. 7, Ch.11, Ch.13) preparation of Chapter 13 wage earner plans, preparation of Chapter 11 Disclosure Statements and Reorganization Plans; drafting and preparation of post-petition pleadings

MATRIMONIAL

Assistance in preparation of Case Information Statement, drafting and preparation of complaints, motions, drafting and preparation of post-judgment pleadings

LEGAL RESEARCH

Determine available case law, brief cases, drafting memoranda of law, drafting briefs

LITIGATION

Assistance in drafting pleading including complaints, answers, counter-claims, etc.; assistance in drafting of all discovery pleadings; assistance with trail preparation, interviewing clients, witnesses, etc.

LAW OFFICE MANAGEMENT

Consultation services with regard to setting up and organizing law office structure including filling systems, diary systems, check writing systems, time and billing systems; streamlining office expenditures, allocating work loads, bookkeeping methods, interviewing prospective employees.

§ 5.4   Profitability Chart

Another aid to help you sell your services is the profitability chart. See **Form 5–5.** This chart can be an efficient method for convincing the attorney of how profitable your services can be. Profitability is bottom line! This is how you sell your services. You are profitable. You are cost-efficient. You will save the attorney money because you will allow the attorney to work on other files while you are performing services in accordance with instructions. As illustrated in the chart, there are examples as to the net profit on a file when the attorney handles the file aided by a legal secretary compared to when the legal assistant handles the file.

The illustration uses a flat fee of $1,000, an hourly rate for the attorney of $200, for the legal assistant $50, and for the legal secretary $15. In the traditional approach, utilizing the services of the legal secretary, the attorney spends five hours interviewing the client, advising and counseling, gathering information, and preparing papers. The legal secretary spends four and one half hours preparing and filing papers. The total cost is $1,067.50; the net profit is $432.50.

In the alternative approach, using the services of the freelance legal assistant, the attorney spends one and a half hours on the matter and the legal assistant spends six hours. The total cost is $900; net profit $600. However, while the legal assistant is working on this file, the attorney is free to work on other billable matters at the hourly rate of $200.

This chart can be reproduced in color; it can be made larger on the photocopier; it can be framed. There are a number of ways you can use this chart to get the point across that your services will be very profitable.

§ 5.5   Projecting a Professional Image

You can't judge a book by its cover—or can you? Publishers spend time and money designing book jackets. Jacket design is a complex art. The front of the jacket must capture the potential reader's attention, the spine must convey information about author, title, and publisher, while the back usually describes the book using catchy phrases and testimonials. The flyleaf summarizes the book without depth. Covers do give information.

People, too, come packaged. A person's cover gives us clues about what is inside. When you first meet people, you can tell a great deal by their appearance, body language, and use of space. Does the person appear neat, clean, and healthy? Are clothes appropriate to the surroundings? What message is the individual's appearance giving you about how the person regards himself?

FORM 5–5
SAMPLE PROFITABILITY CHART

The following is an illustration of how a Legal Assistant may be profitably used on a typical file. Assume the following:

1. A fixed fee of $1,000.00 will be charged.
2. The hourly rate for the lawyer is $200.00.
3. If the lawyer were not actually doing many of the tasks on this file, he could be serving other clients on other matters.
4. In Case I - The Traditional Approach, the secretary receives $15.00 per hour; in Case II - The Legal Assistant Approach, the legal assistant receives $50.00 per hour.

Case I - The Traditional Approach

Functions:	Time Consumed (Hours)	
	Lawyer	Secretary
Interviewing client	1.0	0.0
Advising and counseling	1.0	0.0
Obtaining information	1.0	0.0
Preparing papers	2.0	4.0
Filing papers	0.0	0.5
	5.0	4.5

Cost (measured by economic input)
Total cost   1,067.50
Fee   1,500.00
Net gain over standard
hourly rate $ 432.50

Case II - The Legal Assistant Approach

Functions:	Time Consumed (Hours)	
	Lawyer	Legal Assistant
Interviewing client	0.5	0.5
Advising and counseling	1.0	0.0
Obtaining information	0.0	1.0
Preparing papers	0.0	4.0
Filing papers	0.0	0.5
	1.5	6.0

Cost (measured by economic input)
Total cost $900.00
Fee   1,500.00
Net gain over standard
hourly rate $600.00

In addition to the $600.00 realized in Case II, the Lawyer has 3.5 additional hours to serve other clients on other matters at his hourly rate of $200.00.

What about an individual's posture? Is the body held erect, or is it slumped? Do gestures signal nervousness, anger, or confidence? Does the individual move with authority and confidence in their "territory" or act suspicious and apprehensive? Does the office convey what the workers think about their careers? [3]

People tend to make snap judgments based on appearance. If the image you project is not a favorable one, you may not get the chance to make a viable presentation about your services. Whether you are making a business presentation, conducting a seminar, giving a speech, or being interviewed by a prospective client, your appearance is important. If your appearance is attractive, you will make a good first impression. If it is not, you may alienate your audience.

Picture a rock star, picture a state senator, or a CEO of an important company, picture a fashion model; you instantly conjure up images of what they look like, what they represent.

You and your employees represent to the public the entity now known as "John/Jane Doe, Legal Assistant at Large." You are your own best or worst advertisement for your services. The image you and your staff project is of utmost importance.

Attorneys do a considerable amount of networking; a good word from one attorney to another is the best form of advertising you will ever receive. Attorneys rely upon their peers' opinions. That you project yourself, your services, and most importantly your finished product in a timely and professional manner is vital to the development and continuance of your business.

You must be personally well-groomed and dressed appropriately at all times. This means hair shiny clean and combed, shoes polished, and no worn or scuffed heels. Men should wear business suits or ties and jackets with neatly pressed shirts. Women should wear business suits or dresses with no torn hose or slips showing. You represent your business image. You are asking others to rely upon you and to place their trust in you. Convey an air of professionalism at all times.

Dressing in a classic manner, wearing simple and understated clothes reflects good taste. Individual style is not necessarily lost by adhering to this code of dress. There are many ways in which to individualize your outfit and create your individual style. By accessorizing with jewelry, shoes, or scarves, you can create your own style.

There is more to creating a good image than just dressing. How you see yourself and how you feel about yourself is most important. When you feel good about yourself, you generally feel good about the world around you, and you project that feeling.

When you are dealing with prospective clients you should also be aware of your body language. It is revealing and can tell a great deal about you.

---

[3] Elaina Zuker, Mastering Assertiveness Skills (1983).

When you are relaxed and in control, you transmit that feeling to those around you. When you are tense and under stress, that too will be transmitted.

When you cross your arms, jut out your jaw, and sit rigid and straight, your body is saying "stay away." When you sit relaxed, yet erect, with your arms and legs at ease, your body is communicating openness. If you appear anxious and distant, your body is putting distance between you and with whomever you are speaking.[4]

Your work product must be completed in a timely manner and in accordance with instructions given. If there is ever a question with regard to what your assignment is, do not hesitate to clarify instructions with your supervising attorney. If your finished product is not accurate, you will not have a chance for another assignment.

§ 5.6   Do's and Don'ts in the Business World

In business there is a proper way to behave, a professional way. Here are some suggestions for appropriate behavior:

- Do make yourself visible. Join local organizations and attend meetings.
- Do act, dress, and carry yourself professionally at all times. Project that image!
- Do always identify yourself as a paralegal/legal assistant.
- Do present your work in a timely manner.
- Do join state and local paralegal organizations. Be well informed.
- Do keep up with current changes in the law; attend Continuing Legal Education seminars.
- Do maintain your office with decorum, maintain cogent records, and maintain up-to-date equipment.
- Do know your limitations. If you are given an assignment with which you do not feel comfortable, or don't feel you know the subject matter, don't take the assignment. It is better to refuse than to be embarrassed by an incomplete effort—or worse, an unfinished effort.
- Do develop confidence.
- Do learn to delegate skillfully.
- Do look to the future rather than the past.
- Do strive to improve your personal skills.

- Don't project an unprofessional image. Don't go into an office unprepared.
- Don't ever give legal advice.

---

[4] Lillian Brown, Your Personal Best (1989).

- Don't make a decision with regard to a file without first consulting the attorney responsible for your work product.
- Don't be afraid to ask for clarification so that you fully understand the assignment.
- Don't be afraid to try new ideas providing you clear them with your supervising attorney.
- Don't stagnate; keep up with the business world around you. Consider new equipment. Entertain new ideas, new products.
- Don't be inflexible. There will be many small jobs you will have to complete and new dimensions to old jobs. Be ready to accept what comes.
- Don't set unrealistic goals.
- Don't overextend yourself or your company.
- Don't dwell on who caused a failure, but on what caused it and why.

§ 5.7   Client Selection

As explained in § 5.1, when starting out, you will make a selection of attorneys to whom you feel you would like to contract your services. Depending on your geographic location, there may be other freelance paralegals with whom you are competing. When I started, there was only one other freelance legal assistant in the state. It was exciting to know I was "trail blazing" and I was very aware of everything I did or said. I knew that we (as the first) were setting a standard for all who were to follow. There was no serious competition for the first few years. There were very few legal assistants in my area at that time and no freelance legal assistants. Most attorneys in the community were not even familiar with legal assistants, certainly not freelance legal assistants. I belonged to a state paralegal organization and a national organization and knew that the territory in New Jersey was fairly uncharted regarding legal assistants. The only other freelancer, Brenda Lee Eutsler, was in the southern part of the state an hour and a half away by car, and she specialized in probate work; I had a more generalized practice leaning towards real estate, probate, and corporate law. After a few years there were other freelancers who started businesses in the area. I really feel competition is healthy and as long as you price your services fairly, market well, and produce a quality product, you will have a loyal following. There is competition in all businesses; that is the backbone that free enterprise is built on.

If you are dealing in certain specialty areas, such as real estate, probate, corporate, and so forth, you do not necessarily want to contact only firms handling those specialties. Specialty firms usually have sufficient staff and would not require outside help on a daily or weekly basis. They may need help during vacations or in the event of illness or a leave of absence. The smaller firms, who do not handle specific specialty areas on a daily basis, are usually the firms that need your help and your expertise. There are also smaller firms who handle many different areas of law and who would profit by contracting with you to provide backup to their present staff.

The point is, you must try to talk with as many different firms as possible in order to know who needs your services.

While you are marketing your services and becoming familiar with the needs of the legal community in your area, you can also gather information to help you decide if there are certain areas of law you wish to pursue and certain areas you feel you do not care to handle.

As you interview different firms, your list will change. You will add to and subtract from that list until you feel you have a workable list of attorneys to whom you will advertise and market your services.

From your interviews you will come to understand the different needs of particular firms. You will learn what is needed in the geographic area in which you work and can tailor your business accordingly. Are the firms looking for help with litigation, with real estate, with probate work? Do you have expertise in those areas? Can you obtain that expertise? Can you discern what is needed so that you fill the gap and become not only useful but necessary? You will learn to adopt skills that are needed and eliminate those that are not. You will learn which firms will be most interested in hiring a freelance paralegal and pursue relationships with those firms. You may develop a specialty that is needed that you never considered before. As you perfect your business skills, a sense of self will evolve, a sense of what must be done to accomplish your goals. Perhaps this means ignoring the large firms and only dealing with very small firms, perhaps only sole practitioners. Use whatever works for you in your area. You must be ready and willing to change, to adopt change, and anticipate changes in market areas. It is very different to have a business in the suburbs than it is in the city. Just the sheer numbers of attorneys in a city might overwhelm the paralegal practicing in a suburban town. Tailor your own specific needs to the external landscape.

§ 5.8   Survey Questionnaire

Another method of testing the market is mailing out a short survey questionnaire. This may bring only limited results and could be costly, depending on how large a geographical area with which you are concerned. However, if you want to test the market in a smaller area, it would be advantageous to send this survey to prospective clients with a simple checklist of questions that could be answered very quickly—nothing elaborate. The questions would be framed to help you understand if there is a need for your services and what services are needed. Sample questions are:

1. Do you employ paralegals in your firm?

2. If so, in which areas of substantive law do most paralegals practice?

3. Have you ever used the services of an outside paralegal service?

4. If you were understaffed, would you consider using an outside paralegal service?

5. What specific paralegal services would most interest you?

6. Do you contract with an outside paralegal service at the present time?

Understand that you will receive a very small rate of return on the questionnaires, but whatever feedback you receive, will be helpful. Be creative; think of a way to insure a reply, such as prepaid envelopes or a foldover with prepaid postage. The questions must be short, simple, direct, and easy to answer. They should not require deep thinking. Most of the questions will be answered when first read, on impulse and immediately mailed.

§ 5.9 Advertising

Unless you are fortunate enough to be so busy that you need not ever think about new clients, advertising becomes an important part of your budget and financial planning. You must let your potential clients know you are there. You know what they say, "It pays to advertise."

Although freelance legal assistants have a small market share from which to draw, you still must market yourself in order to keep your business viable. You may have a good client list, however, you never know when an office for whom you have been handling foreclosure matters will employ a full-time paralegal knowledgeable in your field. Perhaps the firm for whom you have been handling real estate closings will employ a legal secretary, or a paralegal who prepares real estate files, and your services will no longer be needed. This happens quite often and when it does, that client must be replaced in order to keep your business lucrative. The best way of advertising your services is by word of mouth; one attorney tells another of your services. Be candid with your attorney clients; ask them to recommend you to friends and associates. If they are happy with your services, they will. When this does occur, be sure to properly thank them and let them know you appreciate the thought and consideration. Ask your suppliers, vendors who deal with attorneys if they know of any attorney who is short-staffed, who might need additional paralegal services. Again, if a recommendation does come, be sure to properly thank your source.

Through hard work you aspire to make your business unique. It is important to communicate that uniqueness to your potential clients so that they will think of you and your services. You may accomplish this in several ways. Consider the following:

- Does your business have a name?
- Is that name easy to remember?
- Is the name always printed in same way on letterheads, billing, brochures, and so forth?
- Do you have a logo?
- Do you use your logo wherever possible?
- Is your address always clear and consistent?
- Is your phone always answered politely, in a friendly way, with the name of your business?

If you have answered most of the above questions with a yes, then you are on your way in establishing an image for your business.[5]

There are several different ways of advertising your services to the local bar.

State Law Journal

I have included (at **Form 5–6**) in this section a sample ad that I ran in the *New Jersey Law Journal* when I started my business. This is a journal published throughout the state. The ad appeared four times for maximum exposure. In terms of business gained it was not very successful. My experience has been that attorneys are hesitant to use someone they don't know. If one attorney tells another attorney about your services, it is the best form of advertising there is.

Local Bar Association

Many local bar associations publish their own newsletters and they publish advertisements. This is less expensive than the *Law Journal* and more meaningful since you get your name across in your own area. This is a much more important way of advertising. Your name will become familiar to the attorneys in your specific geographic location. They are more apt to browse through their local bar newsletter than through state law journals.

You may also consider preparing a seminar for your local bar association on the "proper utilization of legal assistant services", or the "cost effectiveness of legal assistants," or "fee recovery and the legal assistant." There are a number of topics that will be interesting to members of the bar. In working with your local bar association, you will be promoting your company and your services.

---

[5] Sandra Linville Dean, How to Advertise, A Handbook for Small Business (1980).

FORM 5–6
SAMPLE AD

INDEPENDENT PARALEGAL
SERVICES FOR ATTORNEYS

DOROTHY SECOL, CLA
Certified Legal Assistant

Services available in areas of: Litigation - Probate
Real Estate - Corporate - Legal Research - Investigation

Including Document Organization/Review/Preparation

Services performed on an hourly basis in my office or your's

FOR INFORMATION CALL: (201) 542-0711

MIDLANTIC NATIONAL BANK BLDG.
Highway 35 & Wyckoff Road, Eatontown, N.J. 07724

Local Newspaper

Advertising in your local newspaper can be sporadic due to your limited market of only attorneys. However, in a local area or a smaller town, it is a good way for attorneys to recognize and become familiar with your name. An inexpensive way of advertising is through the community newspapers that circulate throughout suburban areas. They don't charge as much for advertising and reach the people in your immediate area.

Direct Mailing

I feel this to be the best form of advertising. Attorneys receiving this information from you may suddenly think of a file they need you for, or will need you for in the future. It is also an excellent way of keeping your name visible. Your mailings should be well thought out, artfully done, and indicative of your professionalism. The brochure contained in this chapter is used in our mailings as well as the letter and résumé included in § **5.3.**

I have also included a mailing that was printed on fluorescent paper—bright yellow, bright red, or orange—meant to be eye-catching. See **Form 5–7.** Every so often I send out the flyer just to remind my clients that I am available. I have also included a mailing to prospective attorneys on the same fluorescent paper with a discount coupon included for first time clients. See **Form 5–8.** It was an idea I decided to try and I only sent out a few. How did I do? No takers! But you have to keep trying.

FORM 5–7
SAMPLE FLYER

<u>REAL ESTATE</u>

<u>PROBATE</u>

<u>CORPORATE</u>

<u>PERSONAL INJURY</u>

Do you need assistence in these areas? Are you suffering from backload and overload?

PARALEGAL SERVICES can help!

Our services are cost efficient, practical and productive.

We do not take up space in your office. You do not have to supply us with furniture, supplies, salaries, vacation pay, health benefits, etc. You pay us an hourly rate for work completed except in the case of real estate which is a flat fee.

Through the use of our services, you can effectively reduce your costs.

> *We conclude that given the appropriate instructions and supervision, paralegals, whether as employees or independent contractors, are valuable and necessary members of an attorney's team in the effective and efficient practice of law.* <u>In re Opinion 24 of the Committee on the Unauthorized Practice of Law</u> 128 N.J. 114 (1992).

PLEASE CALL FOR FURTHER INFORMATION. A LIST OF ALL SERVICES PROVIDED IS ENCLOSED.

FORM 5–8
SAMPLE FLYER WITH COUPON

REAL ESTATE

PROBATE

CORPORATE

PERSONAL INJURY

Do you need assistence in these areas? Are you suffering from backload and overload?

PARALEGAL SERVICES can help!

Our services are **cost efficient**, practical and productive.

We do not take up space in your office. You do not have to supply us with furniture, supplies, salaries, vacation pay, health benefits, etc. You pay us an hourly rate for work completed except in the case of real estate which is a flat fee.

Through the use of our services, you can effectively **reduce** your costs.   Volume discounts given.

> *We conclude that given the appropriate instructions and supervision, paralegals, whether as employees or independent contractors, are valuable and necessary members of an attorney's team in the effective and efficient practice of law.* In re Opinion 24 of the Committee on the Unauthorized Practice of Law 128 N.J. 114 (1992).

PLEASE   CALL   FOR   FURTHER INFORMATION.   A   LIST   OF   ALL SERVICES   PROVIDED   IS   ENCLOSED.

THIS COUPON IS GOOD FOR
FIFTY and no/100 ($50.00)-----------------
toward services rendered by Dorothy Secol, CLA

Miscellaneous Advertising

Use the yellow pages of the telephone book. Ask them to provide a heading under "Paralegal Services" or "Legal Assistant Service," and list your name. In this way when an attorney uses the book, the attorney may see your name.

Have stationery and business cards made. Your stationery is another form of advertising together with your business card, that should match your stationery. Many people don't realize that the printed word leaves a lasting impression. If attorneys are impressed by the originality of your letterhead, they will remember your name, even if they don't have anything for you at the moment. They will associate your letterhead with you. Decide on the type style you prefer, but be clear and professional. Forego a gimmicky letterhead. You want to be taken seriously. You also may want to place a logo on the stationery and on your business cards. Speak to several printers about the mechanics and cost of having a logo made, the quality of paper you could use, the type style for your letterhead and business cards, and whether you will use a less expensive envelope printed on a cheaper grade of paper for returns to your office so that you don't have to waste your good envelopes. See **Forms 5–9** and **5–10.**

Upon the opening of your office you will want to have announcements printed to send to your clients and prospective clients. This is another way of letting them know your location. Formally printed announcements will create a good impression and convey the feeling of professionalism. If you move your office from one location to another, print announcements of the new address.

When Peggy and I moved from our first office into our second, we decided not only to send announcements, but to sponsor an open house. We sent invitations to our clients announcing our move, and invited them to join us for refreshments. We were proud of our new office and wanted everyone to see it. It worked out very well. Not only did we get a chance to meet with our attorney clients, but they got a chance to socialize with each other.

Join community and civic groups such as the Chamber of Commerce, Rotary Club, Kiwanis Club, and Lion's Club and make yourself visible. Many of these organizations have breakfast or lunch meetings. You never know when you will be seated next to a prospective client. Participate in group functions and exhibits in order to keep your company name on everyone's lips. Join professional associations and participate in seminars. Participate in community functions where business cards are collected and exchanged or posted.

Participating in and giving seminars is another form of advertising. The local paralegal organizations hold seminars at their monthly meetings, at their annual conventions, and at the state bar conventions. The national organizations also give seminars on a frequent basis. Let the organizations know you are willing to speak on your area of substantive law. Become involved in

FORM 5–9
SAMPLE LETTERHEAD

Dorothy Secol, CLA
Certified Legal Assistant

100 Main Street
Allenhurst, New Jersey 07711
(908) 517-8555
Fax: (908) 517-8545

Independent Paralegal Services for Attorneys

FORM 5–10
SAMPLE BUSINESS CARD

Dorothy Secol, CLA
Certified Legal Assistant

100 Main Street
Allenhurst, New Jersey 07711
(908) 517 8555
Fax (908) 517 8545

Independent Paralegal Services for Attorneys

speaking to student paralegal organizations at your local colleges. Students always want to know what is prevalent in the profession. Keeping them current is an excellent way for you to practice your public speaking and keep abreast of changes in the profession.

Many companies have experienced growth due to clever and steady advertising. You must let people know you are out there. Let them know how you can help them and how your services will be beneficial to them. To this end perhaps you will need to contact a professional in the field of market research who can help you promote and advertise your business. Those paralegals living in large cities will naturally have more of a client base than those in suburban areas where offices are more spread out and are not as populated with attorneys.

Many small businesses create a logo or identifying symbol for their names so that people will remember them. Large firms spend thousands of dollars creating corporate identification. A clever symbol might enhance the probability that your name will be remembered and with it, the availability of your services.

Free advertising can be obtained through publicity releases to your local newspaper. These releases should be written to create a favorable image and impart a good impression of your company. If you attend a seminar on a specific subject, if you are offering a new service, if you are employing the use of new and state-of-the-art equipment, give your newspaper a publicity release regarding it; perhaps they will want to do a story on your company in the future.

At holiday time we send gifts to our clients. In this way we can thank them for their patronage during the past year and, of course, keep our name out there as a reminder of our services. You can give gifts that will last throughout the year and that will keep your name in front of them, such as pocket calendars printed with a logo of your name, address, and telephone number, ballpoint pens, hand-held calculators—all printed with your business logo.

The best advertising technique we can all employ is to use our clients to advertise for us. Our clients know our services; they are grateful for them, for the fact we are there when they need us. Ask your clients to spread the word. If they don't have any work for you when you are slow, ask them to tell their friends and colleagues about your service. Use word of mouth advertising; it's free!

According to Jerry R. Wilson, in *Word-of-Mouth Marketing,* a client is the continuing loyal customer who keeps coming back because he or she believes in your ability to consistently solve problems or to meet his or her needs.[6]

Once you have cultivated a client list, use that list to gain new clients. Don't be afraid to talk to your clients, explain to them you are geared up to do a larger volume of business and do they have any suggestions, do they know of anyone who might be interested in your services? You might also talk to your suppliers, vendors, and investigative people who work for other attorneys, asking them to mention your services. If a client does recommend you to another attorney, be sure to properly thank them. Write a note or send a little remembrance.

When one of my clients recommends my services to another attorney, I send a single red rose in a bud vase with a thank you note. There are many ways you can let someone know you are grateful that they are thinking of you.

You should always go above and beyond what is expected of you in any particular assignment. This will insure that your services will be sought the next time that attorney needs a project completed. You want clients to think of your services immediately when they have extra work, when someone in their office is leaving, when they are overcommitted and need help.

---

6 Jerry R. Wilson, Word-of-Mouth Marketing, John Wiley & Sons, Inc. (New York 1991).

According to an article published in the Harvard Business Review in 1990, "Companies can boost profits by almost 100% by retaining just 5% more of their customers." This means you can double your profits with just a five percent increase in retention. It is more important to take care of your existing clients, than to spend a good deal of time and money trying to solicit new business.[7]

With this in mind, it is very important to know your client's office staff, work with them, cultivate a relationship with the secretaries and with the in-house paralegals so that there is no resentment towards you. As an outsider, there may be some hostility at first from the in-house office staff. You must do whatever you can to stop any hard feelings before they solidify. Remember the names of the office staff, be courteous to them, ask their opinions, ask their help and their advice. Once you win over the office staff, there may be times when they are overwhelmed with work and they will ask the attorney to call you and ask you to work on a particular project. Office staff can be a major ally in producing work for you. It doesn't hurt to keep a file for each office, or a database in your computer with the names of the office staff, their birthdays, children's names, short important bits of information, that you can look over before going to the office. It is important to recognize people; it makes them feel valued and it makes you a little more special in their eyes.

§ 5.10   Pro Bono Work

Pro bono work, or working without financial compensation, is one aspect of law with which we are all familiar. In many states, lawyers are mandated to fulfill a certain number of hours annually doing pro bono work. Paralegals, through the county bar associations or through their paralegal organizations, also perform pro bono work.

Working without financial compensation may be difficult at times for the freelance paralegal struggling to make ends meet. However, it can be very rewarding. It also serves to keep your name in the public mainstream. Anything positive that you do to keep your name and your business constantly in the public's eye is advertising.

Pro bono work may in done in various ways:

• Seek an appointment to a juvenile conference committee in your municipality. These committees, although called different names in different locations, are set up through the court system to deal with local children under the age of 18, who are charged with minor infractions of the law.

---

[7] Gene Dailey, Secrets of a Successful Entrepreneur (1993).

- Another appointment you may seek, if it is mandated by statute in your area, is serving as a mediator. Mediation has become the way of the '90s, not only in local municipal courts, but also in the family courts and in the law divisions. A mediator helps two people having a problem come to a successful resolution of that problem without going to a formal court hearing. The court system will train you to be an effective mediator. See § **5.10.**

- Volunteer your services on a weekend, or on a day when you are not busy to help the legal services office in your area. You are always dealing with attorneys who could become prospective clients and are filling a desperate need our country has for the delivery of effective legal services.

The Standing Committee on Legal Assistants of the American Bar Association has established a subcommittee on legal assistant pro bono activity. The committee, chaired by Robert Yegge, Esq. has four goals:

1. To prepare for submission and review of the full Standing Committee, of a policy paper defining the appropriate relationship of the legal assistant to the clients in the pro bono programs, including the issues of malpractice responsibility and coverage

2. To compile a list of known pro bono programs involving legal assistants, geographic areas, cross-indexing descriptions of services by type of sponsoring entity, and mode of providing services

3. To provide training guidelines for legal assistants

4. To compile a bibliography of manuals, articles, handbooks, and videotapes as a resource.

There are certain personal qualities you will want to consider before deciding on what type of pro bono with which you wish to become involved:

- Do you wish to become deeply involved in someone's life on an ongoing basis?

- Do you prefer to do paperwork, assist in a legal services office, assist with an intake at a clinic?

- Do you want a long term commitment?

- How much are you willing to work directly with people?

- How much time will you have to give?[8]

Complementary Dispute Resolution (CDR) programs have become an integral part of the superior court and municipal court. These programs are

---

[8] Frances Whiteside, *Pro Bono Publico,* Legal Assistant Today, Mar.–Apr. 1993. James Publishing, Inc. Reprinted with permission.

intended to enhance the quality and performance of the judicial process. Those programs conducted under judicial supervision as well as guidelines and directives from the supreme court, may include:

Settlement proceedings—parties resolve their differences by voluntary agreement

Mediation proceedings—a neutral third party acts facilitate resolution of the dispute by parties

Arbitration proceedings—a neutral third party or panel considers evidence proffered by the parties and renders an arbitration award that may be binding or nonbinding, as provided by statute, rules, or the parties' prior agreement.

For the past year I have been a mediator for the Ocean Township Municipal Court. I was appointed to this position by the Superior Court of New Jersey, Office of the Court Administrator, which oversees the program. For this role, I received 16 hours of training by the Superior Court, and will have to maintain four hours of CLE per year to maintain my status as of mediator.

The municipal courts recognize that minor disputes between parties with ongoing relationships, (neighbors, individuals in a community with an ongoing relationship) do not always require formal judicial resolution. The Municipal Court Mediation programs are designed to remove these cases from the court system for voluntary submission to informal mediation and conciliation.

New Jersey Court Rule 7:3-2 provides that if a complaint is filed charging an offense that may constitute minor disputes, a notice may issue to the person making the charge and to the persons charged requesting their appearance before a person or program designated by the court to provide mediation under Rule 1:40-7. Some of the minor offenses which may be referred to the municipal court are:

Simple assaults (Noninjury)

Trespass

Obstruction (harassment)

Maintaining a nuisance

Harassment

Disorderly persons

Smoking in public

Interference with transportation

Dog and animal complaints

Shoplifting

Malicious destruction of property

Noise complaints

Other minor neighborhood disputes involving merchant/customer, land-lord/tenant, property and family disputes.

Mediation was also designed to help in the family court by resolving dif-ferences that arise between parents with regard to their responsibilities to their children. In family court, the purpose of mediation is to establish a line of communication in which each parent can express their needs and ulti-mately provide a positive plan for the future rearing of their children. Agreements reached through mediation usually last longer and have a higher success rate because it is the parents themselves who create the agreement and are therefore more likely to adhere to it. When parents, working with a mediator, have a hand in making the decisions and developing a program of parenting, they are less likely to sabotage the plan.

In family court, the mediator's role usually consists of the following duties:

- Meeting with the attorneys and/or reviewing the pleadings and parties' information forms so issues can be identified and solutions considered.
- Consulting with the parties individually and/or jointly to discuss the issues and possible resolution of the issues.
- Talking with the children, identifying their needs, and helping them understand how mediation will affect them. The children will feel as if their opinions matter and it will ease some of the tension and pressure felt when their parents fight.
- Helping the parents reach an agreement that benefits the children and incorporates the needs of the parents. The mediator can also confirm each parent's position.
- Putting the terms of the agreement in writing and distributing copies to each attorney, who will then prepare the appropriate order for signature of the parties and the judge.[9]

While mediation is opening new avenues for dispute resolution, it is also opening new doors for legal assistants. Professional mediation services are specializing in different areas of law, such as commercial and business dis-pute resolution. Some law firms are opening mediation services adjunct to

---

[9] Linda Massey, *Preparing Your Client for Mediation,* Legal Assistant Today, Mar.–Apr. 1993. James Publishing, Inc. Reprinted with permission.

their law offices, while other mediation centers are funded by the state, or funded through private resources.

What are the qualities needed to be a mediator?

Be a good listener.

Be able to focus on the issues, cut to the heart of the problem.

Be able to get the parties talking in order to resolve the dispute.

CHAPTER 6

BUSINESS ORGANIZATION

§ 6.1   Choices

You have determined that you are going into business and you have engaged in market research with regard to the firms in your area, their needs, and where you plan to target your advertising. You have studied aspects of looking and acting like a professional and of projecting that image to the world around you. It is time to set up your office.

The first consideration will, of course, be financial. When starting out, you will want to keep your costs to a minimum. If you can rent space in a building where there are law offices or even rent space in an attorney's office, that would be an ideal situation. There you would be able to use the facilities and equipment such as the copy machine, fax machine, and library for a nominal charge. This would be arranged with the attorneys from whom you are renting.

The other alternative is to rent space independent of other law offices and set up your own office starting from scratch. For financial reasons, you will probably want to begin by renting space and sharing equipment with attorneys (or other small businesses). As you grow, and your clientele list grows, you will expand and relocate on your own. At that time you will have to make some decisions about furniture, equipment, a library, and supplies. If you do decide to rent space with an attorney, you will still need certain equipment, furniture, and supplies.

At first you will have some time to visit your attorney client's offices, and it will be economical for you to use their libraries, their forms, and so forth. As you grow, however, you will not have the time to circulate to pick up forms, nor will you have the time to go from office to office to use library facilities. At that point, it means stocking your office with the supplies and equipment necessary for you to do your best work in the best environment.

As described in § **3.3,** I started out in a very small office. I had a desk and chair, a typewriter, another chair, one filing cabinet, and a telephone. I used the photocopy machine in the attorney's office and kept track of my copies. I also used the fax machine and kept track of those copies. As they already had kitchen facilities, I did not need a coffee machine or refrigerator. As my client list grew and I was able to generate more business, I was able to hire a part-time secretary. (Nine hours a week!) I moved out of the very small office into a small office just large enough to accommodate my desk, my secretary's desk, and a filing cabinet. I bought a computer and a printer. I was automated!

About two years later, I came into contact with another paralegal hoping to freelance and we decided to share space. I then hired a secretary for 24 hours a week, bought another computer and printer, more furniture, telephone equipment, and so forth. Today we have expanded to the point mentioned previously in § **3.3.** When I first started I was not sure where this business would lead, how fast it would grow, or if it would grow. Today I occasionally have to hire more personnel to get the job done. I don't feel, at this point, that I want to contain my growth potential. This is a conscious decision. You must decide whether you will be content working alone on a few cases at a time, or whether you will have employees and take on as much as you can. My client list now totals about 30 to 35 attorneys in different areas of law and I employ as many assistants as needed to perform the work.

§ 6.2 Negotiating a Lease

Look to rent space that will fit your present needs as well as allow for expansion. If, for financial reasons, you feel you want to start out small, and consider moving up at a later date, that's certainly acceptable.

There are several factors to consider in renting office space:

Availability to clients

Availability to library facilities, the court house, municipal offices

Parking facilities

Safety factor—Will you be working at night? Is the area well-lighted?

Location. Do you mind being isolated away from the mainstream of a town if necessary?

Use of facilities after hours.

Many landlords want renters to sign a five-year lease. It is in your best interest to sign a lease for no more than a two- or three-year period with an option to rent for an additional two or three years. At the time of the signing of the lease, be certain that the terms for rent for the option periods are included.

Clarify who pays for the utilities. Check to see if janitorial services are included as well as maintenance and repairs. Will there be special assessments for taxes, insurance, and so forth?

There are different types of leases. One lease you may be asked to sign is called a gross lease. This lease includes all of the above items. Another type is the net lease. This type requires the tenant to contribute to the real estate taxes in addition to the rent. A net-net lease requires a base amount for the rent, together with an amount to pay for real estate taxes, insurance, and all operating costs for the building, including maintenance and repairs. It is possible, however to write a limit into the lease addressing your responsibility for these items. You may even want to include a clause that would allow you to cancel the lease if the costs exceed a certain amount.

Will the landlord modify the space to your needs? In some cases, the landlord will renovate the premises to suit your needs in order for you to move in, and in other cases, the landlord will renovate and add the cost of the renovation to your monthly rent payments. When you settle on a monthly figure, ensure that all costs are included. Try to negotiate some incentives into the lease. If you have to paint the office and do any renovation yourself, ask for free or reduced rent until you actually move in. Perhaps you can defer a portion of rent to replace worn items, such as carpeting or linoleum.

If a security deposit is required, clarify how much is due and when it will be returned to you. Inquire as to whether the security deposit will earn interest while it is being held by the landlord.

In buildings where several independent businesses share office suites, your monthly rent could also include secretarial services, the use of conference rooms, security systems, garbage collection, and so forth.

What if you go out of business? What happens to the lease? Depending on the classification of your company, whether sole proprietorship, partnership, or corporation, you will probably be asked to personally sign or guarantee the lease. When that happens, you will be responsible for the balance of the term of the lease. Be sure you have an option to sublet the lease. You may also include a buy-out provision in the lease should you choose to relocate or in case you go out of business.

In the event that you would like to stay in the same building, will your landlord offer a provision for rolling over your lease to a larger facility should you need it?[1]

It is in your best interest to investigate before deciding which office you are going to rent so that you will know what is available to you and how you can negotiate the lease.

---

[1] Gene Dailey, Secrets of a Successful Entrepreneur (1993).

At this point you should decide exactly how you intend to organize and set up your office procedures.

§ 6.3   Office Setup

Your first consideration, as discussed in § **6.2,** is signing a lease for this space of your very own. Do you sign in your individual name or do you incorporate? That question is best answered by your accountant and/or your attorney. Each case is different and requires different considerations. Everyone starting out in business has financial considerations and tax consequences. So too will you. One of your first steps will be discussing your venture with other professionals. Again, your individual needs will dictate the kind of space you need.

Are you working alone?

Do you anticipate secretarial help?

How much equipment do you need and how much room do you need for it?

Do your attorney clients and/or their clients require access to you?

You will also have to decide exactly how you intend to organize the physical set up of your office. As you grow and take on more work, you will change until you find the right order or scheme of things that work for you. However, in the beginning, you must have a plan.

Determine how much space you will have and plan carefully before purchasing your furniture, filing cabinets, and office equipment. You will want to designate areas to perform basic office tasks, process mail, file, and use the fax machine and copy machine.

Create an air of professionalism in the office for your clients and yourself. Minimize personal items. Make sure you have proper lighting and adequate power for lighting and other equipment needs.

Buy or rent good furniture. Have comfortable chairs and ensure that your computer keyboards are positioned at the proper angle.

§ 6.4   Equipment

You are now ready to furnish this wonderful office. Where do you start?

Because many of you have been in the legal field for a years before deciding to go into business independently, you have a fairly good idea of what you need to efficiently run an office. You may also have accumulated sets of model forms, handbooks, and trade books. If your particular state has an Institute for Continuing Legal Education (ICLE), the handbooks it offers are invaluable. They are low in cost and are revised often. You can purchase a book from them on nearly any topic whether it be civil trial preparation, real estate closings, foreclosures, and so forth. These books also include forms. Obtain a copy of your court rules as a minimum. A set of state statutes is also important in any area of law. In New Jersey, a set of books is published by West Publishing Co. called *New Jersey Practice Series.* These books are invaluable and contain forms and information on all areas of law. Try to purchase used books in your area of interest. If your specialty is bankruptcy, you would need books on that subject, and if your specialty is family law, again you would find books on that subject. These resources become very important to you now. Once you start working for different attorneys, you need to become familiar with each individual style of writing and the forms used. Adapt to those forms. This is very beneficial because you will be adding to your ever growing library. A list of items to be considered in your office follows:

Critical items:

- Furniture, that is, desk, chair, chairs for clients, secretarial furniture
- Telephone equipment
- Answering machine
- Copy machine
- Computer equipment, printer
- Typewriter
- Adding machine/calculator
- Stationery
- Supplies, including but not limited to, paper clips, pencils, pens, staplers, stapler removers, scissors, telephone message pads, scratch pads, erasers, white-out, copy paper, plain white paper, envelopes, typewriter ribbons, adding machine tapes, file folders, fasteners, typewriter ribbons, toner for the copy machine, legal pads, Rolodex, index cards, calendars, diary, (preferably a *Lawyer's Diary*), bookkeeping supplies, billing supplies, postage, and certified return receipt cards
- A set of court rules.

Optional items:

- Fax machine (to some a necessity)
- Dictating equipment/transcriber, tapes
- Set of state statutes—practice series books, subscription to state law journal.

§ 6.5   Leasing versus Buying

Whether you decide to lease or buy, you will need to investigate and research all products being considered. Above all, the equipment you are contemplating must fit your individual needs. Whether it is a typewriter, a telephone system, or a photo machine, your projected use and your expectations must be taken into consideration.

In the *Equipment Leasing Market,* Report Number 382 (1976), Frost and Sullivan, Inc. has undertaken a comprehensive survey of the equipment leasing industry. This survey supplies data using sources including trade journals, United States Department of Commerce reports, Survey of Current Business, The Conference Board, annual reports, and data supplied by industry personnel.

The report separates industry into major categories: computer equipment, office equipment and retail store fixtures, machine tools, communications and electronics equipment, and so forth.

When the survey was done in 1976, IBM computers were the dominant force in this market. Lessors are offering total computer packages including software programs.

The office equipment and retail store fixtures market called for items ranging from $2,000 to $17,000. Service is another important aspect of the leasing program. The need for service and the size of the lease prompted the growth of many leasing companies.[2]

Equipment to consider leasing would include typewriters, computers, photocopy machines, printers, fax machines, furniture, telephone equipment, or dictating equipment. There are pros and cons to leasing or buying. Consult with your accountant and/or attorney as to your individual needs.

When leasing:

* Large sums of money do not need to be invested.
* Service on the product is assured.
* Replacement is usually not a problem if something goes wrong with the equipment.
* The option of updating equipment due to changes in technology is yours.
* Leased equipment used in business may be deducted as an expense on your income tax return.
* Option of buying equipment at the end of the lease exists.
* If the life of the equipment is short, you will be better off with a lease.

When buying:

---

[2] 1976 Equipment Leasing Market, Frost & Sullivan, Mountain View, Calif.

- You have a tax advantage in writing off depreciation.
- You own the equipment; you have equity.
- You have trade-in value when you want to sell.
- You pay less in the long run for the equipment; you will not be paying interest on the lease.
- You can always sell if you are unhappy with the product, whereas you would have to wait until the end of the lease to replace equipment.
- If the equipment will endure for many years, a purchase may be better than a lease.

There are also certain factors to evaluate when considering leasing equipment:

- Is there a high risk the equipment will become obsolete before the end of its useful life?
- Is the equipment only needed for a short period of time?
- Is it important to maximize available capital?
- Technical, administrative, or other nonfinancial equipment-related services that are not internally available can be easily secured from the leasing company.
- If you borrow money to buy equipment, you will pay high interest rates.
- Can the tax benefits resulting from ownership be used?
- Will the equipment have a poor market value at the end of its term of use? [3]

It is also possible to rent equipment as needed. This would apply to any equipment needed for a special project, such as a scanner to scan and print material into your computer. Without the scanner you would have to manually input the information, which (depending on the quantity of material) could take days. The advantages to renting are:

You only pay for equipment when needed.

You can rent exactly what you need—no more.

You will not be responsible for major maintenance if the equipment breaks.

There are also disadvantages of which you should be aware:

You will have to schedule pickup and delivery of the rented equipment.

Equipment may not be available when you need it.

---

[3] Richard M. Contino, *Handbook of Equipment Leasing* (1989).

Hourly costs of rental may be so high it may preclude renting the equipment.

With regard to the purchase or lease of a photocopy machine, remember that the finished product you send out (or give to the attorney to send out) must be perfect. That means clean, legible copies and that almost translates to a photocopy machine that has a dual page copy mode, reduction and expansion of text, margin adjustment, automatic stapling, photo imagining and of course, sorting, grouping, and automatic paper feed. If you have to make ten copies of a pleading and you have to hand sort, separate, and staple, time and money are lost. You can charge for photocopies. If the attorney's office were completing the papers, they would make the photocopies, record the number of copies made, and charge the client's account. In your case agree with the attorney on the sum of money to be charged for photocopies.

Whether you decide to lease or purchase a copy machine, negotiate such items as toner, paper, and drums. They can be written into the lease or purchase agreement.

As mentioned in § **7.5** photocopies are reimbursable items; keep track of copies made. Keeping track manually by recording the number of copies for each file is one way to accomplish this. Another method would be to use a copier control device. Equitrac Controller makes such a device for a small office. One other company to consider is Infotech. These systems can also track cost areas other than photocopies. They can track the cost of telephone calls, word processing, LEXIS charges, and computer time.

Inquire as to toner recycling for your copy machine. This will help keep costs down. You can also purchase recycled cartridges for your printers. There are companies in your local area who recycle the cartridges and their names usually may be found in the yellow pages of telephone directories.

All of this equipment may be purchased secondhand. This is an excellent way of starting to build your office.

One piece of equipment to consider leasing is the Pitney-Bowes postage meter and digital scale. You might want to consider the cost, convenience, and professional appearance of the postage meter, not to mention the inconvenience of licking stamps and envelopes. The major benefit of the postage meter is that you can print out the exact postage you need. A very good argument for the use of this equipment is the fact that you will know exactly how much your letter or package weighs and you can therefore put the correct amount of postage on it. If you are using stamps, it is difficult to keep stamps in every denomination and so you tend to put too much postage on your letters. For instance, if you are sending a envelope that requires 98¢ in postage, you might put on four 29¢ stamps that total $1.16. With this letter alone you have overpaid 18¢. This may not seem like much, but multiplied by dozens of oversize envelopes per week, it adds up. The digital scale is the most accurate measure of weight and you are therefore saving money by using the correct and exact amount of postage. There are new postage meters for small offices that track postage by accounts. In this way you can charge back the cost of postage for each outgoing envelope as it is being processed. Many of the postage scales (even for small offices) are programmed to set the meter when you weigh a piece, thereby eliminating the manual step of setting the postage yourself.

A postage meter and electronic scale rent for less than $25 per month (or a postage meter alone for about $15). Get a flat-rate to ensure the cost won't go up simply because you are no longer a first-time user.[4]

Postage costs are reimbursable. If you do not have automatic tracking for letters, it is important to maintain a record by the postage meter so that you may record the amount of postage spent for each case. The record may contain the attorney's name and under the name, the case, or file number, and the amount of postage paid daily. In this way, at the end of the month, you can take the information for billing purposes, and file the sheets with the information in a file or folder marked "Postage Billing."

Telephone equipment is another area in which a decision needs to be made as to buying versus leasing.

Today there are many features to include in your telephone system: conferencing, privacy lines, automatic redial, speed dialing, and much more.

Until the past several years, telephone equipment was leased by the telephone company. One enticing aspect of renting this equipment is the upgrade to newer equipment at the end of the lease term. The high rental cost (including the many features you may want or need) and the lack of ownership of the equipment may determine whether you will want to purchase the equipment or lease with an option to purchase. Again, this is a subject best discussed with your professionals.

Determine the number of telephone lines you will need, including a line for a fax machine and/or a modem. How quickly will your business grow? Will it expand? Will you need more lines? Do you need a telephone jack in or near your file area as well as at each desk?

Another consideration will be a telephone answering machine. When you have an appointment out of the office, at the end of the day, and on weekends have your answering machine on. People are past the stage where no one speaks to the machine. Everybody uses answering machines. Still, some offices prefer to use answering services. There are those who still feel clients would like to hear a human voice. While this may be true, the messages received on the answering machine will be more accurate as they are recorded while spoken. With the advent of voice mail, even the phone company is answering calls for businesses. There are any number of choices

---

[4] Michael L. Vujnovich, *Time for a Postage Meter?*, 11 Office Systems 52 Apr. 1994.

available to receive your messages. It is important to have an answering system that allows you to obtain messages when you are out of the office.

One feature that callers associate with big business is the message board. We recognize it as, "Press 1 for more information; press 2 for a list of options," and so on. Many don't realize that the telephone company offers this service to small businesses.

Another service that telephone companies offer is a service called ISDN (integrated service digital network). This is a method of connecting to outside services without a modem and of transfering information at far greater speeds than are possible using a modem. One of the reasons for the popularity of this service is that small businesses use it to tap into on-line databases.[5]

There are fax machines on the market that double as telephones. At the flick of a switch, the fax machine becomes a telephone and vice-versa. If you are not sure how quickly you will expand and if you suspect that your office arrangement will be temporary, it is possible to buy or lease a fax machine with telephone capabilities. Some fax machines even have answering machines built in and dual lines so that one line can be used for the telephone and one line for the fax machine.

In addition, decide whether you need a thermal paper fax or a plain paper fax. One of the drawbacks to the thermal paper fax is that the paper is not long lasting and constantly curls. Personally, if I intend to keep a fax received on a thermal paper fax, I make a photocopy of it, throw away the thermal paper (which probably has curled up in a ball) and file the plain paper copy. One consideration to be made is the time and extra paper spent in photocopying the fax paper in order to make a lasting copy or even to send it to someone else. If you settle for a thermal paper fax machine, be sure it has a paper cutter so that each copy you receive represents one page, rather than receiving many pages all attached as one long fax that needs to be separated. This can be bothersome and time-consuming.

You can currently purchase a thermal paper fax with a paper cutter for around $350–$500. A plain paper fax, with options, costs between $700–$1,000.

Computers and word processors may be leased or purchased. There are a number of brand name computers being manufactured and a number of generic computers. Naturally, the generic ones are less expensive. Your first consideration is the software you need to use. From there you can choose the computer to support that software. Computers offer a large range of options, including fax cards that transform the computer into a fax machine, modems that allow you to use telephone lines, scanners to facilitate direct input of data from any printed source, a mouse that allows you to move around the screen quickly, and electronic mail.

Small computers, usually called micro-computers, such as the IBM personal computer (PC) are used in most small offices. The larger and more

---

[5] Albert G. Holzinger, *The Right Stuff,* 82 Nation's Business 20, Apr. 1994.

powerful computer is known as the mainframe. These computers will be found only in very large firms since they are expensive and require costly maintenance and upkeep.

Working with a computer will allow you to facilitate your work more quickly. You will be able to accomplish more tasks with a computer than without one and your work product will be neat and cost efficient.

The software that you will need depends on what areas you will be working in, your need for databases, spreadsheets, and word processing. WordPerfect® 5.1 or 6.0 is the software of choice for most offices today. WordPerfect® not only offers a word processing system, but also can be used as a spreadsheet.

How do you choose the right computer equipment?

- Carefully assess your needs and your budget; what do you want and how much can you spend?
- Learn all there is to know about what is available.
- Contact vendors, visit computer stores, ask questions, ask for demonstrations to see how the product works.
- Develop evaluation procedures.
- Make a recommendation based on fulfilling your needs and anticipating future needs and trends. Be sure the equipment you are considering is not outdated by the time it is installed in your office.

For approximately $2,000 you should be able to purchase a 486 system that includes 4MB of RAM which is the minimum you would require for many business programs together with:

- a VL (local bus video) accelerator with at least one megabyte of memory to run a graphics program.
- a 3 1/2 inch disk drive; a SVGA (super video graphics array) monitor that's 14–15 inches in size
- a 200MB or larger disk drive for storage of programs and files.

The disk drive should be preloaded with DOS 6.2, which is the latest version of this operating system software, the current version of 3.1 of Microsoft Corp.'s Windows® graphical user interface (GUI) and at least one business software of your choice.

There are a variety of printers on the market that produce high-quality work for a relatively small outlay of cash. I am most familiar with Hewlett Packard products as I have an HP Desk Jet Plus that I use at home, and a Hewlett Packard HPIIP in the office. I also have an Okidata OL400e printer.

The HP Desk Jet Plus is not a laser printer; however it produces a good quality print and is inexpensive. The paper tray holds 50 pages and can be expanded for legal size paper.

The HPIIP and the OL400e are comparable laser printers. They give you fast four page per minute output at 300 dots per inch resolution and a wide selection of fonts. The OL400e offers four typefaces, (Courier, line printer, Swiss and Dutch) 40 symbol sets, and USPS POSTNET bar codes. A library of font and macro cards is available to expand printing capabilities. The printers have 512 kilobytes of RAM, however you can install four megabytes of additional memory for enhanced graphics printing and down-loading fonts.

The HP Desk Jet Plus can be purchased for under $400. The HPIIP and the OL400e can be purchased for under $600.

More costly is the HPIII laser printer. This printer, which sells for under $1,500, is fast and quiet. The HPIII prints high-quality output up to eight pages per minute with a wide range of media sizes and types, including envelopes, labels, and overhead transparencies. The HPIII also features commands for fully integrated HP-GL/2 vector graphics support, advanced imaging capabilities, and multiple print directions on the same page.

If you decide to lease or buy a computer with a laser printer, it will be possible for you to print your own stationery and envelopes rather than spend the money to have them printed.

If you have several large firms as clients, consider the use of an electronic mail system. This allows your attorney clients to transmit documents to your office. The electronic mail system operates as a service bureau where you would have an electronic mail box in your computer. The attorney's office composes a message by dialing the local telephone number of the system, and then typing in a message. The message is sent to the electronic mail system with your name and address and is held until you dial into the system to pick up your mail.[6]

A good example of a public electronic mail system for legal assistants is NALA Net. NALA members are familiar with the NALA Net facilities which also includes access to legal databases.

The following is a sample of resources written with the small business in mind:

The Office Equipment Advisor by John Derrick. Advice on buying everything from PCs and laser printers to postage meters and shredders. Price: $24.95 from What to Buy for Business, Inc., 1-800-247-2185.

The Small Business Computer Book, A Guide in Plain English by Robert A. Moskowitz. Information on selecting hardware, software and other computing essentials. Price: $19.95 from Upstart Publishing Co., 1-800-235-8866.

---

6 Gary A. Munneke, Law Practice Management (1991).

Tough Times—Tough Tactics by Andrew Johnson. Identifying and finding the proper site for your business and leasing the site as inexpensively as possible. Price: $39.95 from Johnson Commercial Brokerage, 1-800-270-4848.[7]

§ 6.6   Computer Software

The computer software you use can make you efficient, cost-effective, and productive. There is software today for everything—for accounting and bookkeeping, for completing income tax forms, for estate tax returns, for creating wills and powers of attorney. There is real estate software, software to complete closings of title, software for discovery forms, spreadsheets, time management; the list is endless.

WordPerfect® 5.1 and the new 6.0 are the programs that I use for word processing. This software has so many features that it can even be used as a spreadsheet. It performs math functions, creates tables; 6.0 can be used as a desktop publisher and can even create graphics. The obvious benefit of using computers is the ability to sit down to create a form, have it appear before you on the screen, change a few names, addresses, dates, and you have created a new form in less time than it would take to type one-third of that information. And you can do it over and over again. You can also create databases for research and for litigation management, which I will discuss later in this section.

I maintain the statute of limitations list for one law firm. This list records the final date for filing an action on a particular file. For that purpose I created a chart, using the table method (Alt F7) in WordPerfect 5.1. The chart uses headings across the top indicating the file name, file opening date, file number, date of accident, statute of limitations date (SOL), whether the plaintiff is a minor (which would control the SOL date), date complaint was filed, initials of attorney responsible for file, and a small comment box. This way I can keep track of the status of all files at a glance. The chart is reviewed weekly; cases that have been settled are omitted and new cases are added. See **Form 6–1.**

I also use the chart for keeping track of medical bills in personal injury cases. For this chart the headings would be: dates of treatment, name of doctor, amount of bill, amount approved by insurance, amount paid by insurance, balance due. This chart is updated constantly and may be attached to interrogatory answers for a concise list of medical specials. You could also add a column for prescriptions and medical supplies, such as wheelchairs, neck collars, and so forth. See **Form 6–2.**

In conjunction with WordPerfect, I use a program originally called Math Plan®, which is now called Plan Perfect®. Even though WordPerfect has math

---

[7] Albert G. Holzinger, *The Right Stuff,* 82 Nation's Business 23, Apr. 1994.

FORM 6–1

SAMPLE FORM FOR STATUTE OF LIMITATIONS LIST

CLIENT NAME	FILE NO.	FOD	DOA	SOL	MINOR	COMPLAINT FILED	COMMENTS

FORM 6–2
SAMPLE FORM FOR MEDICAL BILLS/PERSONAL INJURY

PROVIDERS	AMOUNT	ALLOWED	INS. PAY	BALANCE

Prepared: April 11, 1994   Total Medical: $

capabilities, I started with Plan Perfect and find it easy to use. Plan Perfect works with WordPerfect to create spreadsheets. This is the program I use for informal accountings and formal accountings to be filed with the court. I can set up different schedules, listing assets, disbursements, distributions, change in assets. The program adds and subtracts and inserts the totals; all I have to do is balance out the account. Of course, this can also be accomplished with spreadsheet programs such as Lotus 1-2-3® or Quatro Pro®. I do use Quatro Pro to produce spreadsheets to monitor the purchase and sale of various stocks and to create charts. Other uses for spreadsheets include analyzing statistical data, tax return preparation, and tracking investments for trusts and estates. One example for the use of a spreadsheet is a project I was working on to summarize depositions in an asbestos case. It was necessary to create a chart to track specific employees, the different jobs they held, places they worked, dates of employment, and whether certain materials were present at their employment sites. It was necessary to record the pages of the depositions where particular references were made. The object of creating the chart was to see the information summarized in columns according to categories across the page. Without the computer, this task would take so much time that the work would be prohibitive. With the computer, changes can be made, information can be inserted and deleted at will, and the chart produced with all the necessary information within a reasonable amount of time.

Another program I use quite often is a real estate program called Easy HUD (RESPA). The program was created by Easy Soft, Inc. in Watchung, New Jersey. When I receive a real estate file, I enter the information with regard to sellers' names, addresses, purchase price, buyers' names, and property address; in fact, all information from the contract goes directly into the computer on a RESPA (closing statement) form. This information is also imputed to form letters, such as requests for payoff of current mortgages, letters to tax offices, county clerk's, title companies, and so forth. The information is also imputed to form deeds, affidavits of title and finally to a ledger sheet that recapitulates all the financial information. The RESPA program calculates all math on the closing statement, calculates the tax apportionment, the sewer and rent apportionments, and the realty transfer fee. When the RESPA form is completed, the program transfers the information to the ledger sheet that shows the amount to be deposited in the attorney's trust account and a list of checks to be drawn down from that deposit. When the correct amounts are placed in the ledger, it will zero out as the checks are subtracted from the deposit to show zero funds left in the account. See **Form 6–3.**

All preclosing and postclosing letters are included in the program as well as the closing documents. This program saves a considerable amount of time, as all of you involved in real estate closings well know. Closing statements can change right up to and including at the closing. With the form in the computer, changes can be made literally in seconds and new forms printed out in perfect condition, no white-outs, no erasures.

Another program designed by Easy Soft, Inc. is the Civil Information Statement (CIS) used in family law practice. This is a form that is quite lengthy, has many math calculations and can take quite a bit of time to complete. The document can be printed on a blank paper or preprinted forms.

Once the program is running, you open a new file with the client name and enter all available information. The program will accumulate column totals, etc. Table lookups for child support and tax withholding calculations are performed and the appropriate fields automatically in. Debt service is computed and placed on page five. See **Form 6–4.**

The program I use to maintain my income and disbursements is Quicken3™. This program allows me to define disbursement categories, that is, rent, telephone, subscriptions, payroll and sub-categories, postage: stamps, postage: couriers; CLE: seminars; CLE: dues, Auto: repairs, Auto: tolls, Auto: gas.

Quicken3™ can analyze all the information that you input and print out a summary of your income and expenses for the month by categories showing net income or loss for the month; by transaction (listing each deposit and check drawn for the month by date), which is virtually a copy of your checkbook, or you can print out a quarterly report, yearly report, whatever you need. For income tax purposes, I print out a yearly statement showing the

FORM 6–3
SAMPLE CLOSING FORM

HUD-1 UNIFORM SETTLEMENT STATEMENT   EASY SOFT, Inc. (C)

A.	U.S. DEPARTMENT OF HOUSING AND URBAN DEVELOPMENT	SETTLEMENT STATEMENT

B. TYPE OF LOAN			6. File Number:	7. Loan Number:
1. FHA	2. FmHA			
3. CONV. UNINS.	4. VA	5. CONV. INS.	8. Mortgage Insurance Case Number	

C. NOTE: This form is furnished to give you a statement of actual settlement costs. Amounts paid to and by the settlement agent are shown. Items marked "(p.o.c.)" were paid outside the closing; they are shown here for informational purposes and are not included in the totals.
NOTE: TIN = Taxpayer's Identification Number

D. NAME AND ADDRESS OF BORROWER:	E. NAME, ADDRESS AND TIN OF SELLER:	F. NAME AND ADDRESS OF LENDER:
RICHARD PURCHASER 22 Main Lane Ocean, New Jersey	PAUL SELLER and NANCY SELLER, H/W 18 Linda Lane Aberdeen, New Jersey	MORTGAGE CITY, INC. 4400 Route 9 South Freehold, New Jersey 07728

G. PROPERTY LOCATION:	H. SETTLEMENT AGENT NAME, ADDRESS AND TIN
18 Linda Lane Aberdeen, New Jersey LOT 6 BLOCK 51	LARRY LAWYER, ESQ.

	PLACE OF SETTLEMENT 100 Main Street Allenhurst, N. J.	I. SETTLEMENT DATE 03/04/94

J. SUMMARY OF BORROWER'S TRANSACTION		K. SUMMARY OF SELLER'S TRANSACTION	
100. GROSS AMOUNT DUE FROM BORROWER:		400. GROSS AMOUNT DUE TO SELLER:	
101. Contract sales price	108,000.00	401. Contract sales price	108,000.00
102. Personal property		402. Personal property	
103. Settlement charges to borrower (Line 1400)	5,816.26	403.	
104.		404.	
105.		405.	
Adjustments for items paid by seller in advance		Adjustments for items paid by seller in advance	
106. City/town taxes 01/01 to 03/04	250.35	406. City/town taxes 01/01 to 03/04	250.35
107. County taxes to		407. County taxes to	
108. Assessments to		408. Assessments to	
109.		409.	
110. Condo Escrow transfer	188.55	410. Condo Escrow transfer	188.55
111.		411.	
112.		412.	
120. GROSS AMOUNT DUE FROM BORROWER	114,255.16	420. GROSS AMOUNT DUE TO SELLER	108,438.90

200. AMOUNTS PAID BY OR IN BEHALF OF BORROWER:		500. REDUCTIONS IN AMOUNT DUE TO SELLER:	
201. Deposit or earnest money	7,000.00	501. Excess deposit	7,000.00
202. Principal amount of new loan(s)	53,000.00	502. Settlement charges to seller (Line 1400)	6,978.00
203. Existing loan(s) taken subject to		503. Existing loan(s) taken subject to	
204.		504. Payoff of first mortgage loan United Jer	82,409.70
205.		505. Payoff of second mortgage loan Bankers S.	2,459.82
206.		506. Certificate of Occ.	40.00
207.		507.	
208.		508.	
209.		509.	
Adjustments for items unpaid by seller		Adjustments for items unpaid by seller	
210. City/town taxes to		510. City/town taxes to	
211. County taxes to		511. County taxes to	
212. Assessments to		512. Assessments to	
213. Sewer Adjustments	46.38	513. Sewer Adjustments	46.38
214. March Condo Maint fee	25.29	514. March Condo Maint fee	25.29
215.		515. Maint. fee arrears	18.92
216. Tax Curr. Yr 1627.28		516. Sewer Cur Yr 129.00	
217. Per Diem 8.94110		517. Per Diem 1.44944	
218. Sellers Paid 813.64		518. Sellers Paid	
219. Seller Owes-Days 63		519. Seller Owes-Days 32	
220. TOTAL PAID BY/FOR BORROWER	60,071.67	520. TOTAL REDUCTION AMOUNT DUE SELLER	98,978.11

300. CASH AT SETTLEMENT FROM/TO BORROWER		600. CASH AT SETTLEMENT FROM/TO SELLER	
301. Gross amount due from borrower (Line 120)	114,255.16	601. Gross amount due to seller (Line 420)	108,438.90
302. Less amount paid by/for borrower (Line 220)	60,071.67	602. Less reduction in amount due seller (Line 520)	98,978.11
303. CASH FROM/TO BORROWER	54,183.49	603. CASH TO/FROM SELLER	9,460.79

SUBSTITUTE FORM 1099 SELLER STATEMENT

The information contained in Blocks E, G, H, and I and on line 401 (or, if line 401 is asterisked, line 403 and 404) is important tax information and is being furnished to the Internal Revenue Services. If you are required to file a return, a negligence penalty or other sanction will be imposed on you if this item is required to be reported and the IRS determines that it has not been reported. If this real estate is your principal residence, file Form 2119, Sale or Exchange of Principal Residence, for any gain, with your income tax return; for other transactions, complete the applicable parts of Form 4797, Form 6252 and/or Schedule D(Form 1040). You are required to provide the Settlement Agent (named above) with your correct taxpayer identification number. If you do not provide the Settlement Agent with your correct taxpayer identification number, you may be subject to civil or criminal penalties imposed by law. Under penalties or perjury, I certify that the number shown on this statement is my correct taxpayer identification number.

(Seller's Signature)

Reprinted with permission.

FORM 6–3 (*continued*)

L. SETTLEMENT CHARGES		PAID FROM BORROWER'S FUNDS AT SETTLEMENT	PAID FROM SELLER'S FUNDS AT SETTLEMENT
700. TOTAL SALES/BROKER'S COMMISSION based on price $108,000.00 @ 6.0 % 6,480.00			
Division of Commission (Line 700) as follows:			
701. $ 6,480.00 to Coldwell Banker Schlott			
702. $ to			
703. Commission paid at Settlement			6,480.00
704			
800. ITEMS PAYABLE IN CONNECTION WITH LOAN			
801. Loan Origination Fee %			
802. Loan Discount 3.000 % 1,590.00		1,590.00	
803. Appraisal Fee to			
804. Credit Report to			
805. Lender's Inspection Fee			
806. Mortgage Insurance Application Fee to			
807. Assumption Fee			
808.			
809.			
810. Attorney Review Fee		500.00	
811.			
900. ITEMS REQUIRED BY LENDER TO BE PAID IN ADVANCE			
901. Interest from 03/04/94 to 03/31/94 @ $ 9.570 /day		267.96	
902. Mortgage Insurance Premium for months to			
903. Hazard Insurance Premium for years to			
904. years to			
905. Second quarter taxes 1994		813.64	
1000. RESERVES DEPOSITED WITH LENDER			
1001. Hazard Insurance months @ $ per month			
1002. Mortgage Insurance months @ $ per month			
1003. City property taxes 1 months @ $ 271.213 per month		271.21	
1004. County property taxes months @ $ per month			
1005. Annual assessments months @ $ per month			
1006. Condo escrow 3 months @ $ 133.150 per month		399.45	
1007. months @ $ per month			
1008. months @ $ per month			
1100. TITLE CHARGES			
1101. Settlement or closing fee to			
1102. Abstract or title search to			
1103. Title examination to			
1104. Title insurance binder to			
1105. Document preparation to			
1106. Notary fees to			
1107. Attorney's fees to LARRY LAWYER, ESQ.		650.00	
(includes above items numbers; 1103, 1105, 1107			
1108. Title Insurance to RED BANK TITLE AGENCY, INC.		638.00	
(includes above items numbers; 1102, 1104, 1108			
1109. Lender's coverage 53,000.00			
1110. Owner's coverage 108,000.00			
1111.			
1112. Condo Maintenance Fee for March		196.00	
1113. Condo Membership Fee		100.00	
1200. GOVERNMENT RECORDING AND TRANSFER CHARGES			
1201. Recording fees: Deed $ 40.00 ; Mortgage $ 40.00 ; Release $ 80.00		80.00	80.00
1202. City/county tax/stamps: Deed $; Mortgage $			
1203. State tax/stamps: Deed $; Mortgage $			
1204. Realty Transfer Fee			378.00
1205. Notice of Settlement (2)		40.00	
1300. ADDITIONAL SETTLEMENT CHARGES			
1301. Survey to Schoor and DePalma, Inc.		200.00	
1302. Pest inspection to			
1303.			
1304. Misc. photos, postage, toll calls, fax etc.		50.00	
1305. Federal Exp/Overnight Mail		20.00	40.00
1400. TOTAL SETTLEMENT CHARGES (enter on lines 103, Section J and 502, Section K)		5,816.26	6,978.00

EASY SOFT, Inc. (C)

CERTIFICATION

I have carefully reviewed the HUD - 1 Settlement Statement and to the best of my knowledge and belief, it is a true and accurate statement of all receipts and disbursements made on my account or by me in this transaction. I further certify that I have received a copy of the HUD - 1 Settlement Statement

_____ Seller	_____ Borrower
PAUL SELLER and	RICHARD PURCHASER
_____ Seller	_____ Borrower
NANCY SELLER	22 Main Lane

To the best of my knowledge the HUD - 1 Settlement Statement which I have prepared is a true and accurate account of the funds which were received and have been or will be used by the undersigned as part of the settlement of this transaction.

_____ Settlement Agent   03/04/94   Date

LARRY LAWYER, ESQ.

WARNING: It is a crime to knowingly make false statements to the United States on this or any other similar form. Penalties upon conviction can include a fine and imprisonment. For details see: Title 18 U.S. Code Section and Section 101.

FORM 6–3 *(continued)*

INITIAL ESCROW ACCOUNT STATEMENT DISCLOSURE

Initial Escrow Account Statement Required by Section 10(c) of the
Real Estate Settlement Procedure Act (RESPA)

The terms of your loan require you to have an escrow account to assure that certain obligations relating to the mortgaged property, such as taxes, insurance premiums and other charges are paid. The amount specified below will be collected along with your mortgage principal and interest payments during the first 12 months after your account is opened in order to pay these anticipated expenses:

Name and Address of Borrower(s)	Property Location	
RICHARD PURCHASER 22 Main Lane Ocean, New Jersey	18 Linda Lane Aberdeen, New Jersey LOT 6 BLOCK 51	
Date 03/04/94	Loan Number	
Beginning Date (First Payment) 05/01/94	Your escrow account payment - per month 271.21	

Payee	Purpose	Anticipated Due Date	Estimated Amount
	HAZARD INSURANCE		
	FLOOD INSURANCE		
	MORT. INSURANCE		
	SCHOOL TAX		
	COUNTY TAX		
	CITY TAX		3,254.56

Annual Total Due | 3,254.56

LARRY LAWYER, ESQ.   RICHARD PURCHASER

                                      22 Main Lane

FORM 6-3 (*continued*)

Ledger Sheet For

RICHARD PURCHASER
22 Main Lane
  PAUL SELLER and   18 Linda Lane
  NANCY SELLER, H/W   Aberdeen, New Jersey

Deposits

	Date	From	Amount
1	03/04/94	Principal amount of loan	$ 53,000.00
2	03/04/94	RICHARD PURCHASER	$ 54,183.49
3			$
4			$
5			$
		Total Deposits	$107,183.49

Withdrawals

	Date	Pay to Order of	Check #	Amount
1	03/04/94	Coldwell Banker Schlott RE Commission	100	$ 6,480.00
2	03/04/94	WENDIE L. ELOCH, ESQUIRE Attorney's fees	101	$ 650.00
3	03/04/94	RED BANK TITLE AGENCY, INC. Title Insurance	102	$ 638.00
4	03/04/94	WYNDAM PLACE ASSOCIATION, INC. Condo Association Escrows	103	$ 714.37
5	03/04/94	WENDIE L. ELOCH, ESQUIRE Reimbursements	104	$ 310.00
6	03/04/94	Monmouth County Clerk Realty Transfer Fee	105	$ 378.00
7	03/04/94	Schoor and DePalma, Inc. Surveyor	106	$ 200.00
8	03/04/94	MORTGAGE CITY, INC.	107	$ 2,629.17
9	03/04/94	Christopher and Nancy Luce Seller	108	$ 9,460.79
10	03/04/94	United Jersey Bank Payoff of first mortgage loan	109	$ 82,409.70
11	03/04/94	Bankers Savings Payoff of second mortgage loan	110	$ 2,459.82
12	03/04/94	Aberdeen Tax Collector Second Quarter Taxes 1994	111	$ 813.64
13	03/04/94	Donna Bruns Certificate of Occupancy	112	$ 40.00
14				$
15				$
16				$
17				$
18				$
19				$
20				$
21				$
22				$
23				$
24				$

Total Withdrawals (For all 24 checks)	$107,183.49
Total Deposits	$107,183.49
Total Withdrawals	$107,183.49
Difference	$ -.00

FORM 6–4
SAMPLE FAMILY COURT FORM

Attorney(s):   JOHN DOE, ESQ.
Office Address & Tel. No.:   15 Main Avenue, Anytown, NJ 07000   201-555-5555
Attorney(s) for

	SUPERIOR COURT OF NEW JERSEY
	CHANCERY DIVISION, FAMILY PART
Plaintiff,	COUNTY
vs.	DOCKET NO.
	CASE INFORMATION STATEMENT
Defendant	OF ....

PART A - CASE INFORMATION:

Date of Statement	**ISSUES IN DISPUTE:**
Date(s) of Prior Statement	Cause of Action ....
....	Custody ....
Your Birthdate	Alimony ....
Birthdate of Spouse	Child Support ....
Date Of Marriage	Equitable Distribution ....
Date of Separation	Counsel Fees ....
Date of Complaint	Other ....

Does an agreement exist between parties relative to any issue?   (   ) Yes (   ) No. If Yes, attach a copy (if written) or a summary (if oral).

1. Name and Address of Parties:

Your Name   ....
Street Address .... City .... State/Zip...............................
Other   Party's   Name   ....
Street Address (if different) .... City .... State/Zip...............................

2. Name, Address, & Birthdate of all Child(ren); Person with whom Child(ren) Resides:

Child's Full Name	Address	Birthdate	Person's Name
....	....	....	....
....	....	....	....
....	....	....	....
....	....	....	....

PART B - MISCELLANEOUS INFORMATION:

1. Name and Address of Your Employer (Provide Name and Address of Co. if Self Employed)

Name of Employer .... Address ....
Name of Employer .... Address ....

2. Name and Address of Your Health Insurance Company (ies); Policy Information:

Name of Company .... Address ....
I.D. Number .... Group Number ....

Coverage Type:	Single ( )	Parent-Child ( )	Family ( )	Optical ( )	
	Hospital ( )	Major-Medical ( )	Dental ( )	Drug ( )	Diagnostic ( )

Check if made available through employment   (   ) or personally obtained(   )

Reprinted with permission.

FORM 6–4 (*continued*)

Name of Company .... Address ....
I D. Number .... Group Number...
Coverage Type: Single   ( )   Parent-Child   ( )   Family ( )   Optical ( )
                  Hospital   ( )   Major-Medical   ( ) Dental ( )   Drug ( )   Diagnostic ( )
Check if made available through employment ( ) or personally obtained ( )

3. Name & Address of Life Insurance Company(ies); Policy Information:

Name of Company   ....   Address ....
Policy Number   ....   Beneficiary ....
Face Amount $ ....   Name of Insured ....
Policy Owner   ....   2nd Beneficiary

Name of Company   ....   Address ....
Policy Number   ....   Beneficiary ....
Face Amount $ ....   Name of Insured ....
Policy Owner   ....   2nd Beneficiary

4. Additional Identification: Social Security Number ....

State Driver's License No ....   Eye Color ....

5. Attach sheet listing all prior/pending family actions involving support, custody, or domestic violence listing Docket Number, County, State and the Disposition reached.   Comments:

PART C - INCOME INFORMATION: Complete this section for self and (if known) for spouse.
Attach to this form a corporate benefits statement as well as a statement of all fringe benefits of employment.

1. LAST YEAR'S INCOME

	Yours	Joint	Spouse or Former Spouse
1. Gross earned income last calendar year (19)	....	....	....
2. Unearned income(same year)	....	....	....
3. Total Income Taxes paid on above income (incl. Fed., State, FICA, and SUI)If Joint Return use middle line	....	....	....
4. Net income (1 + 2 - 3)	0 . 00	0 . 00	0 . 00

Attach a full and complete copy of last year's Federal & State Income Tax Returns. If none has been filed, attach W-2 statements, 1099's, Schedule C's, etc., to show total income plus a copy of the most recently filed Tax Returns. Check if attached. Fed. Tax Return ( ) State Tax Return ( )W-2 ( ) Other ( )

2. PRESENT EARNED INCOME AND EXPENSES

	Yours	Spouse (if known)
1. Average Gross monthly income (based on last 3 pay periods-attach pay stubs)	....	....

Commissions and bonuses, etc., are
(   ) included* (   ) not included* (   ) not paid to you.   Comments:
Attach details of basis thereof, including, but not limited to, percentage overrides, timing of payments, etc. Attach copies of last three statements of such bonuses, commissions, etc.

2. Deductions per month: check all types of withholdings
(   ) Federal   (   ) State   (   )F.I.C.A   ....
(   ) S.U.I   (   ) Other

	Yours	Spouse (if known)
3. Net Income (1 - 2)	0.00	0.00

Comments:

FORM 6–4 (*continued*)

PART C 3.   YOUR YEAR - TO - DATE INCOME   Provide Dates: From .... To ....

1.   GROSS EARNED INCOME: $ ....   Number of Weeks 0.00

2.   TAX DEDUCTIONS: (Number of dependents ....)

    a.   Federal Income Taxes   a. $ ....

    b.   N.J. Income Taxes   b. $ ....

    c.   FICA   c. $ ....

    d.   S.U.I.   d. $ ....

    e.   Estimated tax payment in excess
       of withholding actually made   e. $ ....

    f.   Other (specify)   f. $ ....

                                  TOTAL $ 0.00

3. GROSS INCOME NET OF TAXES $ 0.00

4. OTHER DEDUCTIONS   If mandatory, check box

    a.   Hospitalization/Medical Insurance   a. $ .... ( )

    b.   Life Insurance   b. $ .... ( )

    c.   Pension/Profit Sharing Plan   c. $ .... ( )

    d.   Savings/Bond Plan   d. $ .... ( )

    e.   Wage Execution   e. $ .... ( )

    f.   Retirement Fund Payment   f. $ .... ( )

    g.   Other (specify)   g. $ .... ( )

                                    TOTAL $ 0.00

5. NET YEAR-TO-DATE EARNED INCOME $ 0.00

    NET AVERAGE EARNED INCOME PER MONTH $ 0.00

6. GROSS UNEARNED INCOME

Source	How Often Paid	Year to Date Amount
....	....	....
....	....	....
....	....	....
....	....	....

TOTAL GROSS UNEARNED INCOME YEAR TO DATE $ 0.00

FORM 6–4 (*continued*)

PART C 4. INCOME ANALYSIS UNDER THE CHILD SUPPORT GUIDELINES

To be completed if either parent contends that the child support guidelines apply or should be considered. All amounts must be weekly.

	Mother	Father
1. Gross Taxable Income	1.	1. ....
a. Federal, State, Social Security, Income Taxes	1a	1a. ....
2. Gross Non-Taxable Income	2.	2. ....
3. Income After Taxes (Line 1 - Line 1a + Line2)	3.	3. ....
4. Mandatory Union Dues	4.	4. ....
5. Mandatory Retirement Contribution	5.	5. ....
6. Medical/Dental Insurance Premium	6.	6. ....
7. Child Support and/or Alimony Orders from Other Relationships	7.	7. ....
8. Other Dependent Deduction	8.	8. ....
9. Weekly Available Income (Line 3 minus Lines 4 through 8)	9.	9. ....
Combined Available Income	....	
10. Basic Child Support Amount (From Schedule)	10.	
a. Net Work- Related Child Care Expenses	10a.+	
b. Apportionments to the Child	10b.+	
11. Total Child Support Amount (Line 10 + Line 10a - Line 10b)	11. $	
12. Percentage Share of Income (Line 9 each parent divided by combined available income)	12. ....%	12. ....%
13. Each Parent's Weekly Child Support Obligation (Multiply Line 11 by Line 12)	13.	13. ....
14. Weekly Child Support Order (Non-Custodial Parent)	14.	14. ....
15. Parental Share of Extraordinary Medical/dental Expenses (From Line 12)	15.	15. ....

COMMENTS AND REBUTTALS:

Note: To the extent that you assert that the child support computations set forth above do not take into account all relevant factors append hereto an explanation of what additional factors should be taken into account and what effect said factors should have on the court's determination of child support.

FORM 6–4 (*continued*)

PART D - MONTHLY EXPENSES (computed at 4.3 wks/ mo.)
Should reflect standard of living established during marriage, but not
repeat those income deductions listed on Part C.

	Yours and children (#) residing with you	Expenses paid for spouse and/or children (#) not residing with you

SCHEDULE A: SHELTER

If Tenant:

	Yours and children	Expenses paid
Rent	$............................	$............................
Heat (if not furnished)	....	....
Electric & Gas (if not furnished)	....	....
Renter's Insurance	....	....
Parking (at Apartment)	....	....
Other Charges(Itemize)	....	....
	....	....
	....	....
	....	....

If Homeowner:

Mortgage	$............................	$............................
Real Estate Taxes (unless included w/ mortgage payment)	....	....
Homeowners Insurance (unless included w/ mortgage pymt)	....	....
Repairs & Maintenance	....	....
Heat (unless Electric or Gas)	....	....
Electric & Gas	....	....
Water & Sewer	....	....
Garbage Removal	....	....
Other Mortgages(Specify)	....	....
Snow Removal & Lawn Care	....	....
Maintenance Charges (Condo/co-op)	....	....
Other Charges (Itemize)	....	....
	....	....
	....	....
	....	....

Tenant or Homeowner:

Telephone	$............................	$............................
Service Contracts on Equipment	....	....
Cable TV	....	....
Plumber/Electrician	....	....
Equipment & Furnishings	....	....
Other(itemize)	....	....
	....	....
	....	....
	....	....
TOTAL	$ 0.00	$ 0.00
SHELTER COMBINED TOTAL	$ 0.00	

SCHEDULE B: TRANSPORTATION

Auto Payment	$............................	$............................
Auto Insurance(no. of vehicles)	....	....
Registration, License, Maintenance	....	....
Fuel and Oil	....	....
Commuting Expenses(state frequency and points of travel)	....	....
Other Charges(Itemize)	....	....
TOTAL	$ 0.00	$ 0.00
TRANSPORTATION COMBINED TOTAL	$ 0.00	

FORM 6–4 *(continued)*

SCHEDULE C: **PERSONAL**

	Yours and children (#) residing with you	Expenses paid for spouse and/or children (#) not residing with you
Food at Home & household supplies	$....................	$....................
Prescription Drugs		
Non-prescription drugs, cosmetics, toiletries and sundries		
School Lunch		
Restaurants		
Clothing		
Dry Cleaning, Commercial Laundry		
Hair Care		
Domestic Help		
Medical (exclusive of psychiatric)		
Psychiatric/psychological/counselling		
Dental (exclusive of orthodontic)		
Orthodontic		
Medical Insurance (hospitalization, etc.)		
Club Dues and Memberships		
Sports and Hobbies		
Camps		
Vacations		
Children's Private School Costs		
Parent's Educational Costs		
Children's Lessons (dancing, music, sports, etc.)		
Babysitting		
Day Care Expenses		
Entertainment		
Alcohol and Tobacco		
Newpapers and Periodicals		
Gifts and Contributions		
Payments to Non-Child Dependents		
Prior Existing Support Obligations		
(this family)		
(other families - specify)		
Tax Reserve (not listed elsewhere)		
Life Insurance		
Savings/Investment	Unknown	
Debt Service (from page 7)		
Visitation Expenses		
Professional Expenses (other than this proceeding)		
Other (specify)		
	$.......... 0.00	$.......... 0.00

(bracket at left: *unreimbursed only* — covering Medical through Medical Insurance)

PERSONAL COMBINED TOTAL $.......... 0.00

Summary of Monthly Expenses (Computed at 4.3 w.ks/mo):

	Yours & Children (#) Residing With You	Expenses paid for spouse and/ or Children (#) Not Residing with you	Combined Total Expenses
Schedule A: Shelter	$........0.00 +	$........0.00 =	$........0.00
Schedule B: Transportation	$........0.00 +	$........0.00 =	$........0.00
Schedule C: Personal	$........0.00 +	$........0.00 =	$........0.00
Grand Totals	$........0.00 +	$........0.00 =	$........0.00

FORM 6–4   (*continued*)

PART E - BALANCE SHEET OF ALL FAMILY ASSETS AND LIABILITIES

STATEMENT OF ASSETS Description	Name of Responsible Party (H,W,J)	If you contend liability should not be considered in equitable distribution, state reason	Value $	Date of Evaluation Mo/Day/Yr
1. Real Property				
....	....	....	....	....
....	....	....	....	....
....	....	....	....	....
2. Bank Accounts, Certificates of Deposit				
....	....	....	....	....
....	....	....	....	....
....	....	....	....	....
3. Vehicles				
....	....	....	....	....
....	....	....	....	....
....	....	....	....	....
....	....	....	....	....
4. Tangible Personal Property				
....	....	....	....	....
....	....	....	....	....
....	....	....	....	....
....	....	....	....	....
....	....	....	....	....
5. Stocks and Bonds				
....	....	....	....	....
....	....	....	....	....
....	....	....	....	....
....	....	....	....	....
6. Pension, Profit Sharing, Retirement Plan(s), I.R.A.'s, 401 k's, etc.				
....	....	....	....	....
....	....	....	....	....
....	....	....	....	....
....	....	....	....	....
7. Businesses, Partnerships, Professional Practices				
....	....	....	....	....
....	....	....	....	....
....	....	....	....	....
8. Life Insurance (cash surrender value)				
....	....	....	....	....
....	....	....	....	....
....	....	....	....	....
9. Other (specify)				
....	....	....	....	....
....	....	....	....	....
....	....	....	....	....

TOTAL GROSS ASSETS $ .... 0.00 ....

FORM 6–4 (*continued*)

STATEMENT OF LIABILITIES

Description	Name of Responsi-ble Party (H,W,J)	If you contend liability should not be considered in equitable distribution, state reason	Monthly Payment	Total Owed	Date of Evaluation
1. Mortgage in Real Estate					
....	......	....	....	....	....
....	......	....	....	....	....
....	......	....	....	....	....
....	......	....	....	....	....
....	......	....	....	....	....
....	......	....	....	....	....
2. Other Long Term Debts					
....	......	....	....	....	....
....	......	....	....	....	....
....	......	....	....	....	....
....	......	....	....	....	....
....	......	....	....	....	....
....	......	....	....	....	....
3. Revolving Charges					
....	......	....	....	....	....
....	......	....	....	....	....
....	......	....	....	....	....
....	......	....	....	....	....
....	......	....	....	....	....
....	......	....	....	....	....
....	......	....	....	....	....
4. Other Short Term Debts					
....	......	....	....	....	....
....	......	....	....	....	....
....	......	....	....	....	....
....	......	....	....	....	....
....	......	....	....	....	....
....	......	....	....	....	....
5. Contingent Liabilities					
....	......	....	....	....	....
....	......	....	....	....	....
....	......	....	....	....	....
....	......	....	....	....	....
....	......	....	....	....	....

Items marked with * are not included in Debt Service on page 5.

TOTAL GROSS LIABILITIES: $ ....0.00...........
(Other than Contingent Liabilities)

NET WORTH: $ ....0.00...........
(Other than Contingent Liabilities)

FORM 6–4 (*continued*)

PART F - STATEMENT OF SPECIAL PROBLEMS (Provide a Brief Narrative Statement of Any Special Problems Involving This Case): As example, state if the matter involves complex valuation problems (such as for a closely held business) or special medical problems of any family member, etc.

I certify that the foregoing statements made by are true. I am aware that if any of the foregoing statements made by me are wilfully false. I am subject to punishment.

DATED:..   SIGNED:..

CHECK IF YOU HAVE ATTACHED THE FOLLOWING REQUIRED DOCUMENTS

1. A full and complete copy of your last federal and state income tax returns with all schedules and attachments.   ....

2. Your last calender year's W -2 statements and 1099's.   ....

3. Your three most recent pay stubs.   ....

4. Bonus information including, but not limited to, percentage overrides, timing of payments, etc.; the last three statements of such bonuses, commissions, etc.   ....

5. Your most recent corporate benefit statement or a summary thereof, showing the nature, amount and status of retirement plans, savings plans, income deferral olans, insurance benefits, etc.   ....

6. Any agreements between the parties.   ....

7. A statement of prior/pending cases. (Part B-5).   ....

amount spent in each category and the amount of income I received. By reviewing the amounts spent in each category it also gives me an idea of where I am spending my money for the maintenance of the office. Quicken3® can also be used to maintain your checking accounts, write checks, manage investments, pay bills electronically, and aid in tax preparation.

How many times have you been given an issue to research knowing that you have already done the research but cannot remember where or when? Many times the same issue will occur in different cases. This problem can be solved by creating a simple database that tracks the research you have done in other briefs, memorandums, and motions. The database must be short and easy to use, otherwise you will not enter the information needed after each research project is completed.

Fields you might want to include in the database are:

Research topics (damages)

Subtopic (present value)

Sub-subtopic (reduction of damages)

Case name

Document (Mot. Sum. Judg.1/21/92)

Page number

File number
Other information that would help track this research.

In addition you may want to input slip opinions and unpublished opinions that might have an impact on other types of cases you are handling or will handle in the future.

Periodically you should print an alphabetized list of the research database so that you have it when you begin a research project.[8]

Databases can be used many ways in litigation management. The first step is to decide if you actually need one. How much information do you need to capture and keep track of? How can it best be tracked—manually, using a good word processing program, utilizing a standard database design, or designing a custom database design? A database could:

- Keep track on the docket and litigant's personal history in a massive tort litigation file containing hundreds of thousands of cases
- Assist in summarizing and later accessing 100,000+ documents
- Or it could assist in surveying a single box of financial documents where thorough mathematical analysis of the numerical data is key to the case.

---

[8] Brent D. Roper, *11 Ways Computer Can Make You More Efficient,* 9 Legal Assistant Today 5, May–June 1992.

The following is a checklist for developing a litigation database written by Cynthia L. Patterson, CLAS.

_____ 1. Consideration: What information are you trying to capture and how much is there? How many boxes of documents, pages of information, or individual documents do you anticipate reviewing? Do the documents contain pertinent financial or technical information? Are the documents from numerous critical witnesses? Are they a pertinent part of your production?

Action: Write out your attorney's goals for this case; then write out your goals for this project. Begin to think about, and commit to paper, how a database might accomplish those goals more easily, more quickly, or more efficiently. Relate the information from above into this initial step.

_____ 2. Consideration: How do you anticipate utilizing the information? Is it to more easily assist you in a document production? To produce privilege logs, witness folders, trial exhibits? Or is to analyze financial information, cash flows, invoices and billing? When you print out your first set of reports, how should they physically appear on paper?

Action: You should sketch out precisely how you want your reports to appear and what information should be contained in them, including any numerical totals, calculations or comments.

_____ 3. Consideration: What data should be captured? Will bibliographic data be sufficient or will you need to add subjective data in order for your database to be effective? What various types of documents are present? Will your data requirements be different for these varying types?

Action: List the fields of information you want to include; list the different types of documents you may be working with, if applicable.

_____ 4. Consideration: How will you capture the data? Will you use codes or full text fields? How will you ensure consistency? If subjective information is to be included, who will prepare it?

Action: Prepare a list of fields: will they be coded, alphanumeric, numeric, full text? Are they bibliographic or subjective? Who will develop the codes?

_____ 5. Consideration: How will you accomplish the work in computerizing this case? Are you and your in-house team available and accomplished enough to put together the project? If not, in what areas will you need assistance: organization, programming and design, coding, data entry, etc. What software meets your needs in this project? Does it match your level of computer proficiency, i.e., is it user-friendly?

Action: List your sources and resources; include people, hardware, software, publications, etc. Who will design and program? Who will code? Who will do date entry? Who will oversee and test?

_____ 6. Consideration: Do your reports accurately reflect your posture? Are they correct and complete? Do your totals total and are your calculations accurate? If performing financial analysis, do your numbers accurately reflect that information you wish to portray (i.e. did you really want the median, or do you now realize you should have examined the mean?).

Action: Run test reports; check all the fields on the report against the original documents or coding sheets.

_____ 7. How much will it cost? Breaking the project into manageable segments, how much will each segment cost? How may hours will you need to put into the project? How many hours will the consultant or programmer put into it? Don't be afraid to shop around and get written estimates.

Action: Prepare a proposal for your attorney or client. Include your thought processes and conclusions as you worked through the exercises above. Take this portion of the project seriously; prepare a formal presentation. Don't count on your client accepting a computerization proposal based upon a string of numbers listed on a legal pad; put as much effort into this phase as you would in preparing a brief.[9]

Your personal computer can also be used to organize case management. You will be able to retrieve specific information from a mass of thousands of documents with relative ease. The following information based upon an article by Beth Avant and Pat Elliott, CLAS, explains how the personal computer may be used for organizing your office by maintaining client information, using conflict checks, docket control, time and billing, and case organization.[10]

ABACUS® is a program used by Avant and Elliott for docketing, calendaring and case information. ABACUS can show you a full monthly calendar on the monitor. You can choose a particular day and the itinerary automatically appears for the identified user.

Case information such as the name of the attorney's client, address, telephone number, place of employment, and any other pertinent information can be maintained on the computer. For personal injury cases you can also keep information with regard to wage loss claims, injuries sustained, current medical information, both adverse insurance carrier, adjuster, phone numbers, policy and claim numbers, and importantly, calendar dates.

---

[9] Cynthia L. Patterson, CLAS, *Developing a Database: An Overview,* Facts & Findings. Reprinted with permission of Cynthia L. Patterson, CLAS, and the Nat'l Ass'n of Legal Assistants, Inc., 1516 S. Boston #200, Tulsa, Okla. 74119. This article originally appeared in the Nov. 1993 issue of Facts & Findings, a quarterly journal for legal assistants.

[10] Beth Avant and Pat Elliott, CLAS, *Using Your PC for Case Management,* 19 Facts & Findings 5, Nat'l Ass'n of Legal Assistants, Feb. 1993

ABACUS also may be used for conflict checks. The program runs a cross-check on clients, case names, adverse counsel, or other adversaries to determine whether a new case presents a potential conflict.

Another use of the program is for docket control. The features provided in this area include a system of calculating important dates, alerting to conflicts in scheduling matters, and generating free-time reports.

There are also software programs on the market that produce simple, practical billing systems. It is important that your system provide a variety of means to bill cases, that is, flat rate or hourly rate or fee on a contingency basis. With most billing systems you can also generate management reports, accounts payable and receivable ledgers, trust account reports, and billing summaries for any given period. Another bonus to these types of software packages are spreadsheet programs that are essential to handle payrolls and payroll tax summaries.

One important type of software you will need is a backup program to insure that you don't lose all the information it has taken you so long to compile. You have undoubtedly heard the phrase, "the computer is down." I shudder to think of what would happen in my office if my hard drive crashed and I lost everything in the computer. Everything I do is in that computer—my real estate files, my entire billing system, all my estate accountings, all my discovery forms, briefs, memorandums, motions, and so forth. I would have to start all over again. To insure that does not happen in the event of a sudden power failure, mechanical failure, or user mistake, there are backup programs available to give you peace of mind regarding this. Your DOS program usually contains backup procedures. There are utility programs, as well, such as Norton Utilities or PC Tools that also contain backup programs. These programs backup your disk drive onto disks. Since my assistant and I both use computers and they are not networked together, it is necessary at times for me to have access to her computer. We both have different forms on our computers, however, I do have important forms on disks so that either of us may use them. For my purposes, an external backup works best so that I may backup each computer at the end of the week. The backup I use is Colorado Backup® by Memory Systems, Inc. It is a tape backup and may be installed internally. The tape backup allows you to back up your entire hard drive on one tape. The external backup is small and simply plugs into the back of the computer. It can then be removed and used wherever necessary. It is recommended that you maintain two backup tapes—one to take home and one to keep in the office.

In order to use Colorado Backup, you must have the following hardware requirements:

PC, XT, AT®, PS/1®, PS/2®, laptop, notebook, or compatible computer

Parallel port

DOS 2.1 or higher (to verify your version type VER at the DOS prompt)

420KM of available memory (to check available memory, type CHKDSK at the DOS prompt. Bytes free should be at least 420,000.

The final software programs to investigate are programs for legal research such as LEXIS® or WestLaw®. These programs are expensive and cost-prohibitive for all but the largest law firms. Perhaps the cost of using the programs will decrease to the point where they will become available to all. There have been times when I have used LEXIS or Westlaw for research. The consideration is one of time and money and is to be decided with your attorney client. Your county or state library may have either program; if you have a college or university in your area, with either a law school or paralegal program, they will have one of the programs. If you have a contact in a law firm that has either program, you could ask to use it and pay all charges incurred.

There are several factors to be considered before you make a decision to use computerized legal research:

- What question has been asked and what issues do you need to analyze? You must be very specific and determine whether your question has more than one part, and if so, break it down into separate parts to be researched.
- What limitations do you face in terms of cost, time, and availability of materials? The cost of online time must be considered, that is, the time within which you have to complete the task and where the documents are that need to be retrieved.
- When deciding to use manual or online research, determine your primary source in terms of subject matter. If you are searching for a New Jersey case, you would start by searching West's Digest for New Jersey, rather than the Decennial Digest that covers all states.
- If your research involves a unique term or phrase, it would be advantageous to use online research.
- If your research involves proper names of individuals, corporations, or products, you might consider online research. You do, however, need to add second, limiting terms. For example, if you are researching an issue involving cars, such as a Ford, you would want to add the name Prelude and avoid the retrieval of unrelated documents.

You should not use online research if:

- You need an overview of a subject matter. Manual sources such as legal encyclopedias, hornbooks, and general treatises usually include extensive definitions and invaluable annotations.

- If you are researching commonly used phrases such as "motion for summary judgment," or "request for judgment notwithstanding the verdict (JNOV)," it would be best to manually narrow the field by using key numbers in West's Digest to locate your specific subject.
- If you are researching a broad subject such as "due process" or "equal rights" under a specific amendment, it would be best to start with constitutional law and labor law hornbooks to narrow down the field of research.

The software programs mentioned above represent just a sample. They are programs with which I am familiar and those used by experienced legal assistants in their daily work. There are many programs from which to choose that have different capabilities and uses. Included at **Form 6–5** is a list of software compiled by Brent D. Roper, attorney and former legal assistant, Topeka, Kansas. The list is very complete and comprehensive with regard to software packages for use by lawyers and legal assistants alike.[11]

§ 6.7   Start-up Costs

How much is this venture going to cost? How are you going to pay for the equipment and the supplies you need, the rent and utilities? As in any new business there are start-up costs for the items necessary for you to do business. You do not have an inventory to purchase, however, you need the tools with which to work. Based on current relative costs they are:

Furniture, a desk and chair at the minimum	$500
A telephone system, at least two lines, phones and installation costs	$1,000
Photocopy machine (purchase)	$3,000
Rent security, first month's rent (depending on location)	$1,500
Filing cabinet	$125
Computer/printer—and/or typewriter	$2,000
Library, subscriptions	$350
Miscellaneous supplies with which to work, stationery, photo paper, paper clips, pens, pencils, pads, stapler, staples, mailing envelopes, telephone message pads, post-its, file folders, red folders.	$200
Total	$8,675

---

[11] Excerpted from an article by Brent D. Roper, *11 Ways Computers Can Make You More Efficient,* Legal Assistant Today, James Publishing, Inc. ©1992, Costa Mesa, Calif. Reprinted with permission from Legal Assistant Today. For subscription information call (714) 755-5450.

FORM 6–5
LIST OF SOFTWARE PROGRAMS

IBM-Compatible Software Programs

This is a list of just some of the IBM-compatible software programs that are currently available to help you find the types of programs you are interested in. The inclusion of these programs or the order in which they appear should not be construed as an endorsement of the product by either the author, editors, or publisher. The addresses and telephone numbers were current when this directory was written, but they can change on almost a daily basis.

Pricing Code:

A = Inexpensive (Under $200)

C = Moderately Expensive ($600-$1,000)

B = Moderately Inexpensive ($200-$500)

D = Expensive (over $1,000)

WINDOWS

Windows 3.0	Microsoft Corp., 1 Microsoft Way, Redmond, WA 98053, (800) 426-9400	

WORD PROCESSING

Ami Pro for Windows	Lotus Development Corp., 55 Cambridge Pkwy., Cambridge, MA 02142 (800) 545-6116 or (617) 577-8500	B
Display Write	IBM Corp., Display Write Product Support Center, 5 West Kirkwood Blvd., Roanoke, TX 76299, (800) 237-5511	B
Microsoft Word	Microsoft Corp., 1 Microsoft Way, Redmond, WA 98053, (800) 323-3577	B
Multimate	Borland International, P.O. Box 660001, 1800 Green Hills, Scotts Valley, CA 95067, (800) 437-4329, (800) 331-0877, (416) 229-6000	B
Professional Write	Software Publishing. Co., 3165 Kifer Road, POB 54983, Santa Clara, CA 95056-0983, (800) 336-8360 or (415) 962-8910	B
WordPerfect	WordPerfect Corp., 1555 N. Technology Way, Orem UT 84057, (800) 526-5012 or (801) 225-5000	B
WordStar	WordStar International, Inc., 201 Alameda del Prado, Novato, CA 94949, (800) 227-5609	B

Low Cost Options

Lotus Works	Lotus Development Corp., 55 Cambridge Pkwy., Cambridge, MA 02142, (800) 545-6116 or (617) 577-8500	A
Microsoft Works	Microsoft Corp., 1 Microsoft Way, Redmond, WA 98053, (800) 426-9400	A
PC-Write	Quicksoft, Inc. 219 First Ave. N, #224, Seattle, WA 98109, (206) 282-0452	A
PFS: First Choice	Software Publishing. Co., 3165 Kifer Road, POB 54983, Santa Clara. CA 95056-0983, (800) 336-8360 or (415) 962-8910	A

DATABASES

dBase	Borland International, P.O. Box 660001, 1800 Green Hills, Scotts Valley, CA 95067, (800) 437-4329, (800) 331-0877, (416) 229-6000;	C
Foxbase Plus	Fox Software Inc., 118 W. South Boundary, Perrysburg, OH 43551, (419) 874-0162;	C
Paradox	Borland International, P.O. Box 660001, 1800 Green Hills, Scotts Valley, CA 95067, (800) 437-4329, (800) 331-0877, (416) 229-6000;	C
Q&A	Symantec Corp., 10201 Torre Ave, Cupertino, CA 95014, (408) 252-5700	B
Rbase	Microrim Inc. 15395 S.E. 30th Place, Bellevue, WA 98007, (206) 649-9500	C
Reflex	Borland International, P.O. Box 660001, 1800 Green Hills, Scotts Valley, CA 95067, (800) 437-4329, (800) 331-0877, (416) 229-6000	C

SPREADSHEETS

Framework	Borland International, P.O. Box 660001, 1800 Green Hills, Scotts Valley, CA 95067, (800) 437-4329, (800) 331-0877, (416) 229-6000	C
Lotus 1-2-3	Lotus Development Corp., 55 Cambridge, Cambridge MA 02142, (800) 545-6116 or (617) 577-8500	B
Lucid 3-D	DacEasy Inc., 17950 Preston Rd. #800, Dallas, TX 75252, (800) 877-8088 or (214) 248-0205	A

©1994. James Publishing Inc. Reprinted with permission from *Legal Assistant Today*. For subscription information, call (714) 755-5450.

FORM 6–5 *(continued)*

Microsoft Excel	Microsoft Corp., 1 Microsoft Way, Redmond, WA 98053, (800) 323-3577	B
PlanPerfect	WordPerfect Corp., 1555 N. Technology Way, Orem, UT, 84057, (800) 526-5012	B
Quattro	Borland International, P.O. Box 660001, 1800 Green Hills, Scotts Valley, CA, 95067, (800) 437-4329, (800) 331-0877, (416) 229-6000	C
SuperCalc	Computer Associates International, 711 Stewart Ave, Garden City, NY 11530, (800) 645-3003 or (516) 227-3300	B

DESKTOP PUBLISHING

Legend	NBI, 3450 Mitchell Lane, Boulder, CO 80301, (800) 334-4189	C
The Office Publisher	Laser Friendly, 156 Shorting Rd, Scarborough, Ontario, Canada, M1S 3S6, (416) 291-3736 . . .	B
Pagemaker	Aldus Corp., 411 First Ave. South, Seattle, WA 98104, (800) 332-5387 or (206) 622-5500	C
Ventura Publisher	Ventura Software, 9745 Business Park, San Diego, CA 92131, (800)TEAM-XRX	C

Low Cost Options

GEM Desktop Pub.	Digital Research Inc., Box DRI, Monterey, CA 93942, (800) 274-4374 or (408) 649-3896	B
PFS: First Publisher	Software Publishing. Co., 3165 Kifer Road, POB 54983, Santa Clara, CA 95056-0983, (800) 336-8360 or (415) 962-8910	B
Publish-It	Timeworks, Inc., 444 Lake Cook Rd., Deerfield, IL 60015-4919, (800) 535-9497 or (312) 948-9200	B
Spring Board Publisher	Springboard Software, 7808 Creekridge Circle, Minneapolis MN 55435 (612)944-3915	B

PROJECT MANAGEMENT

Harvard Project Mgr.	Software Publishing. Co., 3165 Kifer Road, POB 54983, Santa Clara, CA 95056-0983, (800) 336-8360 or (415) 962-8910	B
InstaPlan 5000	Micro Planning International, 655 Redwood Hwy., #3311 Mill Valley, CA 94941; (800) 852-7526 or (415) 389-1414	B
Microsoft Project For Windows	Microsoft Corp., 1 Microsoft Way, Redmond, WA 98053, (800) 426-9400	C
Project Scheduler 4	Scitor Corp., 393 Vintage Park Dr., #140, Foster City, CA 94404, (415) 570-7700	C
Timeline	Symantec Corp., 10201 Torre Ave., Cupertino, CA 95014, (408) 253-9600	C

PRESENTATION GRAPHICS

Applause II	Borland International, P.O. Box 660001, 1800 Green Hills, Scotts Valley, CA 95067, (800) 437-4329, (800) 331-0877, (416) 229-6000	B
Freelance Graphics	Lotus Development Corp., 55 Cambridge Parkway, MA 02142, (800) 545-6116 or (617) 577-8500	B
Harvard Graphics	Software Publishing. Co., 3165 Kifer Road, POB 54983, Santa Clara, CA 95056-0983, (800) 336-8360 or (415) 962-8910	B
Microsoft PowerPoint	Microsoft Corp., 1 Microsoft Way, Redmond, WA 98053, (800) 426-9400	B

ART/ILLUSTRATION SOFTWARE

Arts and Letters Graphics Editor	Computer Support Corp., 15926 Midway Rd., Dallas, TX 75244, (214) 661-8960	C
Coreldraw	Corel Systems Corp., 1600 Carling Ave., Ottawa, Ontario, Canada K1Z 8R7, (613) 728-8200 . . .	C
Micrografx Designer	Micrografx, 1303 Arapaho Rd., Richardson, TX 75081, (800) 733-3729	C
Artline	Digital Research Inc., 70 Garden Court, Box DRI, Monterey, CA 93940; (800) 274-4374 or (408) 982-0700	C

TIMEKEEPING & BILLING

Alpine Legal Mgmt.	Alpine Datasystems, 7320 SW Hunziker Rd., Suite 310, Portland, OR 97223, (503) 624-0121, (800) 547-1837	D
Compulaw	Compulaw, Ltd., P.O. Box 67720, Los Angeles, CA 90067, (800) 452-9529	D
Juris	Juris, Inc., 151 Athens Way, Nashville, TN 37228, (615) 242-2870	D

Continued on page 113

FORM 6–5 (*continued*)

11 Ways Computers
Continued from page 51

PC Law	Alumni Computer Group, Ltd., 722-155 N. Michigan Drive, Chicago, IL 60601; (800) 387-9785	D
Rainmaker	Rainmaker Office Information, Inc., 50 Franklin Street, Boston, MA 02110, (617) 426-1040	D
TABS	Software Technology, Inc., 6101 South 58 Street, Suite B, Lincoln, NE 68516; (402) 423-1440	D
Timeslips	Timeslips Corporation, 239 Western Ave, Essex, MA 01929, (800) 338-5314	A
Verdict	Micro Craft, Inc., 688 Discovery Drive, Huntsville, AL 35806, (800) 225-3147	B

DOCKET CONTROL SOFTWARE

Docket	Micro Craft, Inc., 688 Discovery Drive, Huntsville, AL 35806, (800) 225-3147	B
Network Docket	Compulaw, Ltd., P.O. Box 67720, Los Angeles, CA 90067, (800) 452-9529	B
Calendar/Docket	Data Law, 6341 South Troy Circle, Suite E, Englewood, CO 80111, (800) 433-3438	C
Fast Tracker Plus	Abacus Data Systems, Inc., 6725 Mesa Ridge Rd, #204, San Diego, CA 92121, (800) 444-4979	B
Kronos Docket Control	Kubernan, Inc., 321 West Fourth Street, P.O. Box 594, Winston-Salem, NC 27102, (919) 725-1915	B
Legal Calendar	Tussman Programs, Inc., 24 Colorado Ave., Berkley, CA 94707, (800) 228-6589	C

LITIGATION SUPPORT SOFTWARE

askSam	askSam Systems, P.O. Box 1428, Perry, FL 2347, (800) 327-5726	B
BRS/SEARCH	BRS Information Technologies, 800 Westpark Dr., Suite 400, McLean, VA 22102, (800) 235-1209 or (703) 442-3870	C
CAT-Links	CAT-Links, Inc., 2100 No. Broadway, Suite 320, Santa Ana, CA 92706, (714) 834-0563; (800) 825-4657	C
CompuCounsel III	Compulaw, Ltd., P.O. Box 67720, Los Angeles, CA 90067, (800) 452-9529	B
Discovery Base	Data Dynamics, 1465 N. Fiesta Blvd., Suite 107, Gilbert, AZ, 85234, (602) 497-1082	D
Evidence Master	Data Law, 6551 S. Revere Pkwy., Suite 215, Englewood, CO 80111, (303) 790-8193	C
Inmagic	Inmagic Inc., 2067 Massachusetts Ave, Cambridge, MA, 02140-1338; (617) 661-8124	D
Litigator	Micro Craft, Inc., 688 Discovery Drive, Research Park West, Huntsville, AL 35806, (800) 225-3147	B
Litigator's ToolBox	Signum Microsystems, Inc., 3 Regency Dr., Bloomfield, CT 06002, (203) 726-1911	D
MicroText	Document Automation Corp., 481 N. Frederick Ave, Suite 210, Gaithersburg, MD 20877, (800) 446-1028, (301) 990-3480	C
Summation II	Summation Legal Technologies Inc., 595 Market St., Suite 2050, San Francisco, CA 94105, (800) 735-7866, (415) 442-0404	D
ZY Index	ZyLab Corp., 3105-T No. Wilke Rd., Arlington Heights, IL 60004, (800) 544-6339 or (312) 632-1100	B

AMORTIZATION PROGRAMS

Amortization Schedule	Soft Sell, Inc., P.O. Box 136, Hinesburg, VT 05461, (801) 482-2905	B
Amortizer Plus	Good Software Corp., 13601 Preston Road, Suite 500 West, LB 226, Dallas, TX 75240, (214) 239-6085	A
Easy Amortization	Rem Software, P.O. 12010, Reno, NV 89510, (800) 237-7327 or (702) 825-1699	A
Execamort	Electrosonics, 36380 Garfield, Suite 1, Fraser, MI 48026, (313) 791-0770; (800) 858-8448	B
Legal Math Pac	Colorado Custom Legal Software, 3867 Paseo del Prado, Boulder, CO 80301, (303) 443-2634	B
Loan Plus	Advanced Performance, Inc., Authorized Dealer: Vickery Software, 102 St., Pickens, SC 29671, (803) 878-2100	B
The Mortgage Disk	Honeydew Software, Executive Park North, Albany, NY 12203, (518) 459-1115	A
TValue	Time Value Software, P.O. Box 16157, Irvine, CA 92713, (714) 727-1800	B

BANKRUPTCY LAW

Seven/Eleven+ Btcy.	Syntrex Inc., 246 Industrial Way West, Eatontown, NJ, 07724 (404) 551-7800	B
Chapter 13 Bankruptcy	Specialty Software Systems, P.O. Box 7026, Huntington Woods, MI 48070, (313) 398-9930	B

BUSINESS LAW

Business Law Case	Shepard's McGraw-Hill, P.O. Box 1235, Colorado Springs, CO 80901, (800) 525-2474	D

The list includes the bare minimum. You may at any time add to this list by leasing/buying a fax machine, dictating equipment, or hiring a secretary and/or paralegal assistant.

The cost of the above will differ geographically. The cost will also vary depending on whether or not you are willing to purchase used furniture and used equipment. There are many sources for used or rebuilt equipment, most of which come with guaranties. There are business equipment brokers in most major cities, who buy and sell used equipment.

There are several ways in which you can save money on furniture and equipment:

- Attend bankruptcy auctions. Many auctions are advertised in the newspaper. You can also get the names of auctioneers from the telephone book and ask to be placed on their mailing lists.

- Check newspapers for private sales, business liquidations, estate sales, and computer "expos" at which they may be selling demonstration models below retail price.

- Patronize small business fairs and other types of sales events that are advertised through the newspaper.

- Price equipment at your local "superstore," such as Price Club, Sam's, Wal-mart, B J's Wholesale Club, or Staples. Becoming a member of these superchains entitles you to further discounts on merchandise offered to the public. This merchandise is generally well below retail store prices.

- Check the computer magazines for specials in hardware and software. Call and inquire about the offer, ask about the merchandise; it may be a good buy.

- Review the classified sections of your local newspaper for used equipment.

Realistically, you are not going to have much income in the beginning. Unless you are working part-time to maintain a steady income while you build your practice, you must have a considerable start-up sum of money on hand to pay your bills. The rule of thumb is to put away at least one year's worth of expenses. It will take a while to build a client list and generate a steady income. In the meantime you will have to provide for your monthly expenses. If you open an office, furnish it, and employ a secretary, the following monthly expenses will have to be met:

Rent

Telephone

Insurance, including malpractice coverage

Supplies

Postage and/or postage meter

Photocopy machine maintenance, supplies

Fax machine maintenance, supplies

Library

Continuing legal education

Travel expenses

Dues, meetings

Electricity and/or gas (if not included in rent)

Secretary (optional)

Payroll taxes (optional)

Miscellaneous expenses

Monthly expenses should be estimated at between $2,000 and $3,000, depending on the amount of rent you pay and leasing obligations, if any.

You now have an idea of the expense involved in opening and maintaining an office on your own. There are still questions to be asked, however, to ensure you have considered the total financial ramifications:

- How much cash do you have on hand?
- How much will it cost to operate your business for the first year?
- How much during the second year? Until the business can stand on its own?
- Have you provided for additional equipment, maintenance, and repairs? Supplies, additional personnel?
- Have you provided for taxes and insurance?
- Have you provided for your own economic needs?
- How much money should you keep in reserve? [12]

§ 6.8   Financial Help—Raising Money

You may have to borrow money to start your business or to expand your business later. Listed below are prospective sources of financial assistance:

Family Members.   This is a key source of funds, If you borrow from family, you may have little or no interest to pay. You won't have to worry about a credit history; if it's your first time in business, you may not have one.

---

[12] Roger Fritz, Nobody Gets Rich Working for Somebody Else, An Entrepreneur's Guide (1981).

There will be no applications to complete. You are borrowing from people interested in your future.

Private Investors.   Choose someone who may have a knowledge of the profession and of your background and potential. You may find someone who would be willing to be silent partner or invest in your future—someone you may know through a professional association or an alumni association.

Bank.   When you approach your bank with your idea about going into business and your need for capital, be sure the banker understands what your business is all about, exactly how it will work and what security you can offer. In applying for a bank loan you must be very specific with regard to your needs. Do you need a direct loan for a certain sum for a set period of time? Do you want a credit line to provide working capital? Do you want a loan that may be paid monthly over time?

Be sure your presentation to the bank is organized, specific, and complete. Provide a written summary of what it is you are seeking and a statement of your objectives for the business. How do you differ from your competition? Do you have competition? Provide a brief synopsis of your business plan and information on earnings and expenditures for the past three years (if you have this) together with projections for future earnings. Provide a client list if requested and be sure to provide any and all brochures, advertising material, and literature about you and your company.

Money Magazine conducted a random survey of bankers around the country a few years ago, and each responded that the most important financial move a customer can make is to establish a working relationship with a banker. Many business owners have discovered that a strong relationship with a banker can be crucial for avoiding cash crunches.[13]

Small Business Administration (SBA).   If you don't think you can qualify for a loan from a conservative bank, you might want to try the SBA. In order to qualify for a SBA loan, you must fit the definition of "small business." Generally small businesses eligible for SBA loans are those with:

fewer than 250 employees

retailers with less than $2,000,000 in annual sales

service firms with annual receipts not in excess of $2,000,000 to $8,000,000, depending on the industry

---

13 Jeffrey P. Davidson and Charles W. Dean, Cash Traps: Small Business Secrets for Reducing Costs and Improving Cash Flow, John Wiley & Sons, N.Y., N.Y. (1992).

You can see from the above that all freelance paralegals would qualify as a "small business!"

Although the SBA does make special efforts to provide financing to minority-owned businesses, only a small percentage of loans are made to minority firms. When applications to the SBA are properly submitted, a high percentage of them are approved to non-minority firms.

Under the SBA the government guarantees 80 to 90 percent of the loan value. The participating bank services the loan although they can sell the guaranteed portion on the secondary market for a premium price.

Interest rates on SBA loans are competitive; the borrower usually has up to ten years to pay off equipment and up to 25 years to pay off a real estate loan.

Contact the SBA directly or ask your local bank if it participates in SBA loan guarantees. The telephone number may be found in your local telephone directory.

National Association for Female Executives. NAFE will invest up to $50,000 in companies where the owners are all women. This is an investment, not a loan; it does not have to be paid back. If your business shows a profit, a percentage of that profit is paid to NAFE. Contact NAFE, 127 West 24th Street, New York, New York 10011 or call (212) 645-0770.

Women's Business Ownership. The SBA also has an office of Women's Business Ownership that has compiled a list of alternative financing sources. To obtain a free copy of this list write to the Office of Women's Business Ownership, U.S. Small Business Administration, 409 Third Street, Washington, D.C. 20416.[14]

How do you protect and control your cash flow?

- Bill promptly. If you are on a monthly billing cycle, be sure your bills are sent out on the first of each month. Ensure that if a bill is unpaid from the month before, it is rendered the following month.
- If a client asks for a bill upon completion of a project, bill the client. Don't wait until the first of following month.
- Deposit your cash receipts daily, if possible.
- Keep close track of your unpaid bills. Don't let them remain unpaid for too long a period of time before contacting your client.
- Don't pay bills until they become due, unless you receive a discount for doing so.
- Don't pay more estimated tax than you have to on your federal or state returns.

---

[14] Gene Dailey, Secrets of a Successful Entrepreneur (1993).

- Don't carry more supplies than you need so that your cash is not tied up in your inventory.
- Consider using a money market account with check privileges for a portion of your cash in the event your business account does not pay interest.

§ 6.9 Insurance

Consider a hypothetical case. You are retained by an attorney to research bailment in order to respond to a motion for summary judgment. The attorney has asked you to research the question of whether the particular facts in your case fit the theory of bailment and provide a memorandum with your findings. You research the question, however you fail to cite check the cases you have found. You find a case that you believe to be on point and produce your memorandum to the attorney. If you had properly cite checked, you would have discovered the case you depended upon was reversed and overturned. The summary judgment motion is granted, your complaint is dismissed, and the attorney sues you for malpractice. Can it happen? It most certainly can!

Once you are retained by an attorney, you are covered under the attorney's malpractice insurance policy. Inquire whether the attorney has paralegals listed on the malpractice insurance policy and if not, ask the attorney to call the carrier and add this category to the policy. However, this policy protects you as one who is retained by the attorney, from any and all claims made against the attorney by that attorney's client. It does not protect you from a claim made against you by the attorney.

The malpractice insurance referred to in this chapter protects you in a claim by your attorney client against you for an error you've committed. This is highly unlikely as the attorney must review all your work before it goes out, must sign everything you produce, or verify it and give you permission to send it out. However, realistically, if an attorney is sued by the client, the attorney may very well sue you as an independent contractor. You might want to check with an insurance carrier in your area that writes malpractice policies for attorneys. Check to see if they will take a part time lawyer's policy and convert it with a paralegal endorsement. This endorsement will protect you if the attorney sues you.

In 1992 the ABA formed a Commission on Nonlawyer Practice to research the question of nonlawyer practice for society. This committee hoped to reach the subject of malpractice insurance by Spring 1994.

What errors by a paralegal would prompt a claim under a errors and omissions policy?

1. Errors in drafting documents such as pleadings, agreements, contracts
2. Omissions in legal research

3. Failure to maintain a calendar system, missing a deadline
4. Incomplete investigation
5. Omissions and/or errors in title searches.

One of the first areas I checked into when I started my business was malpractice insurance. I felt that the attorneys contracting my services would feel more confident if they knew I carried malpractice insurance. It was one of my selling points. When I started in 1982, I carried $1,000,000 coverage and advertised this in my brochures. I have since dropped the coverage to $500,000 due to the annual cost of the policy. I also carry a $1,000 deductible.

I have been covered by National Union Fire Insurance Co. since the beginning. The policy is a called a Part-time Lawyers Professional Liability Insurance Policy and carries an Independent Paralegal Endorsement. The coverage for the endorsement is as follows:

1. Coverage

    To pay on behalf of the insured all sums which the insured shall become legally obligated to pay as damages because of any claim or claims, including claim(s) for personal injury, first made against the insured and reported to the Company during the policy period, arising out of any act or omission of the insured in rendering or failing to render professional services for others in the capacity as a paralegal, except as excluded or limited by the terms, conditions and exclusions of this policy. . . .

4. The following EXCLUSION is hereby added to the policy:

    (1) any claim arising out of any acts or omissions committed by an insured and arising out of services rendered directly to the insured's client who is not a lawyer or law firm.

The NFPA has recently endorsed an errors and omissions policy issued by Scottsdale Insurance Co., Scottsdale, Arizona; the broker is Meridan General Agency, Chicago, Illinois. Scottsdale issues two policies; one for the employed paralegal and one for the freelance paralegal. The company defines the freelance paralegal as a "self-employed legal assistant doing work under the direction of an attorney client."[15]

As the paralegal profession expands, the issue will be whether paralegals will have individual liability that is not indemnified by the employer/contractor. The fact that you are a freelance legal assistant means you are operating a business, a business that is at risk if you are sued and do not carry insurance. Will the attorney sue you, since the attorney is responsible for what you do? If the facts warrant it, yes. As more and more freelance legal assistants open offices and take on a higher profile, paralegals will be at risk for

---

[15] Phillip M. Perry, *Do You Need Professional Liability Insurance?*, 10 Legal Assistant Today 59, July–Aug. 1993. James Publishing, Inc. Reprinted with permission.

liability to the contracting attorneys. Is it important that you carry malpractice insurance? Some freelance legal assistants carry the insurance; the majority do not. This is an individual choice based on whether you feel you need it, if it is available to you, and if you can afford it.

In addition to malpractice insurance, there are other types of insurance of which you should be aware. When you open your office, you will certainly want to obtain a business owner's policy to insure the contents of your office from fire including your equipment, whether it is leased or owned, that is, your computers, typewriters, telephone systems, fax machines, filing cabinets, postage meters, printers, and furniture. A business owner's policy also insures you for money and/or securities lost or stolen and for loss of valuable papers. Remember, you will have control over your attorney client's files in your office. Depending on the type of file you are handling, you may have exposure to securities and certainly to valuable papers. The business policy will also insure you for liability for personal injury should someone visiting your office fall and injure themselves. There is an annual fee for this policy.

Another policy you should be aware of is workers' compensation and employer's liability policy. This policy will protect you against any claims by an employee for injuries sustained while in the course of employment. There is also an annual fee for this policy and it is determined yearly by the amount of your payroll. An audit statement will be sent to you for completion once each year. This statement consists of your annual payroll records. The insurance company may also visit your office to inspect the workplace. Upon issuance of the policy, the company will send you a poster to be placed in a prominent place in your office, advising your employees of the workers' compensation insurance.

CHAPTER 7

ORGANIZATION

§ 7.1   Office Systems—Organization

Organization is the key to success. Without organization, your time, the direction of your office, and the administration of your business structure will be unmanageable. Decide how to put into practice all the systems you implemented and worked with when you were employed in a law office.

What is a system? Roberta Ramo defines a system as "a documented, logical method or way of handling transactions, procedures or work flow in the law."[1]

Systems are implemented to minimize the waste of time and effort and maximize efficiency. Whether propounding interrogatories, completing a foreclosure procedure, drafting a brief for a summary judgment motion, or preparing a file for a real estate closing, the procedure for each task should be at hand for referral. If you have to start over each time you initiate a procedure, or to find a file you previously worked on to retrieve a form, you lose time and money. These forms and procedures should be accessible to you at all times. When you have completed the work on a file, you may think you will remember that file and the work. You believe you will be able to recall it the next time you have a similar file. You are wrong. It may be one or two years later that you are called upon to repeat the work. It may only be six months, however, hopefully you will have worked on many files in the interim and the name of that file will dim. Another factor to consider is the

---

[1] Gary A. Munneke, Law Practice Management 308 (1991).

fact that copies of the work you performed may be stored in a closed file and not accessible at the time you need them. That is why it is important to have a system—a method of recall—for everyday procedures, unusual procedures, research, administrative tasks, and most everything you do.

In addition to helping you find what you need quickly, it is advantageous to any office staff you may employ. It is much easier to explain a procedure and a form when you can see it in black and white. Research has shown that lawyers who use systems that optimize the involvement of the legal secretary/assistant have increased productivity by 20 to 50 percent. This research also indicates that the productivity of the legal secretary/assistant may increase by as much as 10 to 15 percent through the use of systems.[2] As a freelance legal assistant all work initiates with you, whether doing the work yourself, or whether you have part-time or fulltime help. Systems do make a difference.

These systems described are ones that I use or have used. There is no right or wrong system. Whatever works for you is the best system. The important consideration is that you implement as many systems as you feel necessary to make your service efficient and cost effective.

The important systems you will need follow:

Billing, Time Sheets

Time management is extremely important to you since your product is your service. Only bill for that time you spend performing that service. The administrative task of maintaining your own office is not billable. When you pay your own bills, organize office records, organize files, order supplies, or perform any task for your own individual needs, you will not be paid. You bill only for your services to your clients. Keeping time sheets and setting up billing will be explained in § **7.5** and § **7.6,** however, this is one of the most important functions in your office. If you don't bill, you don't get paid; if you don't get paid, you don't stay in business. It's that simple.

When you begin to work on a file, keep your time sheets in much the same manner as your attorney clients do. If they use .17 for a six-minute charge, or .05 for a five-minute charge, and it is a minimum charge to their clients, then you also can charge that time. If your attorney bills .25 hours or 1/4 hour for a short letter, then you too would bill that time. When it comes to time allocation for pleadings, it depends on how long it takes to review the file, to dictate or produce the document. How complicated is it? How many copies and attachments are there? Watch your time and bill accordingly. Complicated matters tend to take longer; pleadings take longer. Reviewing a file for the first time must be done carefully and could take several hours

---

[2] *Id.*

depending on the size of the file. Learn to judge as you become familiar with the work you are handling. Once you render your bills, whether on a monthly basis or as the job is completed, be sure to follow up every month if the bills are not paid in a timely manner.

One system you may utilize requires producing three copies of your bill, the original for the client, a copy for your file, and a copy for your billing file. All bills that remain unpaid in the billing file at the end of the month are sent out on the first of the following month, and stamped "bill rendered." In this way you have control over your billing and know what is paid or not paid at all times. What do you do if your bill is not paid in a timely manner? Be discreet; be persistent. If more than two months go by without a payment on your bill, do one of two things. Write directly on the bill in your own handwriting the word *Please,* by the balance due amount, or make a telephone call to your attorney client and ask if there is a problem with your bill and that you would appreciate a payment. Your client will not be angered by the call and will most likely send you a check.

Time Management

This is difficult! How do you prioritize? How long should it take to complete a project? In every office you will have tasks to perform that are personal. These tasks could include taking inventory of supplies, ordering supplies, personal telephone calls, bookkeeping for the office, entering income and disbursements, entering information in the computer, examing insurance information, giving instructions to your secretary, paying office bills, reviewing new case law, new rules or statutes, reading law journals or subscription magazines, and attending continuing education seminars. The list is endless. There are many responsibilities you have that are non-billable. That is why time management is critical. Learn to prioritize in order to get all jobs done. There must be time for personal tasks and ample time for the services for which you will bill your clients.

There are effective methods to utilize for time management:

- Screen out interruptions. This may be accomplished if you work with an assistant, or if you are alone, use your telephone answering machine or voice mail. Have a special message that says you are "in conference" or "with a client" and you will get right back to them.
- Work in unbroken blocks of time. Write down the projects you wish to complete, responsibilities you have for the day, and fill in a list:

date	activity	time
4/5	work on interrogatories	9–12
	lunch	12–1
	work on Smith estate	1–3
	routine matters	3–5
4/6	work on Jones estate	9–11
	meet with client	11–12
	lunch	12–1
	review discovery files	1–4
	bookkeeping	4–5

- Monitor your progress. Categorize your efforts and and pay attention to how you allocate your time.
- Standardize and simplify your communications, forms and pleadings.
- Keep only current files—consider color coding them according to use. If you consult a file in your office frequently, perhaps daily, color code it red; if you need a file in your office for review, perhaps weekly, color code it yellow. Color code all other files green.
- Do the job correctly the first time. Be fully prepared and know your material, know your file thoroughly, outline your thoughts.[3]

To effectively handle all tasks, time can be divided into four categories, that is, wasted time, busy work, important work, and urgent work. As your work assignments come in, know which ones fit into the above categories and determine your time accordingly.[4]

The old saying "time is money" is true, as those who have worked for large firms, under the pressure of billing a set number of hours, are well aware. The hours billed will keep your business alive and you must effectively learn to deal with interruptions, distractions, and the delegation of work. Without the billable hours, you will have no income. Plan your time effectively.

There are several ways in which you can consolidate and organize your office for optimum management:

1. Organize your work into categories:
    a. documents you need to review, mail, incoming and outgoing, memos
    b. completed dictation

---

[3] Robert Moskowitz, How to Organize Your Work & Your Life (1993).

[4] Jonathon Lynton, Donna Masinter, and Terri Mick Lyndall, Law Office Management for Paralegals (1992).

      c. documents and materials to be filed or given to someone else

      d. documents you intend to take home to review

2. Do not have more than one file open on your desk at the same time.

3. Write everything down. Don't think you will remember, because you won't. It also makes work easier for other members of your office staff.

4. Take copious notes while speaking on the phone or attending a seminar.

5. Answer mail immediately so that as you read, you dispose of documents except for those that need further review.

6. Stay current or a little ahead of your work. When you are sending out documents, dictate instructions so that when the documents come back, you are ready for the next step.

7. Delegate as much as possible, remembering that you are responsible for all the work that is done.

8. Complete little jobs before tackling the time-consuming ones.

9. Set realistic dates for completion of a project since you must complete your work in a timely fashion.

10. Use the best and newest office equipment available to you.

11. Use messenger services instead of interrupting your day to deliver or pick up files or documents. Time is money.

12. Use checklists, models, and systems whenever possible for speedy completion of your work.

13. When a project is beyond your knowledge, seek help.

14. Organize your day so that you are interrupted as little as possible.

15. Bill as soon as your work is complete.[5]

§ 7.2   Office Systems—Procedures

The implementation of procedural systems will maximize the time you spend in the office. The systems described below will enable you to work efficiently throughout the day.

Calendar Control

Calendar control is an important task in any area of substantive law. Meeting deadlines, statute of limitation dates, inspection dates, and accounting dates, all control an important part of the work performed. If you have ever seen the application attorneys complete for malpractice insurance, you will recall that the subject of calendar control is one of the areas of detailed questioning

---

[5] Gary A. Munneke, Law Practice Management (1991).

on the form. The insurance companies want to know how calendar control is maintained, who maintains it, and any and all safeguards in place to prevent a claim for malpractice because papers weren't filed on time or filed at all.

Just as you diaried filing dates when you were employed, you must now diary or record these dates on your own. You have taken on an obligation to oversee a file or a specific project and it is your job to ensure that every date is diaried, papers filed on time, and dates checked by the attorney. This can be accomplished on computer software or by entering the dates on a calendar on your desk or in your daily diary.

There are various methods for tickler systems aside from using a daily calendar. One method is utilizing an accordion pleated folder with numerical markings representing each day of the month. All information you need to recall on a specific date is put in the appropriate folder. Another method is the use of a 3×5 index card box on your desk with numerical tabs representing days of the month. Written on each card is the information needed for each specific date. Each morning check your index box, or calendar, or the accordion pleated folder, depending on your calendar system. Of course, computer calendar programs can be tailored for your own use. Many have come to depend on the computer for a major part of their office systems. Upon arriving at your office, you will check either your daily desk calendar, computer calendar, or perhaps both. In addition, appointments should be scheduled either in your computer or desk diary, as well as in a pocket diary that you carry with you. If you are in conference at an attorney's office, and depositions are scheduled, or an interview is scheduled with the attorney's client, be ready to advise your availability and record the appointment. Write it down.

Conflict Checking System

When a new file comes into your office, it should be recorded immediately by name of attorney, names of attorney's clients, other parties, and date of happening. (In an estate file, record by the date of death; in a personal injury file by the date of the accident; in a real estate file by the projected date of closing). There are always dates to enter. In this way you can check to see if you have a potential conflict with any prior files on which you have worked. You would then immediately inform your attorney client of any conflict. Conflicts most likely arise for those performing services in the litigation area. Legal assistants doing document retrieval, real estate closings, or probate work (without litigation) would rarely have a conflict problem. However, if your specialty is in the area of litigation, corporate work, or any substantive area of conflict, always check the names of the parties involved in each new matter, to ensure that you have not performed any services for a current attorney client now representing a client on whose file you worked for a different attorney.

The longer you are in practice, the more files you will handle and the more names you will have to remember. You cannot leave conflict control to your memory, especially when you are working for many attorneys at one time. See § **2.4.**

Indexing of Files

When you receive a new file, decide how you intend to set up that file (numerically or alphabetically) and whether you are going to use the attorney's file or open your own file. You might also want to open a general file for each attorney client in which to keep copies of memorandum, correspondence, and billing. You could also insert copies of substantive work completed such as copies of pleadings, notes, and so forth in that attorney's folder. There will be times when your paperwork for some files will necessitate opening your own file to maintain duplicate records. This will occur in larger, complex litigation files that the attorney needs to keep in the office. In order to allow your work to progress, that is to perform legal research, draft answers to interrogatories, and respond to pleadings, you will need the benefit of pleadings filed by the adversary as well as copies of the complaint and any other necessary pleadings filed by your attorney for review.

All files opened should be properly indexed either by computer listing, listing by hand in a looseleaf book, or both. The files can be listed numerically or alphabetically and filed accordingly.

Remember, you will have a number of clients, and will maintain files for each. Setting up a system that will be easy to handle and keep paperwork to a minimum will require some thought. You don't want a room full of files to close within a very short period of time and then have to store them somewhere.

If you are managing litigation files for a firm, for instance, you could possibly be working on 10 to 15 files at a time. This could change from week to week as the assignments change. You may only work on one file a short time, return it, and take back another. If you open your own file for each assignment, you will need a room of filing cabinets in which to maintain all your files.

I don't open a new file for each matter. The paperwork would be voluminous. The first thing I do is index every new file that comes into the office by the attorney's name, the clients' names, dates, kind of matter, file opening date, and so forth. When I receive a copy of a signed real estate contract I do open a file, however that file will go to the attorney for the closing. I retain copies of the closing statement, reconciliation sheet, my notes, payoff letters, and my bill. I then place the copies in a file I maintain in the attorney's name marked John Doe, Real Estate, 1994. In this way, if a question arises at the closing, I have a copy of the closing statement and pertinent information upon which to rely.

For estate files I index the information and open a file for each estate. This file will contain copies of my monthly bills to the attorney and any unusual documents. I don't keep copies of everything I do in the file; it would be impossible. If the tax return is unusual, or if I prepare unusual documents, I maintain copies of them in the file. I also maintain copies of unusual documents in my forms file as explained in § **7.3.**

Litigation files are handled in the same manner, however, when working on a file that involves lengthy research or the drafting of pleadings, I make copies of the pertinent pleadings in the file, so that I have them to refer to while I am working on the matter.

Maintain a file for each attorney client and label those files. (Real Estate, Litigation, Miscellaneous) It will be an effective way to keep copies of documents for easy retrieval.

You will also need a system to close files and be able to subsequently locate them quickly and efficiently. An easy way to do this would be to give each closed file a number. Start a separate looseleaf notebook, or a computer list, with the date the file was closed and number assigned. This number would also be placed in the file open book, or computer list as a cross reference. Simply look in the "file open" book to determine if the file is still open and in the "file closed" book to determine the number. Files can then be boxed according to numbers and stored away.

It does pay to keep good records of your work. You would be surprised how many times attorneys will call you for a copy of work that they cannot locate of which you have a copy. Also many times you will work on a file, some time will pass, and then you will be called upon again to work on that file. You may also need forms in a closed file to refer to in a new matter. It makes life easier when you have the work at your fingertips.

Maintain a brief bank including your research, and a memorandum file for all briefs and memos listed by category to insure that you can find what you want when research and information on a particular subject is required.

This would apply to cases, instructional articles, and information that you read in a law journal or in a subscription journal that may be pertinent to a case. You will need a good system to categorize the articles, along with your research so that you can find it quickly and easily. Even if you put articles or cases in manilla folders properly labeled, (such as threshold injuries, COAH rulings, employment discrimination, broker's commissions) you will be able to locate your research without wasting time.

Bookkeeping

As the owner of a small business you will have monthly bills to pay for rent, equipment, supplies, and personnel, whether on a part-time or fulltime basis. You will have a federal tax identification number and will be required to withhold a percentage of earnings for both the federal and state governments. Tax returns and forms have to be completed monthly, quarterly, and annually, depending on your income. Depending on your income status, employ an accountant to provide these services, or learn to do them yourself. In any event, you will be responsible for the withholding of income, production of tax returns, and payment of monthly bills and payroll. How do you manage it all? You manage it carefully and responsibly. Keep incoming bills in a folder marked unpaid bills. These bills are reviewed every 10 days to see which bills need to be paid immediately and which can be held for 30 days. Once the bill is paid, it is marked paid and put into an alphabetical file folder or a redwell file folder for paid bills. You then have a record of unpaid and paid bills.

There are ledgers that you can purchase in any stationery store in which you can record your expenses and disbursements and income monthly. This information will be required for your income tax return at the end of the year. All income received must be noted by attorney name and date paid. Once incoming bills are paid, they are marked and put into file folders. Expenses for the month will be noted in the ledger by categories such as automobile expenses, rent, telephone, postage, office expense, payroll, and so forth. If you prefer, all this information can be kept on the computer on software programs designed specifically for this purpose. One program you can use easily for keeping track of income and disbursements is Quicken®. You can print out financial information by the month, the quarter, or the year. You can also keep a running list of your daily disbursements. One advantage of using this program is keeping tabs on your financial picture to determine where you are spending your money and where you need to reduce spending.

Library

When you are freelancing, purchase subscriptions to your state law journal, paralegal organization magazines, and bar association newsletters and magazines. Have access to the court rules that are updated periodically. Depending on your practice, you may also need a set of state statutes that are updated annually. Acquire form books, how-to manuals, and books on your particular areas of law. In keeping publications current, you will be amazed at how many books and periodicals you accumulate. Have them properly indexed and convenient for use when needed. Be sure any pocket parts are kept current so that you won't be embarrassed by an out-of-date form or procedure.

Form Files

Over a period of time you will accumulate various forms. In order to be able to secure a particular form at any given time, you must have a system for filing. In a small office, forms may be filed in a cabinet in hanging folders, alphabetically, according to the name of the form. For instance, Deed, Bargain and Sale, will be filed under D. Affidavit of Title may be filed under A. Another method for filing forms is by category. Then the deed and affidavit of title would be filed under Real Estate Forms and in that folder all real estate forms would be found. Certificates of incorporation, change of registered agent, notice of annual meeting would be filed under Corporate Forms, rather than under their individual headings. This is entirely at your discretion. Categories may be color coded and filed alphabetically. Some categories you may have include real estate, corporate forms, negligence, business and commercial forms, and probate forms.

In today's offices, printed forms are slowly being replaced by computerized forms. Many of the forms you produce will be found on the computer, rather than in a form drawer. Years ago, to draw a contract of sale, you used the printed form. Many offices still do, however, many more use a form entitled contract of sale that is on the computer. They simply fill in the pertinent information and produce the form. This encompasses forms in all areas of law, including substitutions of Attorney, stipulations of dismissal, releases, and so forth. If these forms were physically located in a drawer, you would index them. So too, you should have an index for forms contained in the computer. In this way you will know immediately if you need to obtain a printed form or if you have the form already stored and ready for use. Keep a list of all general forms for reference. This list is to be updated periodically.

§ 7.3   Office Systems—Substantive

Substantive systems are the heart of your services. They contain the information, forms, and procedures for the services you perform. The system contains:

Information/Facts.   This section is made up of fact sheets or interview sheets for particular areas of law. The Probate Facts Sheet is a list of questions to be asked upon meeting with the Personal Representative and going over the assets of the estate. This form will assist you in handling the administration of the estate. The Personal Injury Interview is a list of questions to be answered by the plaintiff with regard to the happening of the accident and injuries sustained. You may have an interview sheet for every area of substantive law in which you practice.

When called to meet with an attorney and the client for an initial consultation, (whether it is for estate proceedings, a personal injury claim, organizing and developing a corporation, drafting a pension plan or any new file) bring an interview sheet for that particular area of law. The attorney may not have an effective orderly list of questions, and will be grateful and duly impressed with the fact that you are totally prepared.

Model Letters.   These are letters accumulated as the result of working for different firms. Each attorney may employ a different system of forms. You will also have your own set of form letters for particular areas of law. When needed, they should be available to you or your assistants. Every area of substantive law uses certain letters repeatedly. These are the letters that you send in order to obtain information, give information, or request certain reports and/or documents. They can be letters sent to administrative agencies for filings, to the courts, to doctors, to title companies, and so forth.

Forms.   These are forms drafted in specific files and retained for future use. These would include, for instance, specific forms for foreclosure proceedings, complex agreements, motions, judgments, interrogatories, and contract clauses.

The most important detail about forms is to keep them neatly indexed and arranged so that you don't lose valuable time trying to find something you did last week, last month, or even last year. Indexing your forms correctly, whether on the computer, or in a book, or in a box or drawer can be a valuable time saver. The less time you spend hunting for a form, the more time you can spend producing billable hours.

One way to index your forms is with a looseleaf notebook. Use a notebook for different areas of law, or different types of forms. For example, all real estate forms could go in one book, along with forms on foreclosures, condominium information, and so forth. Another book could contain information on probate, including forms for accountings, guardianships, estate information, and stock transfer information. You could also have litigation forms in separate books. All the forms would be separated by alphabetical index tabs with an index to the forms in the front of the book.

Procedures.   This system involves the maintenance of manuals on procedure in specific areas of law, that is, foreclosure proceedings, proceedings on dissolution of corporations, mergers of corporations, probate manuals, real estate manuals, adoption proceedings, guardianship proceedings, accountings, and so forth.

After completing different procedures for clients, catalog them so that they will be available to draw from the next time you institute that proceeding. One word of caution! Always check court rules and procedures. Rules change; laws change. Check the statutes, check the rules, and make sure you are not embarrassed by an incorrect filing or pleading. Remember, the reason for systems is to organize your office and save time. Saving time is the most important feature of all. Your time is only paid for when you are working for a client. If you spend time trying to locating forms, locating a procedure you have completed in the past, trying to locate a closed file for an attorney or research previously performed and reported, you are losing money.

One easy way to maintain this system is in a looseleaf notebook with divisional tabs or separations. You may have several manuals. Examples of manuals that I maintain are Real Estate, Probate, Corporations, Foreclosure, Miscellaneous, Interrogatories, and Personal Injury Forms. These manuals contain sample forms and procedures together with rule changes, new legislation, and articles I come across that pertain to the subject. In the Miscellaneous manual I have the forms and procedure for adoption, so that when I have to prepare the papers for an adoption, I can refer to the manual. The forms may already be on the computer, however I can research the hard copies to determine exactly what information is needed and what must be done. Organization is the key to good business management.

§ 7.4   Billing and Collection

The most important aspect of business is billing! Remuneration is the reward for the hard work and long hours invested. It is in this area that you have to be the most disciplined—keeping track of your work and billable hours. The time spent on particular files must always be recorded. If you forget to record something you've done, you will not be paid for it.

Freelance paralegals, as well as attorneys, bill for time and skill. Studies show that lawyers who do not keep track of their time, realize 30 to 40 percent less income that the lawyer who does keep track. It is also important for both freelance legal assistants and lawyers to keep records to properly account to their clients and justify their billing.[6]

How do you establish your fees? In any given geographical area, you may know what law clerks and law students charge for hourly work. If you don't have any idea as to the fees they charge, look in your state law journal under "situations wanted" for attorneys, or talk to friends who work for law firms. Inquire about the hourly rates charged by law firms for paralegal time and by temporary agencies for the paralegals they hire. If there are other paralegals in the area who are freelancing, check with them as to their rates. Somewhere will strike a balance within which you feel comfortable. On a flat fee basis, try to estimate your fee to be no less than 25 percent of the fee the attorney will be charging. Quote your rate at your first meeting with the attorney, whether hourly or by the project or file. Sometimes an attorney will ask you how long it will take to complete a project. If you know, state so, if not, overestimate, rather than underestimate—unless you have absolute control over all the work and are not dependent upon the court for filing papers, or third parties such as accountants.

In the 1987 Freelance Paralegal Survey, NALA found that 28 percent of freelancers charged $11 to $20 per hour, 48 percent charged $21 to $30 per

---

6 *Id.* at 353.

hour, 14 percent charged $31 to $40 per hour, and 3 percent charged $41 to $50 per hour.[7] Notice that was a number of years ago.

Charge the attorney for reimbursable items such as copies, toll calls, postage, fax charges, and actual costs advanced. This should be in your retainer agreement. Time and charges for toll calls can be obtained at the time you make the call; postage must be recorded carefully for each client's file as well as for the number of photocopies and fax copies. Costs advanced together with reimbursable items paid on behalf of your attorney client must also be carefully recorded.

At the first meeting with the attorney clearly advise of your fee structure, and the fact that you charge for reimbursable items. In most cases, the attorneys will pass these items through to their clients so they really have no quarrel with paying for these items.

With the cost of postage and the general cost of upkeep of your office, you can't afford to give any of these services away; keep careful records in order to collect your monthly reimbursable items.

Note on the samples provided in § 7.6, there are reimbursements items listed, such as faxes, and photocopies. Be sure to count the numbers of photocopies you make when preparing a project, the number of faxes and the toll calls, as well as any reimbursable items.

For postage spent, keep a pad by the postage meter or by your desk. Each month record the postage spent by attorney name and file worked on, so that at the end of the month when you produce your bill, you have your reimbursable items ready.

You can bill in different ways:

1. Hourly billing at end of assignment
2. Flat fee on special files
3. Hourly billing at end of each month.

When you bill at an hourly rate, keep precise records of the services performed and time spent in order to accurately bill at the end of the assignment or the end of the month. Hourly billing usually means that you will give your attorney clients an itemized, detailed bill for all services. They will then be in a position to properly bill for your services if they so choose.

If given an assignment that consists of a particular job (summarizing depositions, preparing a real estate closing, setting up a corporate minute book) you might quote a flat fee. In this case, although you would not have detailed day-to-day entries, you would also give an itemized bill for your services performed.

Your itemized bill may contain:

---

[7] 1987 National Ass'n of Legal Assistants, Inc. Reprinted with permission.

telephone calls to clients/attorney's clients

telephone calls to third parties

detailed description of services performed by date

disbursements such as postage, photocopies, toll calls, and reimbursable items to you such as monies expended or reimbursable costs.

§ 7.5   Sample Billing—Retainer Agreements

Sample Bill—Flat Fee

This is the form of billing to use when you have a set fee and are not itemizing your services. See **Form 7–1** for a particular bill regarding a real estate closing where the paralegal prepared the closing for the attorney representing a seller.

Another area where a flat fee bill would apply is for projects such as incorporation, dissolution of corporation, summarizing depositions (where the page count is known), real estate closings, and so forth.

Sample Bill—Itemized

This is the form of billing to use when charging an hourly rate and itemizing your work. You are itemizing this work so the attorney can see the services performed and the attorney can bill for your services. This bill is used in all cases where you itemize rather than charge a flat fee. The bill is a synopsis of all work performed month by month. See **Form 7–2.**

Sample Retainer Agreement

Included at **Forms 7–3** and **7–4** are a sample letter and short retainer agreement that can be sent or given to the attorney after the attorney asks for paralegal assistance. The purpose of the letter and agreement is for all parties to understand the fees and costs—what is included and what is not included. If your attorney requires something more detailed, that too can be drawn. This agreement simply defines your fee with regard to the project assigned. It is also important to advise the attorney that you are aware of potential conflicts, and that you will check indexes and advise immediately if a conflict arises. Have the attorney sign the retainer, and sign and mail a copy to the attorney.

FORM 7–1
SAMPLE BILL—FLAT FEE

Dorothy Secol, CLA
Certified Legal Assistant

Cobblestone Plaza
901 West Park Avenue
Ocean, New Jersey 07712
(201) 493-0880

Independent Paralegal Services for Attorneys

BILL FOR FLAT FFEE

December 1, 1990

JOHN P. ATTORNEY, ESQ.

TO   RE: SMITH TO JONES
                            FILE NO. 4567
DOROTHY SECOL, CLA

PROFESSIONAL SERVICES

Professional Services rendered in connection
with closing of title Smith to Jones
                                              $200.00

DISBURSEMENTS

Photo copies, toll calls,
postage $ 10.00   10.00

TOTAL $210.00

FORM 7–2
SAMPLE BILL—ITEMIZED

Dorothy Secol, CLA
Certified Legal Assistant

100 Main Street
Allenhurst, New Jersey 07711
(908) 517-8555
Fax: (908) 517-8545

Independent Paralegal Services for Attorneys

ITEMIZED BILL

December 1, 1990

JOHN P. ATTORNEY, ESQ.

TO   RE: SMITH VS. JONES
                           FILE NO. 4567
DOROTHY SECOL, CLA

PROFESSIONAL SERVICES

Professional Services rendered in connection
with the above from November 1 to December 1 as follows:
office conference with attorney with regard to foreclosure
proceedings on Nov. 3; review of file on Nov. 4; telephone
conference with attorney on Nov. 6, telephone conference with
title company re foreclosure search; office conference with
attorney on Nov. 11 re examination of foreclosure search,
determination of defendants; preparation and drafting of
complaint in Foreclosure on Nov. 15, preparation and drafting
correspondence to court; office conference with attorney with
regard to finalization of pleadings for filing with court on
Nov. 15; attendance to preparation and drafting Summons on Nov.
17, drafting Lis Pendens, telephone conference with title company
with regard to continuation of search; attendance to comletion of
Lis Pendens on Nov. 18, drafting correspondence to county clerk
re Lis Pendens, drafting correspondence to
sheriff re services of Summons and Complaint on defendant.

4 hours @$50.00 $ 200.00

DISBURSEMENTS

Photos 25 @.20 $ 5.00   5.00

TOTAL $205.00

FORM 7-3
SAMPLE RETAINER AGREEMENT LETTER

Dorothy Secol, CLA
Certified Legal Assistant

100 Main Street
Allenhurst, New Jersey 07711
(908) 517-8555
Fax: (908) 517-8545

Independent Paralegal Services for Attorneys

December 1, 1993

John P. Attorney, Esq.
Constitution Avenue
Washington, D. C.

RE: Jefferson v. Lincoln

Dear Mr. Attorney:

This is to confirm our telephone conversation wherein you have asked me to assist you with the regard to the drafting of pleadings for a summary judgment motion in the above matter.

As indicated to you, my hourly rate is $50.00 together with any and all disbursements for photo copies, postage and other out-of-pocket expenses. I am enclosing for your signature, a retainer which embodies our agreement.

I am looking forward to working with you and hope that I will be able to render the services you require in a manner which will be cost efficient and productive to you.

Thank you for the opportunity to work with you.

Very truly yours,

DOROTHY SECOL

DS:S
ENCS.

FORM 7–4
SAMPLE RETAINER AGREEMENT

RETAINER

[date]

I hereby retain [name of paralegal] as a Legal Assistant to assist me with regard to research and writing in the matter of [name of case or project], said assistance to be performed under my direction and supervision.

I agree to pay to the said [name of paralegal] the hourly rate of [$ dollar amount] for all work performed on said file plus any out-of-pocket expenses incurred in connection with said file, including but not limited to postage, photocopies, fax, toll calls, and transportation. I understand I will be billed monthly for said services.

The said [name of paralegal] has advised that she does maintain a conflict check on all files that come into her office and that should she become aware of any conflict she will immediately report it to me as the supervision attorney.

The said [name of paralegal] agrees not to divulge any confidential information she may be privy to while working on any of my files.

I have received a copy of this Retainer.

_____
name of attorney

This above Retainer is hereby accepted on the terms stated.

_____
name of paralegal

We all try to perform services to the best of our abilities. Sometimes, however, mistakes do happen. What do you do in the event of an error?

If you are working on a project and you miss something, or there is an error in the form of a pleading, or a date is in error and it has been missed by both you and the reviewing attorney, the only thing to do is apologize and redo it without charge, hopefully without too much of a problem. When this happens—and it will happen whether you are working in the attorney's office or outside of the office—you cannot charge a fee for the work that is redone. Sometimes you may have to specifiy no charge. This requires a judgment. Remember you are in business to promote good will and maintain satisfied clients. Mistakes do happen and everyone realizes this. There may come a time when you are working on a file that requires extensive pleadings and the time expended on your part is far in excess of the fee the attorney will charge to the client. Here too, you have to know your market, and perhaps discount your bill so that your charges are not cost prohibitive to the attorney.

§ 7.6   Sample Time Sheets

The first sample time record is kept for services on each particular file. See **Form 7–5.** You may have five of these slips for one day for one file, for services performed at different times during the day. All time records are put into a folder at the end of the day. You can then enter them in the computer or on a general record sheet so that you are ready for billing at the end of the month. The time sheets are bound on a pad, 50 to a pad, and the pad is kept on your desk. When you complete a service for a particular file, record your work on the time sheet, tear off the sheet, record your time either manually or in the computer, and file the sheet in your to-be-billed file. At the end of the month, after the bill is drawn, the time sheets are attached to your copy.

FORM 7–5
SAMPLE TIME RECORD

TIME RECORD

DATE: _____ —

CLIENT: _____

SUBJECT: _____

DATE	SERVICE	TIME	CHARGE
	OFFICE CONSULTATION		
	OUTSIDE CONSULTATION		
	APPEARANCES		
	RESEARCH		
	PAPER DRAFTING		
	CLERICAL		
	TELEPHONE		
	TRAVEL		
	DISBURSEMENTS		
	OTHER		
		TOTAL	$

ADDENDA:

SIGNED: _____

The second sample can be used if you handle more than one file for an attorney. See **Form 7–6.** List all files on that one sheet with all services performed. After recording the services and the time, the sheet is also filed in your to-be-billed file until the bill is produced. The sheets are then attached to the copies of the bills for your reference.

At the end of the month, you will have a record of all services performed for each file by you, your secretary, and other paralegals in the office. Your bill is produced from these time records and the records are then filed with a copy of the bills.

The time sheets are your records and are kept by you. If at any time you are questioned by the attorney for any particular service, you can then refer back to your time sheets.

In an office where more than one person may be working on a file, each person keeps a pad of time records or time sheets at each individual's desk. In this way all work performed for a particular file can be recorded at the end of the day, week, or month, whichever is most convenient to you.

There are many different systems for timekeeping. Investigate options and find the system best suited to your needs.

§ 7.7   Office Assistance

Do you know your limitations? How do you handle pressure? Do you have the time to devote solely to your business? Are you willing to give up your free time, social time, and family time? Are you willing to do business alone; can you manage to hire an assistant?

One of the ways to alleviate some of the business pressure is through professional help. If you are fortunate enough to find capable, experienced help, you have half the battle won. A good legal secretary or administrative assistant or junior paralegal, versed in your specialty areas, can take a tremendous burden off your shoulders. However, in the final analysis, the responsibility is all yours.

What do you look for in an assistant? Someone to make your work easier, on whom you can depend to get the job done, promptly, neatly, and correctly. I'm not implying that you will find that perfect someone, but those are the qualities for which you are looking.

When you interview prospective employees, consider those circumstances you disliked when you worked in an office. Keep in mind the manner in which you disliked being treated and the manner in which you liked being treated.

Most readers of this book are probably experienced paralegals. You know what you need to get the job done and what you need in the way of a good assistant. Properly interview prospective employees and know exactly what

FORM 7–6
SAMPLE TIME RECORD—ALTERNATE

DAILY TIME RECORD

DATE:

CLIENT	FILE NO.	SERVICES RENDERED	PHOTOS	TIME

qualifications they actually have—as opposed to those they claim to have—and what their skills really are. This is important. Just because someone graduated from a paralegal program and is certificated does not indicate that they are experienced or qualified for your needs. Before starting the interview, specify what you are looking for. Are you looking for entry-level help? Are you willing to completely train someone? Will you have the time to train and still concentrate on building your business? Everyone is different and in different circumstances. You have a choice; you can seek experienced help for which you will pay a higher salary, or you must be willing to train someone to meet your specific needs.

Here are some questions to consider prior to the interview:

Do you need someone to be computer literate?

Do you need someone with experience in certain areas of law?

Do you need someone who is familiar with dictating equipment?

Do you need someone who can perform legal research?

Do you need someone who can manage your office?

Initially you can hire a part-time employee; you can use temporary employees on an as-needed basis. You can use someone who works at home at night. You can be creative with the assistance as long as it works for you.

When the time comes for you to hire an employee, whether part-time or fulltime, there are considerations:

Do not refer to race or national origins in your ads.

Do not refer to sex classification; you cannot advertise for a girl friday.

Avoid mentioning age references.

Be aware of any anti-discrimination rules that may apply.

You are interested in job qualifications only. Your application, if you use one, should never require personal information such as place of birth, where the individual's parents were born, religious affiliation, race or national origin, union affiliations, or physical characteristics. What is important to you are references you can check, previous experience, and education. See **Form 7–7** for a sample employment application.

FORM 7–7
SAMPLE EMPLOYMENT APPLICATION

Name_____
             Last   Middle   First

Address_____
_____

Telephone No._____

EDUCATION:

High School_____
_____

Graduated? Yes_____ No _____

College _____
_____

Graduated? Yes_____ No _____

If yes, type of degree_____

Certificate Program?_____
_____

Other_____

WORK EXPERIENCE:

List below, all previous employment, starting with the present and/or most recent:

Names & Address of Company	From	To	Type of Work	Reason for Terminating Employment

May we contact the employers listed above?

Yes_____ No_____

Additional information you may want us to be aware of

_____
_____
_____

_____
Applicant's signature

_____
Date

When interviewing a prospective employee, refrain from asking questions with regard to spouse's employment, whether there is a possibility of a transfer or move in the near future, the question of childcare, if there are small children, who will be caring for small children, and whether applicant's religion would interfere with working on certain days of the week or at certain times. Focus on the qualifications of the applicant—previous employment, reasons for leaving, and references given. Is the applicant experienced in the areas in which you are seeking experience? How does the individual's personality fit in with yours? Does the person give references that you can check? Were the reasons for leaving previous employment valid? Is the applicant willing and eager to learn? Do you feel the individual is trainable or does the person seem inflexible?

When and if you do hire an employee, do one of two things—either contact your accountant and advise the accountant to obtain an employer identification number for you or obtain a Form SS-4 from the Internal Revenue Service and complete it. Upon the filing of the form you will receive a federal identification number. See **Form 7–8.** If you are operating your business as a corporation or as a partnership, you must file the SS-4 even though you have no employees. You may request a business tax kit from your local IRS office. The kit will include Circular E, Employer's Tax Guide, which is a publication that explains income tax withholding and social security tax requirements and contains tables to use to determine withholding and social security taxes. Contact your state's division of taxation to obtain a state identification number for state taxes to be withheld.

FORM 7–8
APPLICATION FOR EMPLOYEE INDENTIFICATION NUMBER

Form **SS-4** (Rev. April 1991) Department of the Treasury Internal Revenue Service	**Application for Employer Identification Number** (For use by employers and others. Please read the attached instructions before completing this form.)	EIN OMB No. 1545-0003 Expires 4-30-94

Please type or print clearly.

1   Name of applicant (True legal name) (See instructions.)

2 Trade name of business, if different from name in line 1	**3** Executor, trustee, "care of" name

4a Mailing address (street address) (room, apt., or suite no.)	**5a** Address of business (See instructions.)
4b City, state, and ZIP code	**5b** City, state, and ZIP code

6   County and state where principal business is located

7   Name of principal officer, grantor, or general partner (See instructions.) ▶

8a   Type of entity (Check only one box.) (See instructions.)

☐ Individual SSN ___ : ___ : ___   ☐ Estate   ☐ Trust
☐ REMIC   ☐ Personal service corp.   ☐ Plan administrator SSN ___ : ___ : ___   ☐ Partnership
☐ State/local government   ☐ National guard   ☐ Other corporation (specify) _____   ☐ Farmers' cooperative
☐ Other nonprofit organization (specify) _____   ☐ Federal government/military   ☐ Church or church controlled organization
☐ Other (specify) ▶ _____   If nonprofit organization enter GEN (if applicable) _____

8b If a corporation, give name of foreign country (if applicable) or state in the U.S. where incorporated ▶	Foreign country	State

9   Reason for applying (Check only one box.)
☐ Started new business   ☐ Changed type of organization (specify) ▶ _____
☐ Hired employees   ☐ Purchased going business
☐ Created a pension plan (specify type) ▶ _____   ☐ Created a trust (specify) ▶ _____
☐ Banking purpose (specify) ▶   ☐ Other (specify) ▶

10 Date business started or acquired (Mo., day, year) (See instructions.)	**11** Enter closing month of accounting year. (See instructions.)

12   First date wages or annuities were paid or will be paid (Mo., day, year). Note: *If applicant is a withholding agent, enter date income will first be paid to nonresident alien. (Mo., day, year)* . . . . ▶

13 Enter highest number of employees expected in the next 12 months. Note: *If the applicant does not expect to have any employees during the period, enter "0."* . . . . ▶	Nonagricultural	Agricultural	Household

14   Principal activity (See instructions.) ▶

15   Is the principal business activity manufacturing? . . . . ☐ Yes   ☐ No
If "Yes," principal product and raw material used ▶

16   To whom are most of the products or services sold? Please check the appropriate box.   ☐ Business (wholesale)
☐ Public (retail)   ☐ Other (specify) ▶   ☐ N/A

17a   Has the applicant ever applied for an identification number for this or any other business? . . . . ☐ Yes   ☐ No
Note: *If "Yes," please complete lines 17b and 17c.*

17b   If you checked the "Yes" box in line 17a, give applicant's true name and trade name, if different than name shown on prior application.

True name ▶   Trade name ▶

17c   Enter approximate date, city, and state where the application was filed and the previous employer identification number if known.

Approximate date when filed (Mo., day, year)	City and state where filed	Previous EIN

Under penalties of perjury, I declare that I have examined this application, and to the best of my knowledge and belief, it is true, correct, and complete.	Telephone number (include area code)
Name and title (Please type or print clearly.) ▶	

Signature ▶	Date ▶

Note: *Do not write below this line.   For official use only.*

Please leave blank ▶	Geo.	Ind.	Class	Size	Reason for applying

For Paperwork Reduction Act Notice, see attached instructions.   Cat. No. 16055N   Form **SS-4** (Rev. 4-91)

FORM 7–8 *(continued)*

General Instructions

(Section references are to the Internal Revenue Code unless otherwise noted.)

Paperwork Reduction Act Notice.—We ask for the information on this form to carry out the Internal Revenue laws of the United States. You are required to give us this information. We need it to ensure that you are complying with these laws and to allow us to figure and collect the right amount of tax.

The time needed to complete and file this form will vary depending on individual circumstances. The estimated average time is:

Recordkeeping . . . . 7 min.
Learning about the
law or the form . . . . . 21 min.
Preparing the form . . . . . 42 min.
Copying, assembling, and
sending the form to IRS . . . . 20 min.

If you have comments concerning the accuracy of these time estimates or suggestions for making this form more simple, we would be happy to hear from you. You can write to both the **Internal Revenue Service**, Washington, DC 20224, Attention: IRS Reports Clearance Officer, T:FP; and the **Office of Management and Budget**, Paperwork Reduction Project (1545-0003), Washington, DC 20503. **DO NOT** send the tax form to either of these offices. Instead, see **Where To Apply.**

Purpose.—Use Form SS-4 to apply for an employer identification number (EIN). The information you provide on this form will establish your filing requirements.

Who Must File.—You must file this form if you have not obtained an EIN before and

• You pay wages to one or more employees.

• You are required to have an EIN to use on any return, statement, or other document, even if you are not an employer.

• You are required to withhold taxes on income, other than wages, paid to a nonresident alien (individual, corporation, partnership, etc.). For example, individuals who file Form 1042, Annual Withholding Tax Return for U.S. Source Income of Foreign Persons, to report alimony paid to nonresident aliens must have EINs.

Individuals who file **Schedule C**, Profit or Loss From Business, or **Schedule F**, Profit or Loss From Farming, of **Form 1040**, U.S. Individual Income Tax Return, must use EINs if they have a Keogh plan or are required to file excise, employment, or alcohol, tobacco, or firearms returns.

The following must use EINs even if they do not have any employees:

• Trusts, except an IRA trust, unless the IRA trust is required to file **Form 990-T**, Exempt Organization Business Income Tax Return, to report unrelated business taxable income or is filing Form 990-T to obtain a refund of the credit from a regulated investment company.

• Estates

• Partnerships

• REMICS (real estate mortgage investment conduits)

• Corporations

• Nonprofit organizations (churches, clubs, etc.)

• Farmers' cooperatives

• Plan administrators

New Business.—If you become the new owner of an existing business, **DO NOT** use the EIN of the former owner. If you already have an EIN, use that number. If you do not have an EIN, apply for one on this form. If

you become the "owner" of a corporation by acquiring its stock, use the corporation's EIN.

If you already have an EIN, you may need to get a new one if either the organization or ownership of your business changes. If you incorporate a sole proprietorship or form a partnership, you must get a new EIN. However, **DO NOT** apply for a new EIN if you change only the name of your business.

File Only One Form SS-4.—File only one Form SS-4, regardless of the number of businesses operated or trade names under which a business operates. However, each corporation in an affiliated group must file a separate application.

If you do not have an EIN by the time a return is due, write "Applied for" and the date you applied in the space shown for the number. **DO NOT** show your social security number as an EIN on returns.

If you do not have an EIN by the time a tax deposit is due, send your payment to the Internal Revenue service center for your filing area. (See **Where To Apply** below.) Make your check or money order payable to Internal Revenue Service and show your name (as shown on Form SS-4), address, kind of tax, period covered, and date you applied for an EIN.

For more information about EINs, see Pub. 583, Taxpayers Starting a Business.

How To Apply.—You can apply for an EIN either by mail or by telephone. You can get an EIN immediately by calling the Tele-TIN phone number for the service center for your state, or you can send the completed Form SS-4 directly to the service center to receive your EIN in the mail.

Application by Tele-TIN.—The Tele-TIN program is designed to assign EINs by telephone. Under this program, you can receive your EIN over the telephone and use it immediately to file a return or make a payment.

To receive an EIN by phone, complete Form SS-4, then call the Tele-TIN phone number listed for your state under **Where To Apply.** The person making the call must be authorized to sign the form (see **Signature block** on page 3).

An IRS representative will use the information from the Form SS-4 to establish your account and assign you an EIN. Write the number you are given on the upper right-hand corner of the form, sign and date it, and promptly mail it to the Tele-TIN Unit at the service center address for your state.

Application by mail.—Complete Form SS-4 at least 4 to 5 weeks before you will need an EIN. Sign and date the application and mail it to the service center address for your state. You will receive your EIN in the mail in approximately 4 weeks.

Note: The Tele-TIN phone numbers listed below will involve a long-distance charge to callers outside of the local calling area, and should only be used to apply for an EIN. Use 1-800-829-1040 to ask about an application by mail.

Where To Apply.—

If your principal business, office or agency, or legal residence in the case of an individual, is located in:	Call the Tele-TIN phone number shown or file with the Internal Revenue service center at:
Florida, Georgia, South Carolina	Atlanta, GA 39901 (404) 455-2360
New Jersey, New York City and counties of Nassau, Rockland, Suffolk, and Westchester	Holtsville, NY 00501 (516) 447-4955
New York (all other counties), Connecticut, Maine, Massachusetts, New Hampshire, Rhode Island, Vermont	Andover, MA 05501 (508) 474-9717
Illinois, Iowa, Minnesota, Missouri, Wisconsin	Kansas City, MO 64999 (816) 926-5999
Delaware, District of Columbia, Maryland, Pennsylvania, Virginia	Philadelphia, PA 19255 (215) 961-3980
Indiana, Kentucky, Michigan, Ohio, West Virginia	Cincinnati, OH 45999 (606) 292-5467
Kansas, New Mexico, Oklahoma, Texas	Austin, TX 73301 (512) 462-7845
Alaska, Arizona, California (counties of Alpine, Amador, Butte, Calaveras, Colusa, Contra Costa, Del Norte, El Dorado, Glenn, Humboldt, Lake, Lassen, Marin, Mendocino, Modoc, Napa, Nevada, Placer, Plumas, Sacramento, San Joaquin, Shasta, Sierra, Siskiyou, Solano, Sonoma, Sutter, Tehama, Trinity, Yolo, and Yuba), Colorado, Idaho, Montana, Nebraska, Nevada, North Dakota, Oregon, South Dakota, Utah, Washington, Wyoming	Ogden, UT 84201 (801) 625-7645
California (all other counties), Hawaii	Fresno, CA 93888 (209) 456-5900
Alabama, Arkansas, Louisiana, Mississippi, North Carolina, Tennessee	Memphis, TN 37501 (901) 365-5970

If you have no legal residence, principal place of business, or principal office or agency in any Internal Revenue District, file your form with the Internal Revenue Service Center, Philadelphia, PA 19255 or call (215) 961-3980.

Specific Instructions

The instructions that follow are for those items that are not self-explanatory. Enter N/A (nonapplicable) on the lines that do not apply.

Line 1.—Enter the legal name of the entity applying for the EIN.

Individuals.—Enter the first name, middle initial, and last name.

Trusts.—Enter the name of the trust.

Estate of a decedent.—Enter the name of the estate.

Partnerships.—Enter the legal name of the partnership as it appears in the partnership agreement.

Corporations.—Enter the corporate name as set forth in the corporation charter or other legal document creating it.

Plan administrators.—Enter the name of the plan administrator. A plan administrator who already has an EIN should use that number.

Line 2.—Enter the trade name of the business if different from the legal name.

Note: *Use the full legal name entered on line 1 on all tax returns to be filed for the entity. However, if a trade name is entered on line 2, use only the name on line 1 or the name on line 2 consistently when filing tax returns.*

Line 3.—Trusts enter the name of the trustee. Estates enter the name of the executor, administrator, or other fiduciary. If the entity applying has a designated person to receive tax information, enter that person's name as the "care of" person. Print or type the first name, middle initial, and last name.

Lines 5a and 5b.—If the physical location of the business is different from the mailing address (lines 4a and 4b), enter the address of the physical location on lines 5a and 5b.

CHAPTER 8

PROFESSIONAL GROWTH

§ 8.1   Continuing Education

The law is not static. It changes day by day, year by year. As cases are won and lost, precedents are set, legislators change, and the result is the repeal of a statute, the passage of a new statute, or the change in the court rule. How do you stay current? How will you know when procedures change and what the new procedures will be?

For the freelance paralegal these are important questions. These are questions that will help keep in perspective the importance of being well-informed, of knowing what is current, and when and how changes occur in your areas of substantive law.

Read your law journal! Know when the rules change and when statutes are repealed or passed. Know that you have to read the pocket parts of the statutes when you begin your research. The freelance paralegal must be aware of the latest changes. You are expected to know everything; you must be well-informed at all times. That means being more knowledgeable than most in-house paralegals. You are advertising yourself as an expert in your areas of specialization; you must be that expert.

The most important aspect of your professional career rests on your professional growth, that is, attending continuing legal education (CLE) courses.

Most who freelance have such close ties with attorney offices that when there is a change in a proceeding or court rule, we are informed immediately. By subscribing to the state bar newspaper, or the law journal in your state, you also would be informed of changes in procedure. Keeping up to date by attending continuing legal education seminars is critical. Whether it is a seminar in basic procedure or more advanced procedure, you must keep up to date with your chosen areas of specialization.

181

Both state bar associations and local bar associations present seminars on areas of substantive law. In New Jersey, the state bar association holds an annual meeting each May in Atlantic City. The meeting begins on a Thursday and continues through Saturday morning. During the day there are seminars given by the committees and sections of the bar association as well as seminars given by the Paralegal Committee of the State Bar. Friday is the day designated for paralegals when two or three seminars (depending on the time allotted) chosen by and organized by the Paralegal Committee are presented. There is also a paralegal luncheon on Friday. This is an excellent way to participate in continuing education and to network with peers. If your state bar does not have any paralegal seminars organized and given by paralegals, perhaps those who are members of a state bar association could recommend organizing and setting up seminars by paralegals, given for paralegals, attorneys, and all support staff. In addition to workshops and seminars, there are exhibits to visit that are open for the entire meeting. The exhibitors, including title insurance companies, computer companies, software companies, publishing companies, detective agencies, and subpoena service companies (to mention a few) are informative and usually offer promotional paraphernalia. You can acquire pens, pencils, notepads, coffee mugs, candy, clipboards, and tote bags. The exhibitors demonstrate their products or services and you can pick up information that you can always use. For example, I have located investigation services for personal injury cases and expert witnesses and have been able to purchase Institute of Continuing Education (ICLE) books at a reduced price. You can learn a great deal from the exhibits and speaking with the exhibitors.

Apart from the annual meeting of the state bar, each committee and/or section of the state bar presents its own seminars throughout the year. These seminars are given at a nominal cost and are generally informative and provide written material as to updates and changes in the law in the particular subject. For example the Real Property, Probate and Trust Law Section may combine a seminar with the Corporate and Business Law Section and the Environmental Law Section when the subject is important to all sections. Recently, the three sections combined efforts to give a seminar on the Industrial Site Recovery Act (ISRA) that was signed into law in New Jersey on June 16, 1993. Throughout the year, the sections give seminars to the members of their own sections on various subjects of interest.

The New Jersey State Bar Foundation, the educational and philanthropic arm of the New Jersey State Bar Association, also sponsors public education programs to improve understanding of the law.

In addition to the state and local bar associations, there are other seminars that are important to attend. The Institute for Continuing Education, (ICLE) a nonprofit continuing education service that operates under the auspices of the New Jersey State Bar Association and New Jersey's law schools, offers seminars for attorneys along with a special rate for paralegals. The seminars given by ICLE are either basic skills seminars, refresher courses, or seminars directed to new procedures or rule changes, such as updates on family law, discussions with regard to litigation technology, computer skills, trial preparation, crafting deposition questions, corporate updates, information on foreclosures, and so forth. These seminars are usually given from 6:00 to 10:00 P.M. weeknights, or on Saturdays usually from 9:00 A.M. to 1:00 P.M.

Besides the ICLE, the Practising Law Institute in New York gives seminars for attorneys and paralegals, with a special rate for paralegals. Examples of their workshop subjects are "Environmental Law and Toxic Torts Litigation Workshop for Legal Assistants," "Fundamentals of Medical Malpractice Litigation," and "Basic Patent Law." The American Trial Lawyers Association of America-New Jersey (ATLA) has an educational foundation that offers seminars for litigators. Some of their recent topics included "Winning Verbal Threshold Cases," and "Support Staff: How to Handle Automobile Cases." In the spring, ATLA holds a Boardwalk Seminar in Atlantic City with workshops on personal injury, matrimonial, and criminal law, workers' compensation, toxic torts, the paralegal, and women and the law.

Check with your state or local bar association to determine the name of the continuing education institute in your area. A call to the institute will usually put your name on the mailing list so that you will be aware of upcoming seminars. All of the aforementioned seminars qualify for continuing education credits towards the renewal of your CLA designation.

You can attend seminars of your choice in your area of substantive law, or attend seminars on subjects you are unfamiliar with but would like to learn more about. Whether it is a basic procedures seminar on closing title on residential real estate, or a more complicated subject such as estate planning or preparing fiduciary income tax returns, this is an excellent way to expand your knowledge and to use some marketing skills at the same time. You will be attending seminars where there are attorneys in great number. You want to be visible, make yourself known. It doesn't hurt to be seen attending a seminar where you will be perceived as someone serious about their profession and intent on gaining as much knowledge as possible.

In recent years there have been seminars given that are directed solely to paralegals. The national organizations, National Association of Legal Assistants, the National Federation of Paralegal Associations, National Paralegal Association and Professional Legal Assistants sponsor seminars for legal assistants several times during the year. These seminars or workshops are usually advertised in the association's mailings to their members as well as advertising in the local bar association newsletters or the state law journal and in *Legal Assistant Today,* an excellent monthly publication for paralegals. Local paralegal organizations in your area probably sponsor seminars and workshops. You do not have to be a member of the organizations to attend the seminars. Seminars may run four and a half hours in length—from 9:00 A.M. to 1:30 P.M.—or they may continue all day. In some cases, they may be offered over an entire weekend with several topics being presented concurrently.

In New Jersey there are three paralegal associations—Legal Assistants Association of New Jersey (LAANJ), South Jersey Paralegal Association (SJPA), and Central Jersey Paralegal Association (CJPA). All of these associations sponsor workshops that qualify for CLE credits. Often the programs are equally appropriate for attorneys. The three associations form the Garden State Alliance (GSA) which held its first annual convention in 1993. The convention was administered by the three paralegal associations and members of the three groups conducted the seminars and workshops. The day began at 8:30 A.M. with registration and included concurrent sessions of seminars all morning, a luncheon, and seminars again to 2:30 P.M. The convention was open to the public, including all legal support staff. Examples of seminar offerings were "Employment Law/Americans with Disabilities Act," "Ethics for Paralegals," "Interviewing Techniques/Securing a Paralegal Position," "Military Law/Sexual Preferences and the Military," and "Setting up Shop as an Independent Paralegal," to name a few. These seminars ran concurrently with seminars designed for entry level paralegals and students as well as practicing paralegals seeking alternative practice areas. These seminars, taught by experienced paralegals were entitled "Day in the Life of" and included subjects in administrative law, banking, collection practice, commercial practice, environmental litigation, real estate transactions, personal injury and corporate law. This convention provided an excellent way to improve knowledge of specific areas of law and to network with other legal assistants.

Most community colleges, and many four-year colleges have now instituted paralegal courses in their curriculums. Taking a course in a particular area of substantive law is an excellent way to broaden your knowledge and expand your horizons. The freelance paralegal must be especially competent and aware at all times of changes in the areas of laws in which he or she specializes. You don't want to be in a position of receiving a telephone call from an attorney client, being asked a question about certain procedures, and being unable to answer. You also don't want to be in a position where after you have drafted pleadings, the attorney has filed them with the court, and they are returned due to a change in the rules of which you were not aware.

During the past several years there have been seminars given by the national organizations specifically on the subject of the freelance legal assistant. The local organizations also have had panel discussions on this subject. As the natural outgrowth of the paralegal profession, freelancing is becoming an increasingly popular topic for discussion.

Other sources of CLE include legal newspapers, daily newspapers, law review articles, and magazines and periodicals published by the American Bar Association. Your state bar association and *Legal Assistant Today* contain excellent articles on trends in the profession, articles on substantive law, tips and timesavers, book reviews, opinion polls, grammar reviews, and many interesting and worthwhile articles for the professional legal assistant.

§ 8.2   Paralegal Organizations

The saying "united we stand, divided we fall," is true of any group whether it be a club, organization, or even a profession. The paralegal profession is still in its infancy; only through the efforts of the national and state organizations, have paralegals accomplished all that they have to date.

If you do not belong to a state organization, or national organization, join one! Of course, it is always better to belong to both. If your state organization affiliates with a national organization, you receive a double benefit; however, it is the participation in the organization that is important. Your national organizations have their fingers on the pulse of the profession. They know when it is well and they know when it is ailing. They are watchdogs and guardians and because of their diligence in pursuing satisfactory education and legislation and for creating standards, paralegals have become the fastest growing profession of the 1990s.

National Association of Legal Assistants (NALA)

The National Association of Legal Assistants, Inc. was incorporated in April 1975 as a nonprofit organization in response to the need for a strong national voice to represent legal assistants nationwide. There are over 15,000 members of NALA at the present time.

On May 1, 1975, a Code of Ethics and Professional Responsibility was adopted to serve as a guideline for NALA members and legal assistants. Each member of NALA and of a NALA-affiliated association agrees to be bound by this Code. The Code was revised November 3, 1979, and September 1988. The Code is reproduced in its entirety in **Appendix B** with the permission of the National Association of Legal Assistants, Inc., 1516 S. Boston #200, Tulsa, Oklahoma.

In 1983 the Professional Development Committee was formed to study the professional responsibility and ethical considerations of legal assistants. The committee studies ethical guidelines and opinions adopted or promulgated by various state bar associations. The committee drafted the *NALA Model Standards and Guidelines for Utilization of Legal Assistants.* This document, set forth in **Appendix C,** includes NALA's definition of a legal assistant and provides a model of standards and guidelines for utilization of legal assistants, reference cases, court opinions and state ethical opinions. The *Model Standards and Guidelines* was unanimously adopted in 1984 and revised in 1991. It has been used as an educational tool for bar associations, legal assistant committees, and organizations interested in promulgating standards for legal assistants.

NALA publishes *Facts and Findings,* a bi-monthly publication that features in-depth articles on topics and issues of concern to legal assistants, as well as a membership newsletter published in the months opposite *Facts and Findings*. In addition, NALA makes available numerous brochures, makes presentations to the bar associations on the effective utilization of legal assistants, works with the state governments on issues concerning the legal assistant profession, and works with schools in connection with ongoing legal assistant programs.

NALANet is the first on-line information service for the legal assistant profession. Through NALANet, a paralegal can retrieve information on relevant topics such as ethics, guidelines, membership, case law updates, legislative activities, and bar association activities.

NALA also hosts conferences for state bar representatives to discuss developments within the legal assistant field. These conferences are held semi-annually and provide a forum not otherwise available for bar associations. These bi-annual conferences, first held in 1978, are now known as the NALA Symposium on Legal Assistants. The 1989 conference featured the first presentation of NALA's two amicus briefs filed in the United States Supreme Court. The briefs were filed in the cases, *Blanchard v. Bergeron*[1] and *Missouri v. Jenkins*.[2] Both cases involved the recoverability of legal assistant time in attorney fee awards. Although the Court did not address the issue in *Blanchard* this work resulted in a precedent establishing opinion of the United States Supreme Court in *Missouri* by affirming the recoverability of legal assistant time in attorney fee awards at market rates. The opinion also recognized the professionalism and contribution of the legal assistant career field in the delivery of legal services.

The symposiums are open to legal assistant educators, program directors and representatives of legal assistant associations, and representatives of bar associations legal assistant committees.

Another important aspect of NALA is the affiliated associations. This program allows the affiliation of state and local legal assistant associations, as well as student associations, which subscribe to the same goals and philosophies of NALA. Affiliated associations are also provided with a voice on the NALA Board of Directors and forums, discussion sessions and meetings during the annual and mid-year meetings.

Some of NALA's continuing goals include:

1. establishment of a national voluntary certification program
2. cooperation of local, state and national bar associations in setting standards for legal assistants
3. promotion of the profession of legal assistant, educating the public for the advancement and improvement of the profession.

---

[1] 489 U.S. 87 (1989).

[2] 491 U.S. 274 (1989).

NALA also offers a Certification Examination that is given in certain states during the year. This is a voluntary certification examination lasting two days. The examination has various sections, including communication skills, an understanding of ethics, human relations, judgment and analytical ability, legal research, legal terminology, and substantive law. The substantive law section requires each candidate to complete the section of the American legal system and to choose and complete four of eight sections—litigation, estate planning and probate, real estate, criminal law, bankruptcy, contract, business organizations, and administrative law. This is, of course, an exam on federal rules and regulations. It is not specific to any particular state. Upon passing the exam, you are entitled to use the initials CLA®[3] after your name. See The Certified Legal Assistant Program in **Appendix E.** NALA has also developed a specialty exam that is open to CLAS, offering the title Certified Legal Assistant Specialist (CLAS). These exams are geared to special areas of expertise. This is a four-hour in-depth examination that is administered during the same time as the complete CLA examination. Specialty certifications are available in the following areas of substantive law—civil litigation, probate and estate planning, corporate and business law, criminal law and procedure, and real estate. Other areas of specialty certification will be available in the future.

The CLA designation is a standard to which a paralegal can aspire. Just as the Association of Trial Attorneys (ATLA) certifies attorneys to be Certified Civil Trial Attorneys or Certified Criminal Trial Attorneys, the CLA designation means you have gone that one step further to enhance yourself and increase your knowledge. Of course, not all attorneys are familiar with the designation, however, NALA is confident that within the coming years, there will be states that will adopt the certification exam as a measure of competence for those paralegals who want this recognition. In NALA's 1991 Utilization and Compensation survey,[4] based on a sample of 49 percent CLAS responding, it was reported the average annual salary for CLAS was $29,970 compared to a medium compensation value of $27,700 for non-CLA legal assistants. The NALA survey also showed billing rates for CLAS as $55 per hour compared with non-CLA's medium value at $50 per hour.

After the December 1993 examination, there were 6,159 Certified Legal Assistants and a total of 487 Certified Legal Assistant Specialists as follows:

---

[3] CLA® is a certification mark duly registered with the U.S. Patent and Trademark Office (No. 1131999). CLA® is a registered trademark of the Nat'l Ass'n of Legal Assistants, Inc.

[4] 1991 Nat'l Utilization and Compensation Survey Report, ©1991 Nat'l Ass'n of Legal Assistants, Inc., 1516 S. Boston #200, Tulsa, Okla. 74119.

Civil Litigation Specialists (First introduced July 1982)	264
Probate & Estate Planning Specialists (First introduced July 1982)	62
Corporate & Business Law Specialists (First introduced March 1984)	23
Criminal Law & Procedure Specialists (First introduced July 1984)	26
Real Estate Specialists (First introduced July 1987)	90
Bankruptcy Specialists (First introduced December 1992)	22

A list of the states represented at the time of certification, as of December 1993 are set forth on **Form 8–1.**

FORM 8–1
STATES REPRESENTED AT THE TIME OF CERTIFICATION
CLA EXAMINATION DATA—DECEMBER 1993

76	Alabama	47	Nebraska
57	Alaska	100	Nevada
476	Arizona	2	New Hampshire
39	Arkansas	32	New Jersey
208	California	94	New Mexico
140	Colorado	19	New York
2	Connecticut	100	North Carolina
1	Delaware	64	North Dakota
1	District of Columbia	51	Ohio
1662	Florida	274	Oklahoma
100	Georgia	74	Oregon
1	Hawaii	43	Pennsylvania
29	Idaho	1	Puerto Rico
26	Illinois	4	Rhode Island
33	Indiana	34	South Carolina
88	Iowa	52	South Dakota
127	Kansas	69	Tennessee
10	Kentucky	1386	Texas
95	Louisiana	71	Utah
31	Maine	83	Virginia
3	Maryland	10	Virgin Islands
3	Massachusetts	33	Washington
85	Michigan	25	West Virginia
8	Minnesota	21	Wisconsin
61	Mississippi	24	Wyoming
50	Missouri	6159	Total
34	Montana		

Upon passing the CLA exam, you receive your CLA certification that is valid for five years. During the five-year period, you must maintain five CLE credits (comparable to 50 hours of continuing education) in order to continue your certification. The ways in which you may maintain these credits is found at **Form 8–2** and **Form 8–3.**

FORM 8–2
REQUIREMENTS FOR MAINTAINING
CERTIFIED LEGAL ASSISTANT STATUS

All Certified Legal Assistants must submit evidence of completion of five (5) units of Continuing Legal Assistant Education every five (5) years to maintain valid certification. A completed Recertification Audit Verification plus a fee of $50 will also be required at the time of recertification. Notice of one (1) year probation will be given to all Certified Legal Assistants failing to submit evidence of completion of the five (5) units of CLAE within the five (5) year period. If the Certified Legal Assistant fails to complete the above recertification requirements in this time certification will be revoked, with notice to the legal assistant.

All requests for CLAE credit are subject to Certifying Board approval. Relevancy is subject to approval by the NALA Certifying Board who may request employer attestation.

The categories of CLAE with unit values are:

Category A   Successful completion of a NALA Specialty Examination—2 units per Specialty Examination

Category B   Successful completion (Grade C or better) of a relevant course for a minimum of 3 quarter hours or 2 semester hours at an accredited institution of higher education. Relevancy may be requested by employer attestation and NALA Certifying Board approval—2 units per course.

    Auditing of a relevant course, or completion of a relevant course not meeting above listed minimums — 1 unit per course

    (Clarification of hours: Institutions of higher education generally are organized into quarters—10-12 weeks in length and give "quarter hours" as unit of course measurement or into semesters 14-15 weeks in length and give "semester hours" as unit of course measurement. A 2 semester hour course is usually equal to a 3 quarter hour course. Minimums are specified only.

    Clarification of "accredited": By any nationally recognized accrediting agency.)

Category C   Attendance at conferences, seminars, workshops, etc., on relevant topics for working legal assistants, with actual hours recorded. Minimum content of one hour required for consideration. Actual educational hours will be recorded and copy of brochure and/or program indicating schedule must be attached (unless a NALA-sponsored event.) Units will be recorded on the basis of ten hours of continuing education equalling one CLAE unit.

Category D   Certified Legal Assistants may petition NALA Certifying Board for credit for unusual experiences which may be considered for credit. Examples: teaching experience; extensive research beyond employment requirements on a topic related to the work of a practicing legal assistant which results in publication —limited to 2 units per petition.

Mechanics: It is the obligation of Certified Legal Assistants to secure supporting data (transcripts, employer and coordinator attestations, articles, etc.) to be submitted to NALA Headquarters as events are attended. These documents will be reviewed by the full Certifying Board for action. Request forms are available from NALA Headquarters at the address listed below.

NOTE: Effective October 1982, for recertification purposes, except in Category A, units for attending serninars in areas other than substantive law are limited to one unit maximum for any five year period .

Adopted 10/10/77; Amended 6/81; 8/82; 5/85; 5/87; 2/88; 5/88; 10/88; 3/93

CLA is a certification mark duly registered with the U.S. Patent and Trademark Office (No. 1131999). Any unauthorized use is strictly forbidden.

National Association of Legal Assistants, Inc.
1516 South Boston Avenue, Suite 200
Tulsa, Oklahoma 74119-4013
(918) 587-6828   FAX (918) 582-6772

Aspiring freelance legal assistants want to be recognized as the best in your profession. To that end, be interested in whatever means are at your disposal to make yourself more marketable.

FORM 8–3
CERTIFICATE OF ATTENDANCE

 National Association of Legal Assistants, Inc.
1516 S. BOSTON AVE. ● SUITE 200 ● TULSA, OK 74119
(918) 587-6828

<u>CERTIFICATE OF ATTENDANCE</u>

As a NALA Certified Legal Assistant, proof of continuing education must be submitted for CLAE units. If attending an education event not sponsored by NALA, this form should be completely filled in, including validation and all required signatures, and submitted with other documentation of continuing legal education in accordance with the Requirements to Maintain Certification. The document will be reviewed by the full Certifying Board.

<u>PLEASE COMPLETE THE SPACES BELOW AND ATTACH A PROGRAM</u>

Session Hours	Session Topics (Description and Speakers)	Validation of Attendance
_____	_____	_____
	_____	
_____	_____	_____
	_____	
_____	_____	_____
	_____	
_____	_____	_____
	_____	
	_____	

Name of CLA (Please Print)   Account Number (On Mailing Label)

Signature of CLA   For _____

Address   Authorized Signature of Sponsor

Date of Educational Event: _____

Location: _____

National Federation of Paralegal Associations, Inc.

The National Federation of Paralegal Associations, Inc. was organized in 1974 by eight associations. By 1993 the Federation was an organization representing over 60 member associations whose total membership exceeded 17,500. NFPA is the oldest and largest national organization. Although NFPA began by allowing only associations as members, individuals may now join.

Each voting member association elects or appoints a primary and a secondary representative to participate in NFPA activities, to vote its interests at meetings, and to inform the local membership about national issues.

NFPA is divided into four geographic regions. Regional directors are elected by the representatives within their particular region. These regional directors provide the important link between the member associations and the board of directors.

The NFPA publishes a quarterly newsletter, *The National Paralegal Reporter,* which focuses on paralegal issues. Other publications include *The Alert,* a quarterly newsletter focusing on policy issues, an association directory, a training directory, as well as booklets and pamphlets. NFPA provides a national communications network for addressing the diverse views, professional needs, interests, and responsibilities of paralegals. Like NALA, NFPA works with state and local bar associations, educational facilities, and the legislature for the promulgation of the profession.

Through its Education Task Force, the NFPA works to improve paralegal certificate and degree programs. It also monitors legislation and the court system, maintains liaisons with other professional consumer organizations, monitors issues affecting the profession and the delivery of legal services, and conducts and supports research into these issues.

Some of NFPA's continuing goals are:

1. foster and promote the paralegal profession
2. monitor and participate in developments in the paralegal profession
3. participate in, carry on and conduct research seminars, experiments, investigations, studies, or other work relative to the paralegal profession.

The federation is administered by its Board of Directors. The activities of the Federation are also managed through various committees, including professional development, continuing education, pro bono, career enhancement, consumer liaison, and expansion of professional responsibilities.

In 1975 NFPA adopted the position that it is necessary and advisable that paralegals maintain primary control of the creation of guidelines and standards for the development of the profession. NFPA supports participation by members of the legal community, paralegal educators, and the public with regard to investigatory and policy making activities concerning regulation of the legal assistant profession.

NFPA's annual and mid-year meetings are scheduled in the spring and fall, and are usually hosted by a member organization. The representatives from the member associations vote on issues affecting NFPA's members. Continuing legal education is usually scheduled in conjunction with the meeting.

The NFPA also prepares letters and amicus briefs to educate attorneys and judges on the paralegal's role in the delivery of legal services and the recoverability of paralegal fees. As NALA prepared and filed an amicus brief to aid us in *Opinion 24,*[5] so too did NFPA. They will represent a member's interests at hearings and meetings held by governmental bodies, local and state bar associations, will present written and oral testimony to legislative bodies on issues affecting paralegals at the local, state, and federal levels, will continue to promote the development of our profession at the national level, will work with educators to adopt model curriculum and pursue ABA approval, will develop textbooks for educational programs, and will inform its members of any national concern or issue affecting the paralegal profession today.

The NFPA Mission Statement is as follows:

> The National Federation of Paralegal Associations, Inc. (NFPA) is a non-profit, professional organization comprised of state and local paralegal associations throughout the United States. NFPA affirms the paralegal profession as an independent, self-directed profession which supports increased quality, efficiency and accessibility in the delivery of legal legal services. NFPA promotes the growth, development and recognition of the profession as an integral partner in the delivery of legal services.[6]

Professional Legal Assistants, Inc. (PLA)

The Professional Legal Assistants, Inc. is a newly-formed organization having received its charter in 1985. It is the only national organization that requires a professional standard for membership. Only credentialed legal assistants— those who have successfully completed an academic program that is in "substantial compliance" with the American Bar Association requirements, or who have passed a professional test—are eligible for voting, active membership.

Education is the basis of PLA's definition of a "professional" legal assistant. Those individuals who have successfully completed a paralegal program qualify for active membership status. Those individuals who are not able to obtain a formal paralegal education may receive active membership status by passing a state or national examination. Individuals currently enrolled in a paralegal

---

[5] *Opinion 24,* 607 A.2d 962, 128 N.J. 114 (1992).

[6] NFPA Mission Statement, adopted Mar. 1987, © May 1993, Nat'l Federation of Paralegal Associations, Inc. All rights reserved. Reprinted with permission.

program are designated as student members and others interested in the profession may join PLA as associate members.

Active members are required to complete six hours of continuing education each year to ensure that they will be informed about the profession as it and the law evolves.

Student membership is widely encouraged as PLA believes that these men and women are the future leaders of the profession. It is their philosophy that education is the vehicle to set paralegals apart from other legal support staff and they have a strong desire to better current educational programs. To that end, the Foundation for Professional Legal Assistants, Inc. was chartered. This is a non-profit organization established under § 501(c)(3) of the Internal Revenue Code of 1954, as amended. The Foundation also co-sponsors educational programs for the professsion and funds obtained from these seminars and from contributions are used to establish scholarships for students. The Foundation holds an annual writing contest open to students across the country. They have awarded upwards of $15,000 to students over the past years. This contest is open to any legal assistant student in a legal studies program. Topics are selected by the organization and information is made available publicly to the schools. PLA may be reached at 25 West Creek Drive, Murray, Utah 84107.

PLA is governed by a Board of Directors voted on by the membership. Each director serves for a two-year term and there is no limit to the number of directors that may serve on the board. Presently the board consists of seven members.

PLA has adopted the ABA *Guidelines for the Utilization of Legal Assistant Services* and their members are held to those same standards of ethical conduct as have been established by the ABA in its Model Rules of Professional Conduct. Their members are also subject to the state bar association's rules of professional conduct. PLA is in the process of developing goals and guidelines for personal professional attainment.

The goals and purposes of PLA are as follows:

- To establish a national professional organization for credentialed legal assistants.
- To promote high standards of ethical conduct among its members which are consistent with the Model Code of Professional Responsibility of the American Bar Association.
- To foster, promote, and otherwise encourage the growth and advancement of credentialed legal assistants by recognizing competence and proficiency through schooling or other suitable means.
- To bridge the gap of understanding and meet and fulfil the needs of credentialed legal assistants who are practicing in private law firms, governmental agencies, corporate law departments, and as freelance contractors in the United States, its territories, and Canada.

- To promote and encourage involvement in the profession and meet and fulfill the needs of students enrolled in legal assistant programs.

- To establish a foundation which qualifies as a "public charity" (within the scope and meaning of the Internal Revenue Code) to provide loans and/or scholarships for education and training of legal assistants and/or such other purposes as are set forth in § 501(c)(3) of the Internal Revenue Code of 1954, as amended from time to time.

- To cooperate and work with organized bar associations in developing guidelines for the utilization of legal assistants.

- To cooperate and work with legal assistant educators in the development of curricula for training programs in order to achieve competence and proficiency in the profession.

- To provide a forum for legal assistants to share and exchange experiences, ideas, opinions, and expertise.

- To sponsor state, regional, national, and international seminars, workshops, and other programs for legal assistants designed to improve their capabilities.

- To advance the understanding of the legal community and the general public concerning the use of legal assistants and the delivery of quality legal services performed by qualified legal assistants.

- To serve as a resource for information and assistance to legal assistants, bar associations, and legal assistant educators.

- To promote harmonious relations and mutual understanding and cooperation between its members and other legal assistants throughout the United States, its territories, and Canada.

- To promote a mutually beneficial understanding between the Association and its members and other organizations involved directly or indirectly with the advancement and development of the legal assistant profession.

PLA holds its annual convention in the summer. The organization conducts its business meeting, gives seminars, and discusses the state of the profession.

National Paralegal Association (NPA)

The National Paralegal Association (NPA), Solebury, Pennsylvania, was organized in 1982 and has thousands of members throughout the United States, Canada, and foreign countries. The organization is managed by an Executive Director and has an advisory board consisting of attorneys, paralegals, paralegal educators, and administrators. NPA defines a legal assistant as:

> Any individual or firm trained or educated in legal skills, who provides services to assist an attorney, individual, firm, corporation, government agency,

association or partnership on staff or as an independent contractor, providing such service is not an engagement in the practice of law as defined by the Code of Professional Responsibility of the American Bar Association or federal, state or local statutes governing attorneys and their duties and responsibilities.

NPA publishes a periodic publication entitled *The Paralegal Journal* in addition to the *NPA News,* a regularly issued newsletter. They have a paralegal placement network that is a nationwide network tracking paralegal positions available locally, regionally, and nationally. They also publish a national salary and employment survey, offer a customized NPA Master Card, have a member-loan program, and participate with Quest in obtaining discounts at participating hotel/motel chains nationwide.

NPA has four categories for membership:

Regular Member.   Those who are actively working as paralegals, paralegal supervisors, or legal administrators, or have graduated or completed studies from a proprietary school, university, or other educational program authorized, qualified and approved to extend training to those desiring to become paralegals, or any person who does not fit the above categories but who has successfully completed an examination approved by the American Bar Association, a state or local bar association, or the educational or occupational branch of the state or federal government or such examination which shall be administered by the NPA may be regular members.

Associate Member.   This category is open to attorneys, educators, or schools involved in the training of attorneys, paralegals, or legal assistants. Corporations, schools, or governmental agencies who employ paralegals would fall in this category.

Student Member.   A student in good standing enrolled in a part-time or full-time program that will lead to entrance into the paralegal field qualify for student membership. The curriculum of the school shall be subject to approval by the Association.

Sustaining Member.   Any person, attorney, law firm, corporation, partnership, or institution who supports the paralegal program and concept may become a sustaining member.

Because NPA is a young organization, some of its future goals are the promotion of public relations programs for the advancement of the paralegal profession, regional and national educational seminars and workshops, establishment of special insurance programs, publications of educational material, and the establishment of headquarter consulting services for special problems or applications.

As a freelance paralegal, if you find a number of other freelance parale-gals, you could start your own organization. This could be an offshoot of your state or local organization or a completely separate organization. Freelance paralegals realize there are problems endemic to that specific way of working, problems that the in-house paralegal may not have. By network-ing with other freelance paralegals, all benefit by the exchange of ideas, con-cepts, problem solving, and methods. Belonging to a national organization is absolutely critical. I joined NALA in 1977 and received the CLA designation in June 1978. At that time I was still employed by a law firm. In 1981, when I began to consider freelance work, I contacted NALA to see if I could ethi-cally work outside an office under attorney supervision. Because NALA is a national organization, and had members who were freelancing in other parts of the country, and because of their participation with bar associations in many states, and with the American Bar Association, representatives could comfortably advise me that as long as I worked under the direct supervision of an attorney, I could work for myself, outside the normal law office setting.

In 1982 when I opened my first office, renting space from one of my attor-ney clients, I asked the telephone company to list my name as Dorothy Secol, CLA. The telephone company refused, telling me that they did not have any CLA designation in their list of approved abbreviations and therefore I couldn't be listed that way. I again contacted NALA who sent me literature on NALA in general and on the CLA exam in particular. I forwarded this infor-mation to the telephone company (with a copy to the Board of Public Utilities) and the telephone company agreed to list my CLA designation. I also asked for a listing in the yellow pages, under paralegal. The only problem was there was no listing of paralegal in our yellow pages. With a little more coaxing, the telephone company agreed to a yellow page listing with my name.

Over the years there have been many occasions where I have enlisted the aid of NALA, whether it was a point of information, a question of ethics, or general information on the profession. However, the most important test of my national association coming to my rescue was on November 15, 1990, when the New Jersey Supreme Court Committee on the Unauthorized Practice of Law rendered its opinion that the use of freelance paralegals in New Jersey constituted the unauthorized practice of law. I was out of busi-ness! I made phone calls. The first was to my attorney; the second to NALA. During the next few frantic days, there were many phone calls with NALA, my attorneys, and with other freelance paralegals in New Jersey. When the initial flurry subsided, we had 11 freelance paralegals filing a petition to over-turn the opinion and for a stay of the opinion pending the final outcome. The stay was granted and we were able to work until the supreme court rendered a decision on May 14, 1992. NALA and my local paralegal organization, Legal Assistants Association of New Jersey (a NALA affiliate) filed an amicus brief on our behalf along with NFPA and AFPE (the American Federation of

Paralegal Educators). The paralegal organizations were there to support us during this trying time and I am eternally grateful to them.

In addition to such legal support, my membership keeps me informed as to all the latest trends in the profession as well as legislation and case law in other states. The national associations, through their committees and publications keep their members abreast of the latest changes. NALA and NFPA, as well as the PLA have annual and mid-year meetings during which they report to their members on the latest state of the profession as well as conduct seminars on substantive law. Attending the meetings is an excellent way to meet paralegals from other parts of the country, gather information and new ideas, and generally to interact with peers.

In addition to the national organization, each state has local and state organizations. These associations allow you to meet your peers, network, and meet other paralegals with whom you can exchange ideas and experiences.

§ 8.3   State Bar Associations Membership

In 1981 the State Bar of Texas created a Legal Assistant Division. The by-laws of the division in defining its purposes, state "to enhance legal assistants' participation in the administration of justice, professional responsibility and public service in cooperation with the State Bar of Texas." The Division proved to be very popular and by 1990 had almost 2,000 members.[7]

In 1982 the Standing Committee on Legal Assistants proposed that the ABA create an associate membership category for legal assistants. However, it was not until April 12, 1987, that the House of Delegates of the American Bar Association voted to amend the by-laws to create associate status for legal assistants. This associate membership allows legal assistants to participate in the ABA's various sections, divisions, committees, and other activities.

In the past decade there has been a higher quality of recognition and growth in the paralegal profession. Legal assistants/paralegals have been recognized by the United States Supreme Court as well as many state supreme courts, as an integral part of the legal profession; state bar associations have designated and defined the profession; cases have been decided for paralegal fee recovery and state bar associations have created associate membership categories for paralegals.

The benefits for joining your state or county bar associations are numerous. You will be entitled to a lower membership fee, reduced CLE seminar fees, subscriptions to all bar publications, group insurance rates, and may participate in social functions.

A summary of bar association membership requirements for the state and county bars follows:

---

[7] William P. Statsky, Paralegal Ethics & Regulation 36 2d (1993).

Bar Membership Requirements for Legal Assistants

STATE/ COUNTY	REQUIREMENTS/REMARKS
Alaska	Can join substantive sections
Arizona	
Pima County	1. NALA CLA certification and compliance with all requirements to maintain CLA, and 2. Attorney attestation to employment, and at least three years experience.
Yavapia County	1. NALA CLA certification and compliance with requirements to maintain CLA; or 2. Graduate from ABA approved school.
California	
Santa Barbara County	Legal assistant who meets one of the following: 1. Graduation from ABA approved program or completion of CLA exam. 2. Graduation from courses not ABA approved but accredited institution that requires 60 semester hours of classroom study. 3. Graduation from program not meeting 1 and 2 plus six months in-house training. 4. B.A. degree plus six months in-house training. 5. Three years legal-related experience with six months of in-house training as a legal assistant. 6. Two years in-house training as a legal assistant.
Colorado	Demonstrate job responsibilities contribute to the legal system.
Denver	Demonstrate job responsibilities contribute to the legal system.
Florida	Offered only through individual sections.
Sections:	
Family Law	Must meet one of the following: 1. CLA certification. 2. Graduation from ABA approved school. 3. Graduation from program not accredited nor ABA approved which requires at least 60 semester hours of study. 4. Graduation from a program other than set forth above plus not less that six months in-house training.

STATE/ COUNTY	REQUIREMENTS/REMARKS
General Practice	Must meet one of the following 1. CLA certification. 2. Graduation from ABA approved program. 3. Graduation from accredited institution which requires not less than 60 semester hours of classroom study. 4. Graduation from course not set forth above plus not less than six months in-house training. 5. B.A. degree plus not less than six months in-house training. 6. Three years law-related experience including six months in-house training. 7. Two years in-house training.
Local Government Law	Open to CLA in state of Florida or any member of FLA, Inc.
Health Law Section	Any person who practices a profession dealing with health care.
Practice Management & Technology	Same as General Practice requirements.
Real Property, Probate & Trust	Must meet one of the following 1. CLA certification. 2. Graduation from ABA approved program. 3. Graduation from accredited institution requiring not less than 60 semester hours. 4. Graduation from program other than that above plus not less than six months in-house training. 5. BA degree plus not less than one year in-house training. 6. Five years in-house training as a legal assistant.
Trial Lawyers	Same as General Practice requirements.
Environmental and Land Use	Open to individuals who practice a profession dealing with environment and land use; does not exclude or include paralegals in listing.
Broward County	Requirements not on file.
Orange County	Affiliate membership to legal assistants; no detailed requirements on file.
Illinois	Nonlawyers who are qualified through education, training or work experience, are employed or retained by a lawyer, law office, governmental agency, or other entity in a capacity or function which involves the performance, under the direction and supervision of a lawyer of specifically delegated substantive legal work, which work, for the most part

STATE/ COUNTY	REQUIREMENTS/REMARKS

requires a sufficient knowledge of legal concepts that absent that legal assistant, the lawyer would perform the task.

Must be recommended and sponsored by lawyer member in good standing; applicant must continue to be employed, retained, or supervised by ISBA lawyer to renew membership.

Massachusetts   No further information.

Michigan   (One of two states offering a separate section or division for legal assistants.)

Any person currently employed or retained by a lawyer, law office, governmental agency, or other entity engaged in the practice of law, in a capacity or function which involves the performance under the direction and supervision of an attorney of specifically delegated substantive legal work which work, for the most part requires a sufficient knowledge of legal concepts such that absent that legal assistant the attorney would perform the task, and:

1. Has graduated from an ABA approved program and has baccalaureate degree; or
2. Has received B.A. degree plus not less than two years of in-house training; or
3. Has received associate degree plus not less than two years in-house training; or
4. Has a minimum of four years of in-house training as a legal assistant.

Minnesota
   Hennepin County

Called Organizational Affiliate; attest to membership in good standing or an organization affiliated with the Hennepin County Bar.

Missouri
   Bar Association of Metro St. Louis

1. Hold degree or certificate from college, university or institute in legal assistant or paralegal training.
2. Been employed fulltime a legal assistant or paralegal by any lawyer, law firm or corporation for a period of not less than two years prior to application in the St. Louis Bar Association who supervising attorney certifies to such fulltime employment.

STATE/ COUNTY	REQUIREMENTS/REMARKS
	3. And is sponsored by a member of the Bar Association of Metro St. Louis.
Kansas City Bar Association	Any person not a member of the Missouri Bar or Bar of any other state provided that such person has demonstrated legitimate interest in the promotion or accomplishment of the objects and purposes of the association.
North Dakota	Can join sections as nonvoting member.
Ohio	Not admitted to practice in Ohio. 1. Qualified through education or training; and 2. Employed or retained on an ongoing, regular basis by a lawyer, law firm, governmental agency, or a business entity in a capacity or function which is designated by such employer as that of a paralegal or legal assistant; and 3. Perform legal services under the direction and supervision of a licensed attorney, which services are not primarily clerical or secretarial and which, for the most part, require a sufficient knowledge of legal concepts that, absent such a legal assistant, the attorney would perform the task; and 4. Sponsored by a member of the OSBA who attests to the above. Must maintain employer sponsor to renew annually.
Tennessee Memphis Bar	Established October 1991. Details forthcoming.

Texas	(One of two states offering a separate division or section for legal assistants.)
	Three classes: active, associate, sustaining.
	Active: work as legal assistant under supervision of licensed attorney and meets one of the following:
	1. CLA certification plus one year's experience as a legal assistant.
	2. Bachelor or higher degree plus one year of experience as a legal assistant.
	3. Successful completion of:
	  (1) ABA approved program of education and training, plus one year employment.
	  (2) Program consisting of at least 60 semester hours of which 15 are substantive legal programs, plus one year employment experience.

STATE/ COUNTY	REQUIREMENTS/REMARKS
	(3) Completion of legal assistant program of 15 semester hours of substantive legal courses plus 45 semester hours of general college curriculum plus one year of experience.
	(4) Minimum of three years experience as a legal assistant.
	*Freelance legal assistant must have two letters of recommendation from division members and one from licensed attorney, or if not previously admitted to membership, applicant must present four letters, three from division members and one from licensed attorney.
	Associate: Otherwise meets requirements but does not have one year experience; may change to active with experience.
	Sustaining: Law firm, corporation agency training program institution individual or entity interested supporting the division.
	*Must comply with Code of Ethics.
Virginia	Sections offer nonlawyer membership; Antitrust, Bankruptcy, Corporate Counsel, Environmental, Family, Intellectual, International, Litigation, Real Property, Senior Lawyers
Wisconsin	Must hold membership in organization listed with bar; or performs same tasks as those who are members of listed associations but are not members.

*All experience under direct supervision of licensed attorney.[8]

[8] NALA Net, 1994. Reprinted with permission of the Nat'l Ass'n of Legal Assistants, Inc., 1516 S. Boston #200, Tulsa, Okla. 74119.

CHAPTER 9

RECENT DEVELOPMENTS IN CASE LAW

§ 9.1   Regulation
§ 9.2   Case Law

§ 9.1   Regulation

The question of whether to regulate legal assistants has been debated for many years. On the one hand, legal assistants work under the direct supervision of attorneys; therefore their responsibility is to the attorney and it is the attorney who is responsible for their services. Conversely, as in *In re Opinion 24,* the court stated:

> Although a paralegal's unsupervised work does constitute the unauthorized practice of law, that issue is not unique to independent paralegals. Rather, we emphasize again, it is the lack of educational and regulatory standards to govern their practice at the heart of the problem.[1]

The court went on to state: "We again conclude that regulations and guidelines can be drafted to address adequately the conflict-of-interest problem . . . . Regulation can also remedy any problems resulting from the attendant problem of paralegals sending correspondence directly to clients without the attorney's review and approval."[2]

Because legal assistants are not attorneys, they are not bound by the state codes of ethics for attorneys nor are they subject to sanctions for breaches of those codes. Without certification, licensure, or some form of regulation of the paralegal profession, the legal assistant is bound to comply with high standards of ethical behavior primarily because the attorney for whom the legal assistant works is responsibile for the legal assistant's behavior. It is the attorney who has the strong incentive to see that the legal assistant adheres to

---

[1] 607 A.2d 962, 128 N.J. 114 (1992).

[2] 128 N.J. 114, 130.

a proper code of ethics. There are some states that specifically require that the attorney take affirmative steps to educate the legal assistant about the attorney's ethical obligations and ensure their compliance.

Legal assistants do, however, have one very strong incentive for complying with high standards of conduct—they could become potential defendants in civil legal malpractice suits brought by clients who believe their attorneys have acted in a tortious manner. Legal assistants are subject to the same general tort principles that apply to lawyers and other professionals. They are liable for negligent or intentional misconduct that is injurious to a client.[3]

While it is true that the attorney directly supervises the legal assistant and is responsible for the legal assistant's work product, it is still possible that the legal assistant could be sued for negligence either by the client or by the attorney.

For purposes of clarification, the following definitions identifying individuals working in the paralegal field should be noted. The terms that are being used interchangeably to identify these individuals are legal assistant, paralegal, freelance paralegal, independent paralegal, and legal technician:

Legal Assistant

A nonlawyer working under the direction and supervision of an attorney. It is through this supervisory condition that the client is protected through the confidentiality, work product and attorney-client privileges doctrines. These definitions also refer to the specialized knowledge of these individuals acquired through education and/or experience. The ABA definition further states that a legal assistant performs work that would otherwise be performed by an attorney, absent such legal assistant. Both definitions indicate legal assistants are also known as paralegals.

Paralegal

The terms paralegal and legal assistant are used interchangeably. From the beginning there was a debate with regard to the use of the two terms. One argument advanced was that the term paralegal should be used as an adjective defining the type of work performed, while the term legal assistant should be used as a noun defining an individual in the profession, that is, "legal assistants perform paralegal work." Today the terms are used as a matter of preference describing the individuals.

---

[3] Theresa A. Cannon, Ethics and Professional Responsibility for Legal Assistants at 17 (1992).

Freelance Legal Assistant

A freelance legal assistant is an individual who contracts services to lawyers, or law firms for a specific client matter. This individual is not an employee of the lawyer or law firm but on contract for a specific project. The freelance legal assistant may work in the lawyer's office or off premises in a separate office. The freelance work is supervised, reviewed, and merged into the contracting attorney's final product while the attorney maintains full responsibility for the work. Reference to these freelance individuals is found in the ABA legal assistant definition, which states that legal assistants may be "employed by or retained by" a lawyer.

Independent Paralegal or Legal Technician

These terms are now being used interchangeably to identify nonlawyers delivering services directly to the public, without any intervention or review of work product by an attorney. The legal technician targets only the public for his or her business operations.[4]

Proponents of the strict regulation of the unauthorized practice of law emphasize the increased potential for public harm caused by the ineffective assistance of nonlawyers. Members of the bar are required to pass a state bar examination that ensures a minimum level of legal competency. As members of the bar are subject to state bar disciplinary rules, lawyers also have incentive to perform competently. Furthermore, most state bar associations require members to contribute to a recovery fund that provides reparation to those wronged by a lawyer. Proponents of strict regulation argue that these safeguards are not present, and reparation is uncertain when one is harmed by a nonlawyer.

Although the approaches taken by those who favor strict regulation and those who favor less drastic regulation differ dramatically, they share a common goal. The objective is to create a system that lowers the cost of legal services and allows greater access to the judicial system, while at the same time maintaining a high level of competency and accountability.[5]

A paralegal may have no education or training, but may have work experience in the legal field. A paralegal may have education or training in the legal or any nonlegal field. If the paralegal has legal education or training, the curricula for paralegal training programs varies greatly. The ABA does grant approval of paralegal programs, typically the two-year college degree program with a required number of paralegal courses or a certificate program consisting of a required number of paralegal courses available primarily for

---

[4] Connie Kretchmer, CLA, *The Issues, What Are They? Who Are They Talking About?* 18 Facts & Findings Career Chronicle 52, National Ass'n of Legal Assistants, Inc., (1991).

[5] 34 Ariz. L. Rev. 873 (1994).

students with a four-year degree (the ABA does allow for exceptions to the requirement that certificate students have a four-year degree). However, many non-ABA approved paralegal programs exist with various entrance requirements and curricula.[6]

For purposes of further discussion, the following definitions should also be noted:

Regulation:	The exercise of outside control over a profession or trade.
Licensing:	A mandatory form of regulation that involves the minimum testing of skills for entry into the field of work. Licensure is operated by a governmental agency, not by members of the profession.
Certification:	A voluntary form of regulation that involves the testing of advanced skills for recognition of superior work. The certification board is usually comprised of members of the profession.
Registration:	Identification through a governmental body for the purpose of monitoring, control, and recourse that could be voluntary or mandatory.

Why should legal assistants be regulated if they work under the direct supervision of attorneys?

1. Attorneys are concerned about legal assistants working directly for the public.
2. Without a standard attorneys feel that they are unable to assess an applicant's skills and abilities.
3. Some argue that regulation would protect the public from unscrupulous and unprepared practioners.
4. Regulation would give the legal assistant some level of prestige and increased income.
5. Regulation could limit the duties of legal assistants thereby preserving work for law students and young lawyers.

The arguments against regulation are:

1. Regulation would not protect the public from unethical legal assistants any more than it protects against unethical lawyers.
2. Many services performed by legal assistants are services that attorneys would not undertake.
3. Regulation would impede individual rights and the freedom to follow specific legal interests.

---

[6] Dominic Latorraca, *Regulation of Paralegals: An Upcoming Issue*, 22 Colo. Law. 493 (1994).

4. Legal assistants work under the direct supervision of an attorney whose parameters are already regulated.

5. Regulations would inhibit access to the legal system for low income groups in need of legal services.

6. Attorneys must recognize that certain routine tasks could be handled more efficiently by legal assistants, therefore freeing the attorney for those functions that require an attorney's training. Regulation might inhibit performance of these tasks.

7. Inflexibility as to changes in the profession.[7]

What is licensure? Lawyers are licensed. Licensing requirements for attorneys vary from state to state. Most states require a minimum education at an approved law school and completion and passage of the state bar exam. Licensure requires that the attorney pay annual dues to a bar association and maintain an office and telephone number on file with that association.

The highest court in each state and in the District of Columbia is responsible for making the rules regarding the practice of law and appropriate ethical conduct. The codes of ethical conduct include mechanisms for disciplining lawyers who violate the codes. A few state supreme courts have delegated legislative authority over the practice of law to the legislature.

The immediate problem in licensing paralegals is the lack of a standard in paralegal education. There are many paralegals who obtain a four-year college degree. There are those who obtain a two-year degree. There are also those paralegals who graduate from a proprietary school offering six-month courses, nine-month courses, 12-week courses and home-study programs. There are also those who work in law offices for a certain amount of time and thereafter refer to themselves as paralegals. There is no uniform standardized requirement for education at the present time.

Arguments favoring the licensing of traditional paralegals, working under the supervision of attorneys, center on the benefits to the profession, in terms of establishing it as a separate and autonomous but allied legal career, one with its own identity and a concomitant increase in societal status and rewards.[8]

What is certification? Certification is a voluntary process which enables attorneys to distinguish between those paralegals who have attained a specified level of competency and those who have not:

[A]ssociation credentialing programs address two very important goals:
1. Enabling consumers to recognize a comprehensible and identifiable measure of competency, and

---

[7] Barbara L. Albert, *Paralegal Regulation: Who Will Control the Future of the Profession?*, Legal Assistant Today, Jan.–Feb. 1989.

[8] Theresa A. Cannon, Ethics and Professional Responsbility for Legal Assistants (1992).

2.   Aiding the professional by establishing a means for attaining and recognizing high professional achievement.[9]

Examples of certification programs offered by professional associations
include the Certified Public Accountant (CPA), the trial specialist certification
of the National Trial Advocacy (CTA and CCTA), Certified Life Underwriters
program (CLU), and the Certified Legal Assistant program (CLA).

Due to the proliferation of controversy with regard to regulation, the
American Bar Association has created the Commission on Nonlawyer
Practice to address the issue of nonlawyers administering legal services. The
commission is an outgrowth of the Working Group on Nonlawyer Practice
that studied the expanding role of nonlawyers in the delivery of legal services.
Specifically the purpose of this commission will be to seek information about
the delivery of legal services by persons who are not licensed as lawyers.

The study is to take place over a two-year period. Seven public hearings
were conducted in the first year. These meetings were held in Orlando,
Florida; San Antonio, Texas; Boston, Massachusetts; Sacramento, California;
Chicago, Illinois; New York, New York; and Phoenix, Arizona. During the
second year, 1994, the commission will compile the data from the hearings
and issue a report.

The two major paralegal organizations, NALA and NFPA, each have a
representative on the commission. The issue of regulation has divided these
organizations. NFPA has adopted a resolution that favors licensing and specialty licensing as the preferred form of regulation. The NFPA resolution sets
minimum educational requirements for a paralegal, requires a proficiency-
based examination and includes a standard of character and fitness. NALA,
however, opposes licensure and supports certification.

At the first NFPA mid-year meeting held in September 1992, delegates
passed Resolution 92-M1 endorsing the regulation of paralegals on a state-by-
state basis, provided such measures are consistent with their mission statement, and expanded the role of paralegals in the delivery of legal services.

The resolution adopted a two-tiered licensing system, consisting of licensing and specialty licensing requirements, as NFPA's preferred form of regulation. The system would have to meet minimum standards, expand roles of
qualifying professionals, contain consumer redress provisions, and include
CLE examinations.

The resolution calls for a competency-based core curriculum to be developed to provide the standard for paralegal educational programs and furthermore that a candidate for a license shall meet one of the following minimum
educational requirements:

---

[9] Connie Kretchmer, CLA, *The Issues, What Are They? Who Are They Talking About?,* 18
Facts & Findings Career Chronicle at 53 (1994).

Associate's degree in paralegal studies with 60 semester credit hours or equivalent including a minimum of 24 semester credit hours or equivalent of paralegal specialty courses OR

Associate's degree in any subject (60 semester credit hours or equivalent) PLUS a minimum of 24 semester credit hours or equivalent of paralegal specialty courses OR

Bachelor's degree in paralegal studies, including 24 semester credit hours or equivalent of paralegal specialty courses, OR

Bachelor's degree in any subject plus 24 semester credit hours or equivalent of paralegal specialty courses.

The resolution also calls for any person applying for a license as a paralegal to pass a proficiency examination and meet a standard of character and fitness, that shall include, but not be limited to, no felony convictions and no conviction of unauthorized practice of law.

Resolution 92-M1 further provides that any person seeking a specialty license to practice, including those delivering legal services directly to the public in a specific area of law shall meet the following requirements:

1.   Meet standards for licensing as set out above;
2.   Pass a proficiency-based examination in the specialty/practice area;
3.   Have no ethics violations;
4.   Have a minimum of four years of experience as a licensed paralegal.

The resolution further provides for grandfather clauses for those paralegals currently working in the profession.

In August 1993, NALA submitted its statement to the commission on non-lawyer services. NALA provided the commission with background information on the association, information with regard to the amicus briefs filed in support of the continued growth and development of the legal assistant profession. These briefs include:

1991   *In re Opinion 24*[10] that would have prohibited attorney utilization of freelance legal assistants.

1990   *Dawson v. Phoenix Children's Hospital*[11] discussing the issue of attorney work product and its confidentiality as related to legal assistant work.

1990   *Gluth v. Arizona Department of Corrections*[12] urging the court's reconsideration of use of the terms legal assistant or paralegal to

---

[10] 607 A.2d 962, 128 N.J. 114 (1992).

[11] CV 88-24804 (Ariz. Ct. App. 1990).

[12] 951 F.2d 1504 (9th Cir. 1990).

identify inmates who complete a legal assistant training program established in the Arizona prison system.

1989   *Missouri v. Jenkins*[13] urging the award of legal assistant time in attorney fee awards at market rates; the Court found this to be an acceptable practice.

1989   *Blanchard v. Bergeron*[14] urging the award of legal assistant time in attorney fee awards; this question was not addressed in the Court's opinion.

NALA further provided information with regard to its membership and representation, qualifications and standards, and the CLA examination. NALA explained that the goals and purposes of licensure programs and professional certification programs differ as greatly as those groups responsible for administering the programs. NALA supports the concept of development and promulgation of professional standards through a self-regulatory, voluntary program, including those standards established in the Code of Ethics and Professional Responsibility, NALA's membership requirements as well as the CLA and CLA Specialty credentials. A voluntary certification program establishes the means for career growth and development.

It is NALA's position that licensure controls entry into a profession in addition to limiting the functions, tasks, and responsibilities of the career field. Those who receive a license may only perform those duties as prescribed by statute, and no more. This establishment of limits of responsibility inhibit the growth of a career field.

Furthermore, NALA states that the concept of the legal technician delivering legal services directly to the public has no relationship to the legal assistant or paralegal career field. There are no educational programs in existence today that prepare unsupervised nonlawyers to deliver legal services directly to the public. There is no present consensus as to what these nonlawyers should be allowed to do. The only matter over which there is some agreement among the bills and models is that some sort of licensure must be in place because these individuals would be engaged in an activity that directly affects the public. The legal technician concept is not an expansion of legal assistant functions considering that the duties performed have no relationship to the duties and responsibilities of legal assistants.

NALA supports the expansion of services of legal assistants who work under the supervision of attorneys, whose conduct is compatible with the Rules of Professional Conduct, and who possess special expertise or experience. Legal assistants may perform specifically delegated work under the supervision of an attorney. They may not accept or reject a case, represent a

---

[13] 491 U.S. 274 (1989).
[14] 489 U.S. 87 (1989).

client (unless provided by statutes), set a fee, or give legal advice. These restrictions represent no barrier to the expansion of the legal assistant career field.

§ 9.2 Case Law

During the past five years there has been a proliferation of cases involving legal assistants. Although the profession has been evolving for approximately the past 25 years, it is only in the past several years that the majority of legislation and case law has developed.

To contemporize the state of the profession, decisions are listed by category for easy reference. These recent decisions affect a paralegal's livelihood and the progress of the profession.

Fee Recovery

The legal assistant has become an integral part of the law office staff. The increase in the utilization of legal assistants is due in part to the belief that legal services should be delivered to the public in the most economical manner possible using efficient and cost-effective methods. As a result, legal assistants, at one time used only in large offices, are now emerging in smaller law firms throughout the country. The utilization of legal assistant services has produced a number of significant cases with regard to the award of legal assistant fees.

In *Blanchard v. Bergeron*[15] the United States Supreme Court granted certiorari on June 27, 1988. In the lower court ruling, the 5th Circuit Court of Appeals held that a contingent fee agreement served as a cap on the amount of a fee award under 42 U.S.C. § 1988, and that any billed hours of paralegals or law clerks were included within the contingent fee. There were two questions presented to the Supreme Court.

1. Does an agreement between the client and counsel serve as a cap to limit the award of attorney's fees under the Civil Rights Attorney's Fee Award Act of 1976, 42 U.S.C. § 1988?

2. Should the time of paralegals and law clerks be considered in the award of a reasonable attorney's fee under 42 U.S.C. § 1988?

The Court did not address the questions of paralegal fees in *Blanchard* but chose to address that question in *Missouri v. Jenkins*.[16] On June 19, 1989, in *Missouri,* the United States Supreme Court affirmed the ruling of the district

---

[15] 831 F.2d 563 (1988), *cert. denied,* 489 U.S. 87 (1989).
[16] 491 U.S. 274 (1989).

court, and held that the court had correctly compensated the works of paralegals, law clerks, and recent law graduates at market rates for their services,
rather than compensate them for the actual cost to the attorneys. This case
was most important to the legal assistant profession.

The question before the Court was whether the district court erred in compensating the work of law clerks and paralegals (hereinafter collectively
paralegals) at the market rates for their services, rather than at their cost to
the attorney. *Missouri* argued that the compensation for these personnel
should be included in the fee award, however, it suggests an hourly rate of
$15, which it argued corresponded to their salaries, benefits and overhead,
rather than the $35 to $50 market rate.

The Court explained that the statutory language that provides for "reasonable attorney's fees as part of the cost," 42 U.S.C. § 1988, cannot have been
meant to compensate only work performed personally by members of the
bar. The term must refer to a reasonable fee for the work product of the attorney, including not only the attorney, but secretaries, messengers, librarians,
custodians, and others whose labor contributes to the work product. The
Court further stated that the parties have suggested no reason why the work
of paralegals should not be similarly compensated.

The next question dealt with how to value paralegal time in the fee award.
The Court stated:

> If an attorney's fee awarded under section 1988 is to yield the same level of
> compensation that would be available from the market, the "increasingly wide-
> spread custom of separately billing for the services of paralegals and law stu-
> dents who serve as clerks,". . . must be taken into account. All else being equal,
> the hourly fee charged by an attorney whose rates include paralegal work in
> her hourly fee, or who bills separately for the work of paralegals at cost, will
> be higher than the hourly fee charged by an attorney competing in the same
> market who bills separately for the work of paralegals at "market rates." In
> other words, the prevailing "market rate" for attorney time is not independent
> of the manner in which paralegal time is accounted for. (8) Thus, if the prevail-
> ing practice in a given community were to bill paralegal time separately at
> market fees, fees awarded the attorney at market rates for attorney time would
> not be fully compensatory if the court refused to compensate hours billed by
> paralegals or did so only at "cost." Similarly, the fee awarded would be too
> high if the court accepted separate billing for paralegal hours in a market where
> that was not the custom.[17]

Missouri is a far-reaching decision. The United States Supreme Court has
acknowledged legal assistants and the fact that they are capable of carrying
out many tasks under the supervision of the attorney, who would otherwise
perform the tasks.

---

[17] *Id.* at 286.

In *Baldwin v. Burton*[18] the Supreme Court of Utah allowed the recovery of fees paid to a freelance paralegal. The court held that "allowing recovery for legal assistant fees promotes lawyer efficiency and decreases client litigation costs because a lawyer's time is free from tasks a legal assistant can perform at a lower rate."[19] This matter, did, however, deal with the issue of unauthorized practice of law since the paralegal appeared pro se to argue the fees issue after the winning attorney assigned the paralegal the judgment as payment. The court found that while the paralegal was free to take the assignment and appear on his own behalf to represent the paralegal's interests in the matter, the practice does give rise to at least the appearance of practicing law without a license. The court cited Rule 5.5 of the Utah Rules of Professional Conduct that prohibits lawyers from engaging in or assisting others in activities that constitute the unauthorized practice of law.

Consider *Harris v. Railroad Retirement Board.*[20] Since the plaintiff was the prevailing party in an application for disability benefits, under 28 U.S.C. § 2412, the plaintiff had the right to apply for attorney's fees as well as paralegal fees, which are expenses recoverable under the Act. The paralegal assisted in the legal research and preparation of briefs and "deals with governmental agencies and advises the public in connection with matters falling within her specialized field of expertise."[21] Plaintiff's request for $50 per hour for paralegal expenses was granted.

In *Mains v. Secretary of Health and Human Services*[22] a portion of the attorney and paralegal fees was disallowed. The court's position was that too much time had been billed by both the attorney and the paralegal and that the amount of time spent by the attorney conferring with the paralegal was unreasonable. The court stated that even though an attorney must consult with paralegal staff, it is unreasonable to be compensated for all time spent on such activities. The court also disallowed secretarial services that the attorney attempted to recover. The court held these expenses were not recoverable, just as "rent, electricity or professional subscriptions" are not recoverable.

In South Dakota, *In re Grenoble Apartments II,*[23] an Order re Application for Compensation of Services by a Certified Legal Assistant stated that the fees were reasonable and were based on the prevailing rates in the local market. The application was a good statement of the services of Certified Legal Assistants generally, and specifically outlined the complex nature of this

---

[18] 850 P.2d 1188 (Utah 1993).

[19] *Id. citing* Continental Townhouses E. Unit One Ass'n v. Brockbank, 733 P.2d 1120, 1200 (Ariz. Ct. App. 1986).

[20] 990 F.2d 519 (1993).

[21] *Id.* at 521–22.

[22] 1993 U.S. Cl. Ct. LEXIS 56 (1993).

[23] 145 B.R. 43 (D.S.D. 1993).

particular bankruptcy proceeding, requiring special expertise of the legal assistant.[24]

In *Moody v. EMC Food Services, Inc.*[25] the court set out specific criteria that needed to be established to compensate legal assistant time. The factors to be considered were the education and training or work experience of the legal assistant who performed the work, if the work performed was of a substantive nature and if the work was done under the direction and supervision of an attorney. Also to be considered were the nature of the work performed, the rate charged, and the number of hours expended.

In New Jersey the case of *Argila v. Argila*[26] emphasized the importance of complying with court rules when an application for paraprofessional fees is made. This matter was a cross-appeal from a judgment for counsel fees that directed the defendant to pay plaintiff's attorneys counsel fees of $55,250. The original fee application was in the sum of $85,000. The court upheld the payment of the $55,250 award for counsel fees. However, with regard to the application for paralegal fees, the court found that despite extensive certifications of services provided by the plaintiff, there was no information included that established the prevailing market rate for the locality of counsel's office in Oakhurst, New Jersey. Additionally, regarding the qualifications of the paralegals involved, the certifications of service failed to provide any information as required by Rule 4:42-9(b), other than the paralegals' rates and time spent on the matter. Rule 4:42-9(b) specifically requires that in addition to the time spent and the hourly rate, the certification must include "a summary of the paraprofessionals' qualifications" to ensure that "[n]o portion of any fee allowance claimed for attorney's services . . . duplicate any of the fees claimed by the attorney for paraprofessional services rendered to the client." The Appellate Division concluded the trial court was correct in the reduction of the counsel fees.

In *Cooper v. Secretary of the Department of Health and Human Services*[27] the court recognized the value of the work performed by legal assistants that resulted in fewer hours expended by the attorney at the higher rate. Therefore a lower cost was passed on to the client.

In *Grimes v. Secretary of the Department of Health and Human Services*[28] the court found that by utilizing the services of a legal assistant, it eliminated the need for the attorney to bill the client at a high rate for services performed that did not require the attorney's level of expertise. The court did state, however, that the work of the legal assistant must be substantive in

---

[24] *Case Law Updates,* Membership Newsletter, National Ass'n of Legal Assistants, Inc., July 1993.

[25] 828 S.W.2d 237 (Tex. Ct. App. 1992).

[26] 607 A.2d 142 (N.J. Super. 1992).

[27] 919 F.2d 1317 (1992).

[28] 988 F.2d 1196 (1992).

nature, not merely administrative or clerical, and should not be duplicative in order to be compensable at market or other rates.

In *Yeagers Fuel, Inc. v. Pennsylvania Power & Light Co.,*[29] the court made an unusual ruling. When the attorney time and paralegal time was duplicative and the tasks were "properly delegable to the paralegal" the attorney's fees incurred were disallowed for those tasks.

With *In re Continental Illinois Securities Litigation*[30] the District Court applied a formula that allowed the recovery of a sum equal to the paralegal's salary, plus overhead component in an amount equal to salary, (with a cap of $10 per hour) plus 40 percent profit. In this matter, the Court ruled that the ultimate question is not what the market rate is, but what the reasonable rate is.

In 1992 this decision was reversed. Justice Posner explained that the lower court erred in equating paralegal fees with salaries and referred to *Missouri* wherein the paralegal fee awards were commensurate with market rates:

> The Supreme Court has disapproved the approach of basing reimbursment for paralegal expenses on the "cost" of the paralegal, as distinct from the market value of his services, when it is customary to bill separately for the value of those services. The approach is not only unsound; it is futile from the standpoint of economizing on the expense of litigation. It will lead lawyers to substitute their own time, for which they are entitled to be compensated at market rates rather than at some constructed hourly cost, for that of cheaper paralegals.[31]

In re Superior Beverage/Glass Container Consolidated Pretrial[32] was a class action antitrust case. The court declined to penalize lawyers and paralegals by eliminating hours for which compensation was requested, solely on the basis that entries on their time sheets were vague. The court also held that other than time spent on clerical duties, it was not appropriate to calculate fees for paralegals based on their hourly salaries rather than their normal billing rate.

The court explained:

> There have been suggestions from time to time paralegals are not profit centers and that fees for paralegals should be calculated from their hourly salaries rather than the substantially higher rate at which their work is billed out. In our opinion that is an unfortunate approach. Hourly rates for paralegals are lower than hourly rates for associates. In awarding fees, courts should generally focus on that fact. Disregarding it will result in work now performed by paralegals being returned to associates and, accordingly, in more costly legal services.[33]

---

[29] 804 F. Supp. 700, *cert. denied,* 146 F.R.D. 110 (1992).
[30] 750 F. Supp. 868 (1990), *rev'd,* 962 F.2d 566 (1992).
[31] 962 F.2d 566, 569 (1992).
[32] 133 F.R.D. 119 (N.D. Ill. 1990).
[33] *Id.* at 131.

In *Decibus v. Woodbridge Township Police Department*[34] the defendant objected to the hourly rates claimed by plaintiff's counsel, the number of hours spent, and the use of paralegals and attorneys to perform nonlegal work, such as transporting witnesses. The court ruled that in this case both attorneys and paralegals were utilized to perform work that could have been performed in a much more cost efficient manner through the use of secretaries or messengers. Citing the Third Circuit, the court stated that reductions of fee awards were justified when clerical or administrative tasks have been billed at a high rate.

The court also cited *Missouri* stating "rates should be in direct correlation to the test performed. Consequently a clerical task should be billed at a lower rate than a paralegal task, no matter who performed it."

The plaintiff's application for fees included paralegal fees at $100 per hour when they were billed at $45 per hour. The court allowed paralegal time of $60 in order to align the rates in accordance with market rates.

Regarding bankruptcy in *In re Hobbs,*[35] the court set forth three considerations for dealing with paralegal compensation:

1. Paralegals should be compensated as paraprofessionals, not as part of general overhead expense, pursuant to Bankruptcy Code provision 11 U.S.C. § 330(a)(1).

2. The application for compensation of a paralegal should establish that the work done by the paralegal should be charged to the estate and not as a part of the nonprofessional, clerical overhead costs for the trustee that remains the trustee's responsibility.

3. There is a clear need for both economy of effort and utilization of more cost-efficient personnel to do the work required. The purpose is to lower overall costs of administration and thereby increase the available proceeds to serve as dividends to estate creditors.[36]

Price v. Cole[37] held that hourly charges from $175 for lead counsel to $90 for an associate and $60 for paralegal and law clerks were reasonable.

Privileged Communication

Paralegals are familiar with the attorney-client relationship, that is, an attorney cannot divulge information confided by a client. The courts have now determined that an attorney may act through a legal assistant without violating

---

[34] 1991 WL 59428 (D.N.J. 1991).

[35] 108 B.R. 93 (D. Md. 1989).

[36] *Id.*

[37] 574 N.E.2d 403 (Mass. App. Ct. 1991).

the attorney-client privilege. In *Samaritan Foundation v. Dawson,*[38] the court held:

> A lawyer does not forfeit the attorney-client privilege by receiving otherwise privileged communications through the conduit of a properly supervised paralegal employee. Further, that paralegal status did not strip the communications received of whatever attorney-client privilege might otherwise attach.[39]

In *Dawson* the court discussed the fact that a lawyer is responsible for any nonlawyer employee, retained or associated with the attorney and furthermore, that freelance legal assistants are covered by the work product and confidentiality doctrines.

In *Waldron v. Lesza*[40] the court found that the attorney-client privilege extends not only to correspondence from attorneys, but also to legal assistants.

In *Lanari v. State*[41] the court held that a legal assistant could not be examined with regard to information and facts acquired without obtaining the consent of both the attorney and the attorney's client.

In *Czaokowski v. City of Chicago*[42] the court ruled that legal assistants have the same privilege protection as attorneys in review of confidential information in a case.

In *Mountain States Telephone & Telegraph v. DiFede*[43] and *B.B. v. State*[44] the courts held that legal assistants are included in the attorney-client privilege and specifically in *B.B.* that the privilege extends to communications between the client and the agent of the attorney (legal assistant).

Conflict

Although most of the opinions set forth in § 9.2 apply to in-house paralegals working in the traditional law office, all decisions may be related to the freelance paralegal. In this category, monitoring conflict when an employee moves from one firm to another, an analogous situation certainly may arise for the freelance paralegal working for various attorneys. Section 2.4 covers the importance of conflict control by listing the plaintiffs' and defendants' names and cross-checking when approached to handle new matters.

---

[38] 844 P.2d 593 (Ariz. Ct. App. 1992).

[39] *Id.* at 599, 600.

[40] 1992 U.S. Dist. LEXIS 2694 (Mar. 10, 1992).

[41] 827 P.2d 495 (Colo. 1992).

[42] 810 F. Supp. 1428 (N.D. Ill. 1992).

[43] 780 P.2d 583 (Colo. 1989).

[44] 785 P.2d 132 (Colo. 1990).

In *Jacob v. Norris, McLaughlin & Marcus*[45] former members of the law firm sued the firm for compensation allegedly owing under service termination agreement governing withdrawal of partners from the firm. The Superior Court, Chancery Division, entered partial summary judgment invalidating provisions of the agreement upon which firm relied to deny compensation. The firm sought interlocutory review. The Appellate Division affirmed in part and reversed in part. On appeal the Supreme Court held that:

1. service termination agreement's provision barring compensation to departing members of firm if services were rendered to clients of firm within one year of their termination date, violated public policy
2. provision discouraging withdrawing partners from contacting firm's professional and paraprofessional staff violated public policy
3. court could sever offending portion of agreement and enforce the remainder.[46]

The court further stated that restrictive covenants have a similiarly unfair effect on paraprofessionals. Paraprofessionals, no less than lawyers, should not have career mobility inhibited, especially when not a party to the action. The ABA has addressed the problem of conflict-of-interest issues in paraprofessional hiring in Opinion 88-1526 that states in part:

> [i]t is important that non-lawyer employees have as much mobility in employment opportunity as possible consistent with the protection of client's interests. . . . [A]ny restrictions on the non-lawyer's employment should be held to the minimum necessary to protect confidentialty of client information.[47]

The court concluded that the unrestricted "practice of law"[48] included the right to solicit both attorneys and paraprofessionals that the attorney believed were necessary to provide the best legal services for their clients.

In *Widger v. Owens-Corning Fiberglass Corp. (In re Complex Asbestos Litigation)*[49] the question of what ethical standards apply and what rules govern in protecting the client communications when the nonlawyer employee moves from one firm to another was addressed. This case involved a paralegal, formerly employed by a law firm representing defendants in complex asbestos-related personal injury ligation, presently working for the law firm representing the plaintiffs. The defense firm was concerned about confidential information acquired by the paralegal in the course of employment with

---

[45] 607 A.2d 142, 128 N.J. 10 (1992).

[46] *Id.*

[47] Op. 88-1526 at 31, American Bar Ass'n (1988).

[48] Jacob v. Norris, McLaughlin, & Marcus, 607 A.2d 142, 147, 128 N.J. 10 (1992).

[49] 283 Cal. Rptr. 732 (Ct. App. 1991).

the firm. If the confidential information was shared with the new employer, it would not only violate a previous confidence, but might also give the plaintiff a tactical advantage in settlement discussions and trial prosecution.

The Court of Appeals recognized that while courts have frequently considered the problem of attorneys moving from firm to firm that "Considerably less attention has been given to the problem posed by nonlawyer employees of the law firms who do the same."

The court felt that certain restrictions must be placed on attorneys hiring opposing counsel's employees, to insure that confidentiality be maintained, that is, obtain a waiver from the former employee, or construct a cone of silence around the newly-hired employee, meaning the employee will not be allowed to work on or become involved with any cases involving former employers.

In *Widger* it was determined that written consent be obtained from the former employer to hire an individual in order to eliminate any basis for disqualification. The court also required that the hiring firm effectively screen newly-employed legal assistants from any involvement in litigation in which they had taken part with their former firms, by erecting what is known as a Chinese wall, indicating that the newly-hired legal assistant will not come into contact at all with any cases involving the former employer and the present employer.

Similarly, in *Rivera v. Chicago Pneumatic Tool Co.*[50] it was decided that a Chinese wall be erected to insure the preservation of confidences, that is, to effectively screen the employee from any involvement with the litigation. This determination should be made as a matter of routine during the hiring process. The proposed Chinese wall should incorporate the following:

1. The legal assistant would not be allowed to disclose or discuss any information acquired while employed by defendant's counsel concerning the cases.

2. The files in questions would be locked and not accessible to the legal assistant.

3. The legal assistant would not be permitted in the vicinity of the files when others were working on them.

4. The legal assistant's supervisors would not work on the cases in question.

5. The legal assistant would sign an affidavit and agreement to have no contact with the files, or discuss the files with anyone in plaintiff's firm, or disclose any information acquired in a former position.

6. The attorney handling the files would have no direct contact with the legal assistant.[51]

---

[50] 1991 WL 151892 (1991) (unreported).

[51] *Case Law Updates,* Membership Newsletter, National Ass'n of Legal Assistants, Inc., July–Sept. 1991.

In *Rivera* the court found that the Chinese wall erected was sufficient and reasonable and that defendant did not meet the burden of proof necessary to show that the legal assistant had disclosed any confidential information to her new employer.

Fee Splitting

State Bar of Texas v. Faubion[52] involved an allegation of fee splitting by a lawyer and a paralegal/investigator. The paralegal was paid a salary, given a transportation allowance and an incentive bonus. The attorney's fees from the cases worked on by the paralegal were deposited into the attorney's firm operating account and the paralegal's compensation was computed at 20 percent to 33 1/3 percent of the gross fees calculated by the paralegal's time involvement in the case. The court ruled that the attorney shared legal fees with the paralegal and that the fees were a percentage of particular fees and not based on an hourly wage. Thus the arrangement violated Disciplinary Rule 3-102.

Gallagher v. Weiner,[53] decided on October 19, 1993, involved a feesharing agreement between a lawyer and a nonlawyer that the court deemed to be void.

---

[52] 1991 WL 155568 1991 (unreported).

[53] 1993 U.S. Dist. LEXIS 15709 (Oct. 19, 1993).

APPENDIXES

THE AMERICAN BAR ASSOCIATION MODEL GUIDELINES FOR THE UTILIZATION OF LEGAL ASSISTANT SERVICES

Reprinted with the permission of the American Bar Association

Preamble

State courts, bar associations, or bar committees in at least seventeen states have prepared recommendations[1] for the utilization of legal assistant services.[2] While their content varies, their purposes appears uniform: to provide lawyers with a reliable basis for delegating responsibility for performing a portion of the lawyer's tasks to legal assistants. The purpose of preparing model guidelines already adopted or to suggest that other guidelines may be more appropriate in a particular jurisdiction. It is the view of the Standing Committee on Legal Assistants of the American Bar Association, however, that a model set of guidelines for the utilization of legal assistant services may assist many states in adopting or revising such guidelines. The Standing Committee is of the view that guidelines will encourage lawyers to utilize

---

[1] An appendix identifies the guidelines, court rules, and recommendations that were reviewed in drafting these Model Guidelines.

[2] On February 6, 1986, the ABA Board of Governors approved the following definition of the term "legal assistant":

> A legal assistant is a person, qualified through education, training or work experience, who is employed or retained by a lawyer, law office, governmental agency, or other entity in a capacity or function which involves the performance, under the ultimate direction and supervision of an attorney, of specifically delegated substantive legal work, which work, for the most part, requires a sufficient knowledge of legal concepts that, absent such assistant, the attorney would perform the task.

> In some contexts, the term "paralegal" is used interchangeably with the term legal assistant.

APPENDIXES

legal assistant services effectively and promote the growth of the legal assistant profession.[3] In undertaking this project, the Standing Committee has attempted to state guidelines that conform with the American Bar Association's Model Rules of Professional Conduct, decided authority, and contemporary practice. Lawyers, of course, are to be first directed by Rule 5.3 of the Model Rules in the utilization of legal assistant services, and nothing contained in these guidelines is intended to be inconsistent with that rule. Specific ethical considerations in particular states, however, may require modification of these guidelines before their adoption. In the commentary after each guideline, we have attempted to identify the basis for the guideline and any issues of which we are aware that the guideline may present; those drafting such guidelines may wish to take them into account.

Guideline 1: A lawyer is responsible for all of the professional actions of a legal assistant performing legal assistant services at the lawyer's direction and should take reasonable measures to ensure that the legal assistant's conduct is consistent with the lawyer's obligations under the ABA Model Rules of Professional Conduct.

Comment to Guideline 1: An attorney who utilizes a legal assistant's services is responsible for determining that the legal assistant is competent to perform the tasks assigned, based on the legal assistant's education, training, and experience, and for ensuring that the legal assistant is familiar with the responsibilities of attorneys and legal assistants under the applicable rules governing professional conduct.[4]

Under principles of agency law and rules governing the conduct of attorneys, lawyers are responsible for the actions and the work product of the non-lawyers they employ. Rule 5.3 of the Model Rules[5] requires that partners

---

[3] While necessarily mentioning legal assistant conduct, lawyers are the intended audience of these Guidelines. The Guidelines, therefore, are addressed to lawyer conduct and not directly to the conduct of the legal assistant. Both the National Association of Legal Assistants (NALA) and the National Federation of Paralegal Associations (NFPA) have adopted guidelines of conduct that are directed to legal assistants. See NALA, "Code of ethics and Professional Responsibility of the National Association of Legal Assistants, Inc." (adopted May 1975, revised November 1979 and September 1988); NFPA, "Affirmation of Responsibility" (adopted 1977, revised 1981).

[4] Attorneys, of course, are not liable for violations of the AMA Model Rules of Professional Conduct ("Model Rules") unless the Model Rules have been adopted as the code of professional conduct in a jurisdiction in which the lawyer practices. The are referenced in this model guideline for illustrative purposes; if the guideline is to be adopted, the reference should be modified to the jurisdiction's rules of professional conduct.

[5] The Model Rules were first adopted by the ABA House of Delegates in August of 1983. Since that time many states have adopted the Model Rules to govern the professional

and supervising attorneys ensure that the conduct of non-lawyer assistants is compatible with the lawyer's professional obligations. Several state guidelines have adopted this language, *e.g.,* Commentary to Illinois Recommendation (A), Kansas Guidelines III(a), New Hampshire Rule 35, Sub-Rule 9, and North Carolina Guideline 4. Ethical Consideration 3-6 of the Model Code encouraged lawyers to delegate tasks to legal assistants provided the lawyer maintained a direct relationship with the client, supervised appropriately, and had complete responsibility for the work product. The adoption of Rule 5.3, which incorporates these principles, implicitly reaffirms this encouragement.

Several states have addressed the issue of the lawyer's ultimate responsibility for work performed by subordinates. For example, Colorado Guideline 1.c, Kentucky Supreme Court Rule 3.700, Sub-Rule 2.C, and Michigan Guideline I provide: "The lawyer remains responsible for the actions of the legal assistant to the same extent as if such representation had been furnished entirely by the lawyer and such actions were those of the lawyer." New Mexico Guideline X states "[the] lawyer maintains ultimate responsibility for and has an ongoing duty to actively supervise the legal assistant's work performance, conduct and product." Connecticut Recommendation 2 and Rhode Island Guideline III state specifically that lawyers are liable for malpractice for the mistakes and omissions of their legal assistants.

Finally, the lawyer should ensure that legal assistants supervised by the lawyer are familiar with the rules governing attorney conduct and that they follow those rules. *See* Comment to Model Rule 5.3; Illinois Recommendation (A)(5), New Hampshire Supreme Court Rule 35, Sub-Rule 9, and New Mexico, Statement of Purpose; see also NALA's Model Standards and Guidelines for the Utilization of Legal Assistants, guidelines IV, V, and VIII (1985, revised 1990) hereafter "NALA Guidelines").

The Standing Committee and several of those who have commented upon these Guidelines regard Guideline I as a comprehensive statement of general principal governing lawyers who utilize legal assistant services in the practice of law. As such it, in effect, is a part of each of the remaining Guidelines.

Guideline 2: Provided the lawyer maintains responsibility for the work product, a lawyer may delegate to a legal assistant any task normally performed by the lawyer except those tasks proscribed to one not

---

conduct of lawyers licensed in those states. Since a number of states still utilize a version of the Model Code of Professional Responsibility ("Model Code"), which was adopted by the House of Delegates in August of 1969, however, these comments will refer to both the Model Rules and the predecessor Model Code (and to the Ethical Considerations and Disciplinary Rules found under the canons in the Model Code).

licensed as a lawyer by statute, court rule, administrative rule or regulation, controlling authority, the ABA Model Rules of Professional Conduct, or these Guidelines.

<u>Comment to Guideline 2:</u> The essence of the definition of the term legal assistant adopted by the ABA Board of Governors in 1986 is that, so long as appropriate supervision is maintained, many tasks normally performed by lawyers may be delegated to legal assistants. Of course, Rule 5.5 of the Model Rules, DR 3-101 of the Model Code, and most states specifically prohibit lawyers from assisting or aiding a non-lawyer in the unauthorized practice of law. Thus, while appropriate delegation of tasks to legal assistants is encouraged, the lawyer may not permit the legal assistant to engage in the "practice of law." Neither the Model Rules nor the Model Code define the "practice of law." EC 3-5 under the Model Code gave some guidance by equating the practice of law to the application of the professional judgment of the lawyer in solving clients' legal problems. Further, ABA Opinion 316 (1967) states: "A lawyer can employ lay secretaries, lay investigators, lay detectives, lay researchers, accountants, lay scriveners, non-lawyer draftsmen or non-lawyer researchers. In fact, he may employ non-lawyers to do any task for him except counsel clients about law matters, engage directly in the practice of law, appear in court or appear in formal proceedings as part of the judicial process, so long as it is he who takes the work and vouches for it to the client and becomes responsible for it to the client."

Most state guidelines specify that legal assistants may not appear before courts, administrative tribunals, or other adjudicatory bodies unless their rules authorize such appearances; may not conduct dispositions; and may not give legal advice to clients, *e.g.* Connecticut Recommendation 4; Fla. EC 3-6 (327 So. 2d at 16); and Michigan Guidelines II. Also *See* NALA Guidelines IV and VI. But it is also important to note that, as some guidelines have recognized, pursuant to federal or state statute legal assistants are permitted to provide direct client representation in certain administrative proceedings. *e.g.,* South Carolina Guidelines II. While this does not obviate the attorney's responsibility for the legal assistant's work, it does change the nature of the attorney supervision of the legal assistant. The opportunity to use such legal assistant services has particular benefits to legal services programs and does not violate Guideline 2. *See generally ABA Standards for Providers of Civil Legal Services to the Poor;* Std. 6.3, at 6.17-6.18 (1986).

The Model Rules emphasize the importance of appropriate delegation. The key to appropriate delegation is proper supervision, which includes adequate instruction when assigning projects, monitoring of the project, and review of the completed project. The Supreme Court of Virginia upheld a malpractice verdict against a lawyer based in part on negligent actions of a legal assistant in performing tasks that evidently were properly delegable. *Musselman v. Willoughby Corp.* 230 Va. 337, 337 S.E. 2d 724 (1985). *See* also C. Wolfran, *Modern Legal Ethics* (1986), at 236, 896. All state guidelines refer to the requirement that the lawyer "supervise" legal assistants in the performance of their duties. Lawyers should also take care in hiring and choosing a legal assistant to work on a specific project to ensure that the legal assistant has the education, knowledge, and ability necessary to perform the delegated tasks competently. *See* Connecticut Recommendations 14, Kansas Standards I, II and III, and New Mexico Guideline VIII. Finally, some states describe appropriate delegation and review in terms of the delegated work losing its identity and becoming "merged" into the work product of the attorney. *See* Florida EC 3-6 (327 So. 2d at 16).

Legal assistants often play an important role in improving communication between the attorney and the client. EC 3-6 under the Model Code mentioned three specific kinds of tasks that the legal assistants may perform under appropriate lawyer supervision: factual investigation and research, legal research, and the preparation of legal documents. Some states delineate more specific tasks in their guidelines, such as attending client conferences, corresponding with and obtaining information from clients, handling witness execution of documents, preparing transmittal letters, maintaining estate guardianship trust accounts, etc. *See, e.g.,* Colorado (lists of specialized functions in several areas follow guidelines); Michigan, Comment to Definition of Legal Assistant; New York, Specialized Skills of Legal Assistants; Rhode Island Guidelines II; and NALA Guidelines IX. The two-volume *Working with Legal Assistants,* published by the Standing Committee in 1982, attempted to provide a general description of the types of tasks that may be delegated to legal assistants in various practice areas.

There are tasks that have been specifically prohibited in some states, but that may be delegated in others. For example, legal assistants may not supervise will executions or represent clients at real estate closings in some jurisdictions, but may in others. *Compare* Connecticut Recommendation 7 and Illinois State Bar Association Position Paper on Use of Attorney Assistants in Real Estate Transactions (May 16, 1984), which proscribe legal assistants conducting real estate closings, *with* Georgia "real estate job description," Florida Professional Ethics Committee Advisory Opinion 89-5 (1989), and Missouri Comment to Guideline I, which permit legal assistants to conduct real estate closings. *Also compare* Connecticut Recommendation 8 (prohibiting attorneys from authorizing legal assistants to supervise will executions) *with* Colorado "estate planning job description," Georgia "estate, trusts, and wills job description," Missouri Comment to Guideline I, and Rhode Island

Guideline II (suggesting that legal assistants may supervise the execution of wills, trusts and other documents).

Guideline 3: A lawyer may not delegate to a legal assistant:
(a) Responsibility for establishing an attorney-client relationship.
(b) Responsibility for establishing the amount of a fee to be charged for a legal service.
(c) Responsibility for a legal opinion rendered to a client.

Comment to Guideline 3: The Model Rules and most state codes require that lawyers communication with their clients in order for clients to make well-informed decisions about their representation and resolution of legal issues. Model Rule 1.4, Ethical Consideration 3-6 under the Model Code emphasized that "delegation [of legal tasks to non-lawyers] is proper if the lawyer maintains a direct relationship with his client, supervise the delegated work and has complete professional responsibility for the work product." (Emphasis added.) Accordingly, most state guidelines also stress the importance of a direct attorney-client relationship. *See* Colorado Guideline 1, Florida EC 306, Illinois Recommendation (A)(1), Iowa EC 3-6(2), and New Mexico Guideline IV. The direct personal relationship between client and lawyer is necessary to the exercise of the lawyer's trained professional judgment.

An essential aspect of the lawyer-client relationship is the agreement to undertake representation and the related fee arrangement. The Model Rules and most states require that fee arrangements be agreed upon early on and be communicated to the client by the lawyer, in some circumstances in writing. Model Rule 1.5 and Comments. Many state guidelines prohibit legal assistants from "setting fees" or "accepting cases." *See, e.g.,* Colorado Guideline 1 and NALA Guideline VI. Connecticut recommends that legal assistants be prohibited from accepting or rejecting cases or setting fees "if these tasks entail any discretion on the part of the paralegals." Connecticut Recommendation 9.

EC 3-5 states: "[T]he essence of the professional judgment of the lawyer is his educated ability to relate the general body and philosophy of law to a specific legal problem of a client: and thus, the public interest will be better served if only lawyers are permitted to act in matters involving professional judgment." Clients are entitled to their lawyers' professional judgment and opinion. Legal assistants may, however, be authorized to communicate legal advice so long as they do not interpret or expand on that advice. Typically, state guidelines phrase this prohibition in terms of legal assistants being forbidden from "giving legal advice" or "counseling clients about legal matters." *See, e.g.,* Colorado Guideline 2, Connecticut Recommendation 6, Florida DR 3-104, Iowa EC 3-6(3), Kansas Guideline I and Guideline VI. Some states have more expansive wording that prohibits legal assistants from engaging in any activity that would require the exercise of independent legal judgment. Nevertheless, it is clear that all states, as well as the Model Rules, encourage direct communication between clients and a legal assistant insofar as the legal assistant is performing a task properly delegated by a lawyer. It should be noted that a lawyer who permits a legal assistant to assist in establishing the attorney-client relationship, communicating a fee, or preparing a legal opinion is not delegating responsibility for those matters and, therefore, may be complying with this guideline.

Guideline 4: **It is the lawyer's responsibility to take reasonable measure to ensure that clients, courts, and other lawyers are aware that a legal assistant, whose services are utilized by the lawyer in performing legal services, is not licenses to practice law.**

Comment to Guideline 4: Since, in most instances, a legal assistant is not licensed as a lawyer, it is important that those with whom the legal assistant deals are aware of the fact. Several state guidelines impose on the lawyer responsibility for instructing a legal assistant whose services are utilized by the lawyer to disclose the legal assistant's status in any dealings with a third party. *See, e.g.,* Michigan Guideline III, part 5, New Hampshire Rule 35, Sub-Rule 8, and NALA Guideline V. While requiring the legal assistant to make such disclosure is one way in which the attorney's responsibility to third parties may be discharged, the Standing Committee is of the view that it is desirable to emphasize the lawyer's responsibility for the disclosure and leave to the lawyer the discretion to decide whether the lawyer will discharge that responsibility by direct communication with the client, by requiring the legal assistant to make the disclosure, by a written memorandum, or by some other means. Although in most initial engagements by a client it may be prudent for the attorney to discharge this responsibility with a writing, the guideline requires only that the lawyer recognize the responsibility and ensure that it is discharged. Clearly, when a client has been adequately informed of the lawyer's utilization of legal assistant services, it is unnecessary to make additional formalistic disclosures as the client retains the lawyer for other services.

Most state guidelines specifically endorse legal assistants signing correspondence so long as their status as a legal assistant is indicated by an appropriate title. *e.g.,* Colorado Guidelines 2; Kansas, Comment to Guideline IX; and North Carolina Guideline 9; *also see* AMA Informal Opinion 1367 (1976). The comment to New Mexico Guideline XI warns against the use of the title "associate" since it may be construed to mean associate-attorney.

Guideline 5: **A lawyer may identify legal assistants by name and title on the lawyer's letterhead and on business cards identifying the lawyer's firm.**

Comment to Guideline 5: Under Guideline 4, above, an attorney who employs a legal assistant has an obligation to ensure that the status of the legal assistant as a non-lawyer is fully disclosed. the primary purpose of this disclosure is to avoid confusion that might lead someone to believe that the legal assistant is a lawyer. The identification suggested by this guideline is consistent with that objective, while also affording the legal assistant recognition as an important part of the legal services team.

Recent ABA Informal Opinion 1527 (1989) provides that non-lawyer support personnel, including legal assistants, may be listed on al law firm's letterhead and reiterates previous opinions that approve of legal assistants having business cards. *See* also ABA Informal Opinion 1185 (1971). The listing must not be false or misleading and "must make it clear that the support personnel who are listed are not lawyers."

Nearly all state guidelines approve of business cards for legal assistants, but some prescribe the contents and format of the card. *E.g.,* Iowa Guideline 4 and Texas Guideline VIII. All agree the legal assistant's status must be clearly indicated and the card may not be used in a deceptive way. New Hampshire Supreme Court Rule 7 approves the use of business cards so long as the card is not used for unethical solicitation.

Some states do not permit attorneys to list legal assistants on their letterhead. *e.g.,* Kansas Guideline VIII, Michigan Guideline III, New Hampshire Rule 35, Sub-Rule 7, New Mexico Guideline XI, and North Carolina Guideline 9. Several of these states rely on earlier ABA Informal Opinion 619 (1962), 845 (1965), and 1000 (1977), all of which were expressly withdrawn by ABA Informal Opinion 1527. The earlier opinions interpreted the predecessor Model Code and DR 2-102(A), which, prior to *Bates v. State Bar of Arizona,* 433 U.S. 350 (1977), had strict limitations on the information that could be listed on letterheads. States which do not permit attorneys to list names of legal assistants on their stationery, if the listing is not deceptive and the legal assistant's status is clearly identified, include Arizona Committee on Rules of Professional Conduct Formal Opinion 3/90 (1990); Connecticut Recommendation 12; Florida Professional Ethics Committee Advisory Opinion 86-4 (1986); Hawaii, Formal Opinion 78-8-19 (1978, as revised 1984); Illinois State Bar Association Advisory Opinion 87-1 (1987); Kentucky Sub-Rule 6; Mississippi State Bar Ethics Committee Opinion No. 93 (1984); Missouri Guideline IV; New York State Bar Association Committee on Professional Ethics Opinion 500 (1978); Oregon, Ethical Opinion No. 349 (1977); and Texas, Ethics Committee Opinion 436 (1983). In light of the United States Supreme Court opinion in *Peel v. Attorney Registration and Disciplinary Commission of Illinois,* -U.S.-, 110 S. Ct. 2281 (1990), it may be that a restriction on letterhead identification of legal assistants that is not deceptive and clearly identifies the legal assistant's status violated the First Amendment right of the lawyer.

Guideline 6: **It is the responsibility of a lawyer to take reasonable measures to ensure that all client confidences are preserved by a legal assistant.**

Comment to Guideline 6: A fundamental principle underlying the free exchange of information in a lawyer-client relationship is that the lawyer maintain the confidentiality of information relating to the representation. "It is a matter of common knowledge that the normal operation of a law office exposes confidential professional information to non-lawyer employees of the office. This obligates a lawyer to exercise care in selecting and training his employees so that the sanctity of all confidences and secrets of his clients may be preserved." EC 4-2, Model Code.

Rule 5.3 of the Model Rules requires "a lawyer who has direct supervisory authority over the non-lawyer [to] make reasonable efforts to ensure that the person's conduct is compatible with the professional obligations of the lawyer." The Comment to Rule 5.3 makes it clear that lawyers should give legal assistants "appropriate instruction and supervision concerning the ethical aspects of their employment, particularly regarding the obligation not to disclose information relating to the representation of the client." DR 4-101(D) under the Model Code provides that: "A lawyer shall exercise reasonable care to prevent his employees, associates and others whose services are utilized by him from discharging or using confidences or secrets of a client . . ."

It is particularly important that the lawyer ensure that the legal assistant understands that all information concerning the client, even the mere fact that a person is a client of the firm, may be strictly confidential. Rule 1.6 of the Model Rules expanded the definition of confidential information ". . . not merely to matters communicated in confidence by the client but also to all information relating to the representation, whatever its source."[6] It is therefore the lawyer's obligation to instruct clearly and to take reasonable steps to

---

[6] rule 1.05 of the Texas Disciplinary Rules of Professional Conduct (1990) provides a different formulation, which is equally expansive:

> "Confidential information" includes both "privileged information" and "unprivileged client information." "Privileged information" refers to the information of a client protected by the lawyer-client privilege of Rule 503 of the Texas Rules of Evidence or of Rule 503 of the Texas Rules of Criminal Evidence or by the principles of attorney-client privilege governed by Rule 501 of the Federal Rules of Evidence for United States Courts and Magistrates. "Unprivileged client information" means all information, acquired by the lawyer during the course of or by reason of the representation of the client.

ensure the legal assistant's preservation of client confidences. Nearly all states that have guidelines for the utilization of legal assistants require the lawyer "to instruct legal assistants concerning client confidences" and "to exercise care to ensure that legal assistants comply" with the Code in this regard. Even if the client consents to divulging information, this information must not be used to the disadvantage of the client. *See, e.g.,* Connecticut Recommendation 3; New Hampshire Rule 35, Sub-Rule 4; NALA Guideline V.

Guideline 7: A lawyer should take reasonable measures to prevent conflicts of interest resulting from a legal assistant's other employment for interests insofar as such other employment or interests would present a conflict of interest if it were that of the lawyer.

Comment to Guideline 7: A lawyer must make "reasonable efforts to ensure that [a] legal assistant's conduct is compatible with the professional obligations of the lawyer." Model Rule 5.3. these professional obligations include the duty to exercise independent professional judgment on behalf of a client, "free of compromising influences and loyalties." ABA Model rules 1.7 through 1.13. Therefore, legal assistants should be instructed to inform the supervising attorney of any interest that could result in a conflict of interest or even given the appearance of a conflict. The guideline intentionally speaks to other employment rather than only past employment, since there are instances where legal assistants are employed by more than one law firm at the same time. The guideline's reference to "other interests" is intended to include personal relationships as well as instances where a legal assistant may have a financial interest (i.e., as stockholder, trust beneficiary or trustee, etc.) that would conflict with the client's in the matter in which the lawyer has been employed.

"Imputed Disqualification Arising from Change in Employment by Non-lawyer Employee," ABA Informal Opinion 1526 (1988), defines the duties of both the present and former employing lawyers and reasons that the restriction son legal assistants' employment should be kept to "the minimum necessary to protect confidentiality" in order to prevent legal assistants from being forced to leave their careers, which "would disserve clients as well as the legal profession." The Opinion describes the attorney's obligations (1) to caution the legal assistant not to disclose any information and (2) to prevent the legal assistant from working on any matter on which the legal assistant worked for a prior employer or respecting which the employee has confidential information.

If a conflict is discovered, it may be possible to "wall" the legal assistant from the conflict area so that the entire firm need not be disqualified and the legal assistant is effectively screened from information concerning the matter. The American Bar Association has taken the position that what historically has been described as "Chinese wall" will allow non-lawyer personnel (including legal assistants) who are in possession of confidential client information to accept employment with a law firm opposing the former client so long as the wall is observed and effectively screens the non-lawyer from confidential information. ABA Informal Opinion 1526 (1988). *See* also Tennessee Formal Ethics Opinion 89-F 118 (March 10, 1989). The implication of this Informal Opinion is that if a wall is not in place, the employer may be disqualified from representing either party to the controversy. One court has so held. *In re: Complex Asbestoses Litigation,* No. 828684 (San Francisco Superior Court, September 19, 1989).

It is not clear that a wall will prevent disqualification in the case of a lawyer employed to work for a law firm representing a client with an adverse interest to a client of the lawyer's former employer. Under Model Rule 1.10, when a lawyer moves to a firm that represents an adverse party in a matter in which the lawyer's former firm was involved, absent a waiver by the client, the new firm's representation may continue only if the newly employed lawyer acquired no protected information and did not work directly on the matter in the former employment. The new Rules of Professional Conduct in Kentucky and Texas (both effective on January 1, 1990) specifically provide for disqualification. Rule 1.10(b) in the District of Columbia, which became effective on January 1, 1991, does so as well. The Sixth Circuit, however, has held that the wall will effectively insulate the new firm from disqualification if it prevents the new lawyer-employee from access to information concerning the client with the adverse interest. *Manning v. Waring, Cox, James, Sklar & Allen,* 849 F.2d 222 (6th Cir. 1988). [As a result of the Sixth Circuit opinion, Tennessee revised its formal ethics opinion, which is cited above, and now applies the same rule to lawyers, legal assistants, law clerks, and legal secretaries.] *See generally* NFPA, "The Chinese Wall - Its Application to Paralegals" (1990).

The states have guidelines that address the legal assistant conflict of interest issue refer to the lawyer's responsibility to ensure against personal business or social interests of the legal assistant that would conflict with the representation of the client or impinge on the services rendered to the client. *e.g.,* Kansas Guideline X, New Mexico Guideline VI, and North Carolina Guideline 7. Florida Professional Ethics Opinion 86-5 (1986) discusses a legal assistant's move from one firm to another and the obligations of each not to disclose confidences. *See also* Vermont Ethics Opinion 85-8 (1985) (a legal assistant is not bound by the Code of Professional Responsibility and, absent an absolute waiver by the client, the new firm should not represent client if legal assistant possessed confidential information from old firm).

Guideline 8: A lawyer may include a charge for the work performed by a legal assistant in setting a charge for legal services.

Comment to Guideline 8: The U.S. Supreme Court in *Missouri v. Jenkins,* 491 U.S. 274 (1989), held that in setting a reasonable attorney's fee under 28 U.S.C. §1988, a legal fee may include a charge for legal assistant services at "market rates" rather than "actual cost" to the attorneys. This decision should resolve any question concerning the propriety of setting a charge for legal services based on work performed by a legal assistant. Its rationale favors setting a charge based on the "market" rate for such services, rather than their direct cost to the lawyer. This result was recognized by Connecticut Recommendation 11, Illinois Recommendation D, and Texas Guideline V prior to the Supreme Court decision. *See also* Fla. Stat. Ann §57.104 (1991 Supp.) (adopted in 1987 and permitting consideration of legal assistant services in computing attorneys' fees) and Fla. Stat. Ann. §744.108 (1991 Supp.) (adopted in 1989 and permitting recovery of "customary and reasonable charges for work performed by legal assistants" as fees for legal services in guardianship matters).

It is important to note, however, that *Missouri v. Jenkins* does not abrogate the attorney's responsibilities under Model Rule 1.5 to set a reasonable fee for legal services and it follows that those considerations apply to a fee that includes a fee for legal assistant services. Accordingly, the effect of combining a market rate charge for the services of lawyers and legal assistants should, in most instances, result in a lower total cost for the legal service than if the lawyer had performed the service alone.

Guideline 9: A lawyer may not split legal fees with a legal assistant nor pay a legal assistant for the referral of legal business. A lawyer may compensate a legal assistant based on the quantity and quality of the legal assistant's work and value of that work to a law practice, but the legal assistant's compensation may not be contingent, by advance agreement, upon the profitability of the lawyer's practice.

Comment to Guideline 9: Model Rule 5.4 and DR 3-102(A) and 3-103(A) under the Model Code clearly prohibit fee "splitting" with legal assistants, whether characterized as splitting of contingent fees, "forwarding" fees, or other sharing of legal fees. Virtually all guidelines adopted by state bar associations have continued this prohibition in one form or another.[7] It appears

---

[7] Connecticut Recommendation 10: Illinois Recommendation D; Kansas Guideline VI; Kentucky Supreme Court Rule 3.700, sub-rule 5; Michigan Guideline III, part 2; Missouri Guideline II; New Hampshire Rule 35, Sub-Rules 5 and 6; New Mexico Guideline IX; Rhode Island Guideline VIII and IX; South Carolina Guideline V; Texas Guideline V.

clear that a legal assistant may not be compensated on a contingent basis for a particular case or paid for "signing up" clients for a legal practice.

Having stated this prohibition, however, the guideline attempts to deal with the practical consideration of how a legal assistant properly may be compensated by an attorney or law firm. The linchpin of the prohibition seems to be the advance agreement of the lawyer to "split" a fee based on a pre-existing contingent arrangement.[8] There is no general prohibition against a lawyer who enjoys a particularly profitable period recognizing the contribution of the legal assistant to that profitability with a discretionary bonus. Likewise, a lawyer engaged in a particularly profitable specialty of legal practice is not prohibited from compensating the legal assistant who aids materially in that practice more handsomely than the compensation generally awarded to legal assistants in that geographic area who work in law practices that are less lucrative. Indeed, any effort to fix a compensation level for legal assistants and prohibit greater compensation would appear to violate the federal antitrust laws. *See, e.g., Goldfarb v. Virginia State Bar,* 421 U.S. 773 (1975).

Guideline 10: A lawyer who employs a legal assistant should facilitate the legal assistant's participation in appropriate continuing education and pro bono publico activities.

Comment to Guideline 10: While Guideline 10 does not appear to have been adopted in the guidelines of any state bar association, the Standing Committee on Legal Assistants believes that its adoption would be appropriate.[9] For many years the Standing Committee on Legal Assistants has advocated that the improvement of formal legal assistant education will generally improve the legal services rendered by lawyers employing legal assistants and provide a more satisfying professional atmosphere in which legal assistants may work. *See, e.g.,* ABA, Board of Governors, Policy on Legal Assistant Licensure and/or Certification, Statement 4 (February 6, 1986);

---

[8] In its Rule 5.4, which became effective on January 1, 1991, the District of Columbia will permit lawyers to form legal service partnerships that include non-lawyer participants. Comments 5 and 6 to that rule, however, state that the term "non-lawyer participants" should not be confused with the term "non-lawyer assistants" and that "[n]on-lawyer assistants under Rule 5.3 do not have managerial authority or financial interests in the organization."

[9] While no state has apparently adopted a guideline similar to Model Guideline 10, parts 4 and 5 of NALA Guidelines VIII suggest similar requirements. Sections III and V of NFPA's "Affirmation of Professional Responsibility" recognize a legal assistant's obligation to "maintain a high level of competence" (which "is achieved through continuing education . . .") and to "serve the public interest." NFPA has also published a guide to assist legal assistant groups in developing public service projects. See NFPA, "Pro Bono Publico (For the Good of the People)" (1987).

ABA, Standing Committee on Legal Assistants, "Position Paper on the Question of Legal Assistant Licensure or Certification" (December 10, 1985), at 6 and Conclusion 3. Recognition of the employing lawyer's obligation to facilitate the legal assistant's continuing professional education is, therefore, appropriate because of the benefits to both the law practice and the legal assistants and is consistent with the lawyer's own responsibility to maintain professional competence under Model Rule 1.1. *See also* EC 6-2 of the Model Code.

The Standing Committee is of the view that similar benefits will accrue to the lawyer and legal assistant if the legal assistant is included in the *pro bono publico* legal services that a lawyer has a clear obligation to provide under Model Rule 6.1 and, where appropriate, the legal assistant is encouraged to provide such services independently. The ability of a law firm to provide more *pro bono publico* services will be enhanced if legal assistants are included. Recognition of the legal assistant's role in such services is consistent with the role of the legal assistant in the contemporary delivery of legal services generally and is consistent with the lawyer's duty to the legal profession under Canon 2 of the Model Code.

> **THE STANDING COMMITTEE ON
> LEGAL ASSISTANTS OF THE
> AMERICAN BAR ASSOCIATION**
> May 1991
>
> Adopted by the American Bar Association
> House of Delegates August 1991[10]

---

[10] Reprinted with permission of the Standing Committee on Legal Assistants of the American Bar Association.

CODE OF ETHICS AND PROFESSIONAL RESPONSIBILITY OF NATIONAL ASSOCIATION OF LEGAL ASSISTANTS, INC.

Reprinted with permission of the Association of Legal Assistants, Inc., 1516 South Boston Avenue, Suite 200, Tulsa, Oklahoma 74105

Preamble

It is the responsibility of every legal assistant to adhere strictly to the accepted standards of legal ethics and to live by general principles of proper conduct. The performance of the duties of the legal assistant shall be governed by specific canons as defined herein in order that justice will be served and the goals of the profession attained.

The canons of ethics set forth hereafter are adopted by the National Association of Legal Assistant as a general guide, and the enumeration of these rules does not mean there are not others of equal importance although not specifically mentioned.

Canon 1 - A legal assistant shall not perform any of the duties that lawyers only may perform nor do things that lawyers themselves may not do.

Canon 2 - A legal assistant may perform any task delegated and supervised by a lawyer so long as the lawyer is responsible to the client, maintains a direct relationship with the client, and assumes full professional responsibility for the work product.

Canon 3 - A legal assistant shall not engage in the practice of law by accepting cases, setting fees, giving legal advise or appearing in court (unless otherwise authorized by court of agency rules).

Canon 4 - A legal assistant shall not act in matters involving professional legal judgment as the services of a lawyer are essential in the public interest whenever the exercise of such judgment is required.

Canon 5 - A legal assistant must act prudently in determining the extent to which a client may be assisted without the presence of a lawyer.

Canon 6 - A legal assistant shall not engage in the unauthorized practice of law and shall assist in preventing the unauthorized practice of law.

Canon 7 - A legal assistant must protect the confidences of a client, and it shall be unethical for a legal assistance to violate any statute now in effect or hereafter to be enacted controlling privileged communication.

Canon 8 - It is the obligation of the legal assistant to avoid conduct which would cause the lawyer to be unethical or even appear to be unethical, and loyalty to the employer is incumbent upon the legal assistant.

Canon 9 - A legal assistant shall work continually to maintain integrity and a high degree of competency throughout the legal profession.

Canon 10 - A legal assistant shall strive for perfection through education in order to better assist the legal profession in fulfilling its duty of making legal services available to clients and the public.

Canon 11 - A legal assistant shall do all other things incidental, necessary, or expedient for the attainment of the ethics and responsibilities imposed by statute or rule of Court.

Canon 12 - A legal assistant is governed by the American Bar Association code of Professional Responsibility.

THE NATIONAL ASSOCIATION OF LEGAL ASSISTANTS, INC. MODEL STANDARDS AND GUIDELINES FOR UTILIZATION OF LEGAL ASSISTANTS ANNOTATED

1516 South Boston Road, Suite 200
Tulsa, Okla. 74119
(918) 582-6772

INTRODUCTION

The purpose of this annotated version of the National Association of Legal Assistants, Inc. (NALA) Model Standards and Guidelines for the Utilization of Legal Assistants is to provide references to the existing case law and other authorities where the underlying issues have been considered. The authorities cited will serve as a basis upon which conduct of a legal assistant may be analyzed as proper or improper.

The Guidelines represent a statement of how the legal assistant may function in the law office. The Guidelines are not intended to be a comprehensive or exhaustive list of the proper duties of a legal assistant. Rather, they are designed as guides to what may or may not be proper conduct for the legal assistant. In formulating the Guidelines, the reasoning and rules of law in many reported decisions of disciplinary cases and unauthorized practice of law cases have been analyzed and considered. In addition, the provisions of the American Bar Association's Model code or Professional Conduct, as well as the ethical promulgations of various state courts and bar associations have been considered in development of the Guidelines.

While the Guidelines may not have universal application, they do form a sound basis for the legal assistant and the supervising attorney to follow in the operation of a law office. The Model will serve as a definitive and well-reasoned guide to those considering voluntary standards and guidelines for legal assistants. If regulation is to be imposed in a given jurisdiction the Model may serve as a comprehensive resource document.

I   PREAMBLE

Proper utilization of the services of legal assistants affects the efficient delivery of legal services. Legal assistants and the legal profession should be assured that some measures exist for identifying legal assistants and their role in assisting attorneys in the delivery of legal services. Therefore, the National Association of Legal Assistants, Inc., hereby adopts these Model Standards and Guidelines as an educational document for the benefit of legal assistants and the legal profession.

COMMENT

The three most frequently raised questions concerning legal assistants are (1) How do you define a legal assistant; (2) Who is qualified to be identified as a legal assistant; and (3) What duties may a legal assistant perform? The definition adopted answers the first question insofar a legal assistants serving attorneys are concerned. The Model sets forth minimum education, training, and experience through standards which will assure that one denominated as a legal assistant has the qualifications to be held out to the public in that capacity. The Guidelines identify those acts which the reported cases hold to be proscribed and give examples of services which the legal assistant may perform under the supervision of an attorney.

The three fundamental issues in the preceding paragraph have been raised in various cases for the past fifty years. In *Ferris v. Snively,* 19 P.2d 942 (Wash. 1933), the Court, stated work performed by a law clerk to be proper and not the unauthorized practice of law required supervision by the employing attorney. The Court stated:

We realize that law clerks have their place in a law office, and we recognize the fact that the nature of their work approaches in a degree that of their employers. The line of demarcation as to where their work begins and where it ends cannot always be drawn with absolute distinction or accuracy. Probably as nearly as it can be fixed, and it is sufficient to say that it is work of a preparatory nature, such as research, investigation of details, the assemblage of data and other necessary information, and such other work as will assist the employing attorney in carrying the matter to a completed product, either by his personal examination and approval thereof or by additional effort on his part. The work must be such, however, as loses its separate identify and becomes either the product, or else merged in the product, of the attorney himself. (19 P.2d at pp. 945-46) (See Florida EC3-6, infra at, Section IV.)

The NALA Guidelines constitute a statement relating to services performed by non-lawyer employees as approved by court decisions and other sources of authority. The purpose of the Guidelines is not to place limitations or restrictions on the legal profession. Rather, the Guidelines are intended to outline for the legal profession an acceptable course of conduct. By voluntary recognition and utilization of the Model Standards and Guidelines the legal profession will avoid many problems.

II DEFINITION

Legal assistants* are a distinguishable group of persons who assist attorneys in the delivery of legal services. Through formal education, training, and experience, legal assistants have knowledge and expertise regarding the legal system and substantive and procedural law which qualify them to do work of a legal nature under the supervision of an attorney.

---

*Within this occupational category some individuals are known as paralegals.

COMMENT

This definition has been used to foster a distinction between a legal assistant as one working under the direct supervision of an attorney and a broader class of paralegals who perform tasks of similar nature, but not necessarily under the supervision of an attorney. In applying the standards and guidelines it is important to remember that they in turn were developed to apply to the legal assistant as defined herein.

III   STANDARDS

A legal assistant should need certain minimum qualifications. The following standards may be used to determine an individual's qualifications as a legal assistant:

1.   Successful completion of the Certified Legal Assistant certifying ("CLA") examination of the National Association of Legal Assistants, Inc.;

2.   Graduation from a ABA approved program of study for legal assistants;

3.   Graduation from a course of study for legal assistant which is institutionally accredited but not ABA approved, and which requires not less than the equivalent of 60 semester house of classroom study.

4.   Graduation from a course of study for legal assistants, other than those set forth in (2) and (3) above, plus not less than six months of in-house training as a legal assistant.

5.   A baccalaureate degree in any field, plus not less than six months in-house training as a legal assistant;

6.   A minimum of three years of law-related experience under the supervision of an attorney, including at lease six months of in-house training as a legal assistant; or

7.   Two years of in-house training as a legal assistant.

For purposes of these Standards, "in-house training as a legal assistant" means attorney education of the employee concerning legal assistant duties and these Guidelines. In addition to review and analysis of assignments the legal assistant should receive a reasonable amount of instruction directly related to the duties and obligations of the legal assistant.

COMMENT

The Standards set forth suggested minimum qualifications for a legal assistant. The minimum qualifications as adopted recognize legal related work backgrounds and formal education backgrounds, both of which should provide the legal assistant with a broad base in exposure to knowledge of the legal profession. The background is necessary to assure the public and the legal profession that the one being identified as a legal assistant is qualified.

The Certified Legal Assistant ("CLA") examination offered by the NALA is the only voluntary nationwide certification program for legal assistants. The "CLA" designation is a statement to the legal profession and the public that the legal assistant has met the high levels of knowledge and professionalism required by NALA's certification program. Continuing education requirements, which all certified legal assistants must meet, assure that high standards are maintained. Certification through NALA is available to any legal assistant meeting the educational and experience requirements.

IV   GUIDELINES

The guidelines relating to standards of performance and professional responsibility are intended to aid legal assistants and attorneys. The responsibility rests with an attorney who employs legal assistants to educate them with respect to the duties they are assigned and to supervise the manner in which such duties are accomplished.

COMMENT

In general, a legal assistant is allowed to perform any task which is properly delegated and supervised by an attorney, as long as **the attorney is ultimately responsible to the client and assumes complete professional responsibility for the work product.**

The Code of Professional Responsibility of the American Bar Association, EC3-6 states:

ABA Model Rules of Professional Conduct, Rule 5.3 provides:

With respect to a non-lawyer employed or retained by or associated with a lawyer:

(a) a partner in a law firm shall make reasonable efforts to ensure that the firm has in effect measures giving reasonable assurance that the person's conduct is compatible with the professional obligations of the lawyer;

(b) a lawyer having direct supervisory authority over the non-lawyer shall make reasonable efforts to ensure that the person's conduct is compatible with the professional obligations of the lawyer; and

(c) a lawyer shall be responsible for conduct of such a person that would be a violation of the rules of professional conduct if engaged in by a lawyer if:

(1) the lawyer orders or, with the knowledge of the specific conduct ratifies the conduct involved; or

(2) the lawyer is a partner in the law firm in which the person is employed, or has direct supervisory authority over the person, and knows of

the conduct at time when its consequences can be avoided or mitigated but fails to take reasonable remedial action.

The Florida version of EC3-6 provides:

A lawyer or law firm may employ non-lawyers such as secretaries law clerks, investigators, researchers, legal assistants, accountants, draftsmen, office administrators; and other lay personnel to assist the lawyer in the delivery of legal services. A lawyer often delegates tasks to such persons. Such delegation is proper if a lawyer retains a direct relationship with his client, supervises the delegated work, and has complete professional responsibility for the work product.

The work which is delegated is such that it will assist the employing attorney in carrying the matter to a completed product either by the lawyer's personal examination and approval thereof or by additional effort on the lawyer's part. The delegated work must be such, however, as loses its separate identity and becomes either the product or else merged in the product of the attorney himself.

The Kentucky Paralegal Code defines a legal assistant as:

...a person under the supervision an direction of a licensed lawyer, who may apply knowledge of law and legal procedures in rendering direct assistance to lawyers engaged in legal research; design, develop or plan modifications or new procedures, techniques, services, processes or applications; prepare or interpret legal documents and write detailed procedure for practicing in certain fields of law; select, compile and use technical information from such references as digests, encyclopedias or practice manuals; and analyze and follow procedural problems that involve independent decisions.

Kentucky became the first state to adopt a Paralegal Code, which sets forth certain exclusions to the unauthorized practice of law:

For purpose of this rule, the unauthorized practice of law shall not include any service rendered involving legal knowledge or advice, whether representation, counsel or advocacy, in or out of court, rendered in respect to the acts, duties, obligations, liabilities or business relations of the one requiring services where:
A. The client understands that the paralegal is not a lawyer;
B. The lawyer supervises the paralegal in the performance of his duties; and
C. The lawyer remains fully responsible for such representation, including all actions taken or not taken n connection therewith by the paralegal to the

same extent as if such representation had been furnished entirely by the
lawyer and all such actions had been taken or not taken directly by the attor-
ney. Paralegal Code, Ky.S.Ct. R 3.700, Sub-Rule 2.

While the Kentucky rules is an exception, it does provide a basis for
expanding services which may be performed by legal assistants.

There are many interesting and complex issues involving the use of legal
assistants. One issue which is not addressed in the Guidelines is whether a
legal assistant, as defined herein, may make appearances before administrative agencies. This issue is discussed in Remmer, *Representation of Clients*
Before Administrative Agencies: Authorized or Unauthorized Practice of
Law? 15 Valparaiso Univer. L. Rev. 567 (1981). The State Bar of California
Standing Committee on Professional Responsibility and conduct, in opinion
1988-103 (2/8/89) has stated a law firm can delegate authority to a legal
assistant employee to file petitions, motions and make other appearances
before the Workers Compensation Appeals Board provided adequate supervision is maintained by the attorney and the client is informed and has con-
sented to the use of the legal assistant in such fashion.

In any discussion of the proper role of a legal assistant attention must be
direct to what constitutes the practice of law. The proper delegation of work
and duties to legal assistants if further complicated and confused by the lack of
adequate definition of the practice of law and the unauthorized practice of law.

In *Davis v. Unauthorized Practice Committee,* 431 S.W.2d 590 (Texas,
1968), the Court found that the defendant was properly enjoined from the unauthorized practice of law. The Court, in defining the "practice of law," stated:

According to the generally understood definition of the practice of law, it
embraces the preparation of pleadings and other papers incident to actions of
special proceedings, and the management of such actions in proceedings on
behalf of clients before judges in courts. However, the practice of law is not
confined to cases conducted in court. In fact, the major portion of the practice
of any capable lawyer consists of work done outside of the courts. The prac-
tice of law involves not only appearance in court in connection with litigation,
but also services rendered out of court, and includes the giving of advice or
the rendering of any service requiring the use of legal skill or knowledge,
such as preparing a will, contract or other instrument, the legal effect of which
under the facts an conclusions involved must be carefully determined.

The important distinguishing fact between the defendant in Davies and a
legal assistant is that the acts of the legal assistant are performed under the
supervision of an attorney.

EC3-5 of the Code of Professional Responsibility states:

It is neither necessary nor desirable to attempt the formulation of a single, specific definition of what constitutes the practice of law. Functionally, the practice of law relates to the rendition of services for others that call for the professional judgment of a lawyer. The essence of the professional judgment of the lawyer is his educated ability to relate the general body and philosophy of law to a specific legal problem of a client; and thus, the public interest will be better served if only lawyers are permitted to act in matters involving professional judgment. Where this professional judgment is not involved, non-lawyers, such as court clerks, police officers, abstracters, and many governmental employees, may engage in occupations that require a special knowledge of law in certain areas. But the services of a lawyer are essential in the public interest whenever the exercise of professional legal judgment is required.

There are many cases relating to the unauthorized practice of law, but the most troublesome ones in attempting to define what would or would not form the unauthorized practice of law for acts performed by a legal assistant are those such as *Crawford v. State Bar of California,* 355 P.2d 490 (Calif. 1960) which states that any act performed in a law office is the practice of law because the clients have sought the attorney to perform the work because of the training and judgment exercised by attorneys.

See also, Annot. "Layman's Assistance to Parties in Divorce Proceedings as Unauthorized Practice of Law," 12 ALR4 656; Annot. "Activities of Law Clerks as Illegal Practice of Law," 13 ALR3 1137; Annot. "Sale of Books or Forms Designed to Enable Layman to Achieve Legal Results Without Assistance of Attorney as Unauthorized Practice of Law," 71 ALR3 1000; Annot. "Nature of Legal Services or Law-Related Services Which May Be Performed for Others By Disbarred or Suspended Attorney," 87 ALR3 272. See also, Karen B. Judd, CLA, "Beyond the Bar: Legal Assistants and the Unauthorized Practice of Lat," *Facts and Findings,* Vol. VIII, Issue 6, National Association of Legal Assistants, May-June, 1982.

V

LEGAL ASSISTANTS SHOULD:

1. Disclose their status as legal assistants at the outset of any professional relationship with a client, other attorneys, a court or administrative agency or personnel thereof, or members of the general public;

2. Preserve the confidences and secrets of all clients; and

3. Understand the attorney's Code of Professional Responsibility and these guidelines in order to avoid any action which would involve the attorney in a violation of that Code, or give the appearance of professional impropriety.

COMMENT

Routine early disclosure of the legal assistant's status when dealing with persona outside the attorneys status when dealing with persons outside the attorney's office is necessary to assure that there will be no misunderstanding as to the responsibilities and role of the legal assistant. Disclosure may be made in any way that avoids confusion. If the person dealing with the legal assistant already knows of his or her status, further disclosure is unnecessary. If at any time written or in oral communication the legal assistant becomes aware that the other person may believe the legal assistant is an attorney, it should be made clear that the legal assistant is not an attorney.

The attorney should exercise care that the legal assistant preserves and refrains from using any confidence or secrets of a client, and should instruct the legal assistant not to disclose or use any such confidences or secrets.

DR 4-101(D), ABA Code of Professional Responsibility, provides in part that:

A Lawyer shall exercise reasonable care to prevent his employees, associates, and others whose services are utilized by him from disclosing or using confidences or secrets of a client...

This obligation is emphasized in EC4-2:

It is a matter of common knowledge that the normal operation of a law office exposes confidential professional information to non-lawyer employees of the office, particularly secretaries and those having access to the files; and this obligates the lawyer to exercise care in selecting and training his employees so that the sanctity of all confidences and secrets of his clients may be preserved.

The ultimate responsibility for compliance with approved standards of professional conduct rests with the supervising attorney. *In the Matter of Martinez,* 107 N.M. 171, 754 P.2d 842 (N.M. 1988). However, the legal assistant should understand that he may or may not do. The burden rests upon the attorney who employs a legal assistant to educate the latter with respect to the duties which may be assigned and then to supervise the manner in which the legal assistant carries such duties. However, this does not relieve the legal assistant from an independent obligation to refrain from illegal conduct.

Additionally, and not withstanding that the code is not binding upon non-lawyers, the very nature of a legal assistant's employment imposes an obligation not to engage in conduct which would involve the supervising attorney in a violation of the Code. NALA has adopted the ABA Code as a part of its Code of Ethics.

VI

Legal assistants should not:

1. Establish attorney-client relationships; set legal fees, give legal opinions or advice; or represent a client before a court; nor

2. Engage in, encourage, or contribute to any act which could constitute the unauthorized practice of law.

COMMENT

Reported cases holding which acts can and cannot be performed by a legal assistant are few:

The legal assistant cannot create the attorney-client relationship. *DeVaux v. American Home Assur. Co.,* 444 N.E. 2d 355 (Mass. 1983).

The legal assistant cannot make court appearances. The question of what constitute a court appearance is also somewhat vague. See, for example, *People v. Alexander,* 53 111, App.2d 299, 202 N.E. 2d 841 (1964), where preparation of a court order and transmitting information to court was not the unauthorized practice of law, and *People v. Belfor,* 611 P.2d 979 (Colo. 1980), where the trial court found that the acts of a disbarred attorney did not constitute an appearance and the Supreme Court of Colorado held that only the Supreme Court could make the determination of what acts constituted an appearance and the unauthorized practice of law.

The following cases have identified certain areas in which an attorney has a duty to act, but it is interesting to note that none of these cases state that it is improper for an attorney to have the initial work performed by a legal assistant. This again points out the importance of adequate supervision by the employing attorney.

Courts have found that attorneys have the duty to check bank statements, preserve a client's property, review and sign all pleadings, insure that all communications are opened and answered, and make inquiry when items of dictation are not received. *Attorney Grievance Commission of Maryland vs.*

Goldberg, 441 A.2d 338, 292 Md. 650 (1982). See also *Vaughn v. State Bar of California,* 100 Cal. Reptr. 713, 494 P.2d 1257 (1972).

The legal assistant cannot exercise professional legal judgment or give legal advice. In Louisiana State Bar v. Edwins, 540 So.2d 294 (La. 1989)

Attorneys have the responsibility to supervise the work of associates and clerical staff. *Moore v. State Bar Association,* 41 Cal. Rptr. 161, 396 P.2d 577 (1964); *Attorney Grievance Committee of Maryland v. Goldberg, supra.*

An Attorney must exercise sufficient supervision to insure that all monies received are properly deposited and disbursed. *Black v. State Bar of California,* 103 Cal. Rptr. 288, 499 P.2d 968 (1972); *Fitzpatrick v. State Bar of California,* 141 Cal. Rptr. 169, 569 P.2d 763 (1977).

The attorney must insure that his staff is competent and effective to perform the work delegated. *In re Reinmiller* 325 P.2d 773 (Oregon, 1958). See also, *State of Kansas v. Barrett,* 483 P.2d 1106 (Kansas, 1971); *Attorney Grievance Committee of Maryland v. Goldberg, supra.*

The attorney must make sufficient background investigation of the prior activities and character and integrity of his employees to insure that legal assistants have not previously been involved in unethical, illegal, or other nefarious schemes which demonstrate such person unfit to be associated with the practice of law. See *In the Matter of Shaw,* 88 N.J. 433, A.2d 678 (1982), wherein the Court announced that while it had no disciplinary jurisdiction over legal assistants, it directed that disciplinary hearings make specific findings of fact concerning paralegals' collaboration in nefarious schemes in order that the court might properly discipline any attorney establishing an office relationship with one who had been implicated in unscrupulous schemes.

VII

Legal assistants may perform services for an attorney in the representation of a client, provided:

1.   The services performed by the legal assistant do not require the exercise of independent professional legal judgment;

2.   The attorney maintains a direct relationship with the client and maintains control of all client matters;

3.   The attorney supervises the legal assistant;

4.   The attorney remains professionally responsible for all work on behalf of the client, including any actions taken or not taken by the legal assistant in connection therewith; and

5.   The services performed supplement, merge with and become the attorney's work product.

COMMENT

EC3-6, ABA Code of Professional Responsibility, recognizes the value of utilizing the services of legal assistants, but provides certain conditions to such employment:

A lawyer often delegates tasks to clerks, secretaries, and other lay persons. Such delegation is proper if the lawyer maintains a direct relationship with his client, supervises the delegated work, and has complete professional responsibility for the work product. This delegation enables a lawyer to render legal services more economically and efficiently.

VIII

In supervision of a legal assistant, consideration should be given to:

1.   Designating work assignments that correspond to the legal assistant's abilities, knowledge, training and experience.

2.   Educating and training the legal assistant with respect to professional responsibility, local rules and practices, and firm policies;

3.   Monitoring the work and professional conduct of the legal assistant to ensure that the work is substantively correct and timely performed;

4.   Providing continuing education for the legal assistant in substantive matters through courses, institutes, work shops, seminars and in-house training; and

5.   Encouraging and supporting membership and active participation in professional organizations.

COMMENT

Attorneys are responsible for the actions of their employees in both malpractice and disciplinary proceedings. The attorney cannot delegate work to a legal assistant which involves activities constituting the unauthorized practice of law. See *Louisiana State Bar v. Edwins,* 540 So.2d 294 (La. 1989), and

People of the State of Colorado v. Felker, 770 P.2d 402 (Col. 1989). In the vast majority of the cases, the courts have not censured attorneys for the particular act delegated to the legal assistant, but rather have been critical of an imposed sanctions against attorneys for failure to adequately supervise the legal assistants. See e.g., *Attorney Grievance Commission of Maryland v. Goldberg, supra.*

The attorney's responsibility for supervision of legal assistants must be more than a willingness to accept responsibility and liability for the legal assistant's work. The attorney must monitor the work product and conduct of the legal assistant to insure that the work performed is substantively correct and competently performed in a professional manner. This duty includes the responsibility to provide continuing legal education for the legal assistant.

Supervision of legal assistants must be offered in both the procedural and substantive legal areas in the law office.

In *Spindell v. State Bar of California,* 118 Cal. Rptr. 480, 530 P.2d 168 (1975), the attorney was suspended from practice because of the improper legal advise given by a secretary. The case illustrates that it is important that both attorneys and legal assistants confirm all telephonic advice by letter.

In all instances where the legal assistant relays information to a client in response to an inquiry from the client, the advice relayed telephonically by the legal assistant should be confirmed in writing by the attorney. This will eliminate claims if the client acts contrary to the advice given. It will establish that the legal advice given is in fact that of the attorney, not the legal assistant, and obviate any confusion resulting from transmission of the advice through the legal assistant.

The *Spindell* case is an example of an attorney's failure to supervise and educate his staff. Not only was the secretary uneducated as to the substantive provisions of the law, but more importantly, she was uneducated as to her duty and authority as an employee of the attorney.

IX

Except as otherwise provided by statute, court rule or decision administrative rule or regulations, or the attorney's Code of Professional Responsibility; and within the preceding parameters and proscriptions, a legal assistant may perform any function delegated by an attorney, including but not limited to the following:

1. Conduce client interviews and maintain general contact with the client after the establishment of the attorney-client relationship, so long as the client is aware of the status and function of the legal assistant, and the client contact is under the supervision of the attorney.

2. Locate and interview witnesses, so long as the witnesses are aware of the status and function of the legal assistant.

3. Conduct investigations and statistical and documentary research for review by the attorney.

4. Conduct legal research for review by the attorney.

5. Draft legal documents for review by the attorney.

6. Draft correspondence and pleadings for review by and signature of the attorney.

7. Summarize depositions, interrogatories, and testimony for review by the attorney.

8. Attend executions of wills, real estate closings, depositions, court or administrative hearings and trials with the attorney.

9. Author and sign letters provided the legal assistant's status is clearly indicated and the correspondence does not contain independent legal opinions or legal advice.

COMMENT

The United States Supreme Court has recognized the variety of tasks being performed by legal assistants and has noted that use of legal assistants encourage cost effective delivery of legal services, *Missouri v. Jenkins,* 491 U.S. 274, 109 S. Ct. 2463, 2471, n.10 (1989). In Jenkins the Court further held that legal assistant time should be included in compensation for attorney fee awards at the prevailing practice in the relevant community to bill legal assistant time.

Except for the specific proscription contained in Section VI, the reported cases, such as *Attorney Grievance Commission of Maryland v. Goldberg,* supra, do not limit the duties which may be performed by a legal assistant under the supervision of the attorney. The Guidelines were developed from generally accepted practices. Each supervising attorney must be aware of the specific rules, decisions and statutes applicable to legal assistants within his jurisdiction.

NFPA
MODEL CODE OF ETHICS
AND PROFESSIONAL
RESPONSIBILITY

PREAMBLE

The National Federal of Paralegal Associations, Inc. ("NFPA") is a professional organization comprised of paralegal associations and individual paralegals throughout the United States. Members of NFPA have varying types of backgrounds, experience, education and job responsibilities which reflect the diversity of the paralegal profession. NFPA promotes the growth, development and recognition of the paralegal profession as an integral partner in the delivery of legal services.

NFPA recognizes that the creation of guidelines and standards for professional conduct are important for the development and expansion of the paralegal profession. In May 1993, NFPA adopted this Model Code of Ethics and Professional Responsibility ("Model Code") to delineate the principles for ethics and conduct to which every paralegal should aspire. The Model Code expresses NFPA's commitment to increasing the quality and efficiency of legal services and recognizes the profession's responsibilities to the public, the legal community, and colleagues.

Paralegals perform many different functions, and these functions differ greatly among practice areas. In addition, each jurisdiction has its own unique legal authority and practices governing ethical conduct and professional responsibilities.

It is essential that each paralegal strive for personal and professional excellence and encourage the professional development of other paralegals as well as those entering the profession. Participation in professional associations intended to advance the quality and standards of the legal profession is of particular importance. Paralegals should possess integrity, professional skill and dedication to the improvement of the legal system and should strive to expand the paralegal role in the delivery of legal services.

CANON 1.

A PARALEGAL[1] SHALL ACHIEVE AND MAINTAIN A HIGH LEVEL OF COMPETENCE.

EC-1.1   A paralegal shall achieve competency through education, training, and work experience.

EC-1.2   A paralegal shall participate in continuing education to keep informed of current legal, technical and general developments.

EC-1.3   A paralegal shall perform all assignments promptly and efficiently.

CANON 2.

A PARALEGAL SHALL MAINTAIN A HIGH LEVEL OF PERSONAL AND PROFESSIONAL INTEGRITY.

EC-2.1   A paralegal shall not engage in an ex parte[2] communications involving the courts or any other adjudicatory body in an attempt to exert undue influence or to obtain advantage for the benefit of only one party.

EC-2.2   A paralegal shall not communicate, or cause another to communicate, with a party the paralegal knows to be represented by a lawyer in a pending matter without the prior consent of the lawyer representing such other party.

EC-2.3   A paralegal shall ensure that all timekeeping and billing records prepared by the paralegal are thorough, accurate, and honest.

EC-2.4   A paralegal shall be scrupulous, thorough and honest in the identification and maintenance of all funds, securities, and other assets of a client and shall provide accurate accountings as appropriate.

---

[1] "Paralegal" is synonymous with "Legal Assistant" and is defined as a person qualified through education, training, or work experience to perform substantive legal work that requires knowledge of legal concepts and is customarily, but not exclusively performed by a lawyer. This person may be retained or employed by a lawyer, law office, governmental agency or other entity or may be authorized by administrative, statutory or court authority to perform this work.

[2] "Ex Parte" denotes actions or communications conducted at the instance and for the benefit of one party only, and without notice to, or contestation by, and person adversely interested.

EC-2.5 A paralegal shall advise the proper authority of any dishonest or fraudulent acts by any person pertaining to the handling of the funds, securities or other assets of a client.

CANON 3.

A PARALEGAL SHALL MAINTAIN A HIGH STANDARD OF PROFESSIONAL CONDUCT.

EC-3.1 A paralegal shall refrain from engaging in any conduct that offends the dignity and decorum of proceedings before a court or other adjudicatory body and shall be respectful of all rules and procedures.

EC-3.2 A paralegal shall advise the proper authority of any action of another legal professional which clearly demonstrates fraud, deceit, dishonesty, or misrepresentation.

EC-3.3 A paralegal shall avoid impropriety and the appearance of impropriety.

CANON 4.

A PARALEGAL SHALL SERVE THE PUBLIC INTEREST BY CONTRIBUTING TO THE DELIVERY OF QUALITY LEGAL SERVICES AND THE IMPROVEMENT OF THE LEGAL SYSTEM.

EC-4.1 A paralegal shall be sensitive to the legal needs of the public and shall promote the development and implementation of programs that address those needs.

EC-4.2 A paralegal shall support bonafide efforts to meet the need for legal services by those unable to pay reasonable or customary fees; for example, participation in pro bono projects and volunteer work.

EC-4.3 A paralegal shall support efforts to improve the legal system and shall assist in making changes.

CANON 5.

A PARALEGAL SHALL PRESERVE ALL CONFIDENTIAL INFORMATION[3] PROVIDED BY THE CLIENT OR ACQUIRED FROM OTHER

---

[3] "Confidential Information" denotes information relating to a client, whatever its source, which is not public knowledge nor available to the public. ("Non-Confidential

SOURCES BEFORE, DURING, AND AFTER THE COURSE OF THE PROFESSIONAL RELATIONSHIP.

EC-5.1   A paralegal shall be aware of an abide by all legal authority governing confidential information.

EC-5.2   A paralegal shall not use confidential information to the disadvantage of the client.

EC-5.3   A paralegal shall not use confidential information to the advantage of the paralegal or of a third person.

EC-5.4   A paralegal may reveal confidential information only after full disclosure and with the client's written consent; or, when required by law or court order; or, when necessary to prevent the client from committing an act which could result in death or serious bodily harm.

EC-5.5   A paralegal shall keep those individuals responsible for the legal representation of a client fully informed of any confidential information the paralegal may have pertaining to that client.

EC-5.6   A paralegal shall not engage in any indiscreet communications concerning clients.

CANON 6.

A PARALEGAL'S TITLE SHALL BE FULLY DISCLOSED[4]

EC-6.1   A paralegal's title shall clearly indicate the individuals status and shall be disclosed in all business and professional communications to avoid misunderstandings and misconceptions about the paralegal's role and responsibilities.

EC-6.2   A paralegal's title shall be included if the paralegal's name appears on business cards, letterhead, brochures, directories, and advertisements.

Information" would generally include the name of the client and the identity of the matter for which the paralegal provided services.)

[4] "Disclose" denotes communication of information reasonably sufficient to permit identification of the significance of the matter in question.

CANON 7.

A PARALEGAL SHALL NOT ENGAGE IN THE UNAUTHORIZED PRACTICE OF LAW.

EC-7.1   A paralegal shall comply with the applicable legal authority governing the unauthorized practice of law.

CANON 8.

A PARALEGAL SHALL AVOID CONFLICTS OF INTEREST AND SHALL DISCLOSE ANY POSSIBLE CONFLICT TO THE EMPLOYER OR CLIENT, AS WELL AS TO THE PROSPECTIVE EMPLOYERS OR CLIENTS.

EC-8.1   A paralegal shall act within the bounds of the law, solely for the benefit of the client, and shall be free of compromising influences and loyalties. Neither the paralegal's personal or business interest, nor those of other clients or third persons, should compromise the paralegal's professional judgment and loyalty to the client.

EC-8.2   A paralegal shall avoid conflicts of interest which may arise from previous assignments whether for a present or past employer or client.

EC-8.3   A paralegal shall avoid conflicts of interest which may arise from family relationships and from personal and business interests.

EC-8.4   A paralegal shall create and maintain an effective recordkeeping system that identifies clients, matters, and parties with which the paralegal has worked, to be able to determine whether an actual or potential conflict of interest exists.

EC-8.5   A paralegal shall reveal sufficient non-confidential information about a client or former client to reasonably ascertain if an actual or potential conflict of interest exists.

EC-8.6   A paralegal shall not participate in or conduct work on any matter where a conflict of interest has been identified.

EC-8.7   In matters where a conflict of interest has been identified and the client consents to continued representation, a paralegal shall comply fully with the implementation and maintenance of an Ethical Wall.[5]

---

[5] "Ethical Wall" refers to the screening method implemented in order to protect a client from a conflict of interest. An Ethical Wall generally includes, but is not limited to, the following elements: (1) p paralegal from having any connection with the matter: (2) ban discussions with or the transfer of documents to or from the paralegal; (3) restrict access to files; and (4) educate all members of the firm, corporation or entity as to the separatof the paralegal (both organizationally and physically) from the pending matter. For more information regarding the Ethical Wall, see the NFPA publication entitled "The Ethical Wall" - Its Application to Paralegals."

NATIONAL ASSOCIATION OF LEGAL ASSISTANTS, INC. THE CERTIFIED LEGAL ASSISTANT PROGRAM— SELECTED PROVISION

National Association of Legal Assistants, Inc.

THE
Certified Legal Assistant
PROGRAM

TABLE OF CONTENTS

CERTIFICATION -- A PROFESSIONAL GOAL

Certification bestows a measure of professional recognition to those persons who achieve significant competence in the field.

This opportunity for the legal assistant profession is provided by the National Association of Legal Assistants, Inc., through its national certification program. The CLA Certifying program consists of successful completion of a comprehensive two day examination. Thereafter, evidence of continuing legal education must be submitted periodically in order to maintain certification. The program is administered by the National Association of Legal Assistants through its Certifying Board which consists of a minimum of five legal assistants who have the Certified Legal Assistant designation, two attorneys and two paralegal educators. In 1991, the number of Certified Legal Assistants throughout the nation surpassed 4,000 -- legal assistants in 47 states, the District of Columbia and the Virgin Islands have been certified by NALA.

Although the goal of becoming a Certified Legal Assistant is a voluntary commitment, the Certified Legal Assistant designation is recognized in the legal field as denoting high standards of professionalism and excellence. The legal community recognizes Certified Legal Assistants have proven that their experience and knowledge are not restricted to a few limited areas but that they have a general knowledge and understanding of the entire profession and capabilities far exceeding minimal requirements.

The NALA CLA Certifying examination program involves successful completion of a two day examination administered in the Spring; in conjunction with the NALA Annual Convention in July; and in cooperation with NALA Affiliated Associations in December. The body of knowledge required to attain the Certified Legal Assistant designation is great. Although the NALA Certifying Board recognizes the expertise required of a legal assistant cannot be reduced to a formula, certain basic skills common to the profession are measurable: verbal and written communication skills; judgment and analytical abilities; and an understanding of ethics, human relations, legal terminology and legal research. The examination covers these areas as well as substantive knowledge of law and procedures. The substantive law section requires each candidate to complete a section on the American legal system and to choose and complete four of eight sections: litigation; estate planning and probate; real estate; criminal law; bankruptcy; contract; business organizations; and administrative law. As a standardized national examination, all sections are on the federal level -- no state laws or procedures are tested.

As with all NALA programs, the purpose of the examination program is to help the legal assistant profession by serving as a means of distinguishing and recognizing excellence among legal assistants and by serving as a stabilizing force and directional tool in the growth of the profession. The Certified Legal Assistant program is not rigid -- its foundation allows methodical and thoughtful change. It helps by attesting to the competency of certified legal assistants and by serving as a guideline for colleges and schools offering legal assistant programs. While the profession grows the individuals within must, too. Legal assistants are an integral part of the legal team and must strive to improve the profession. NALA's voluntary certification program is one answer to those needs.

THE CERTIFIED LEGAL ASSISTANT EXAMINATION -- OUTLINE

Each section of the examination contains objective questions, such as multiple choice, true/false and matching. Most sections contain essay and/or short answer questions.

Communications

This section of the Certified Legal Assistant examination covers the following areas of communications:

Word Usage   Rules of Composition
Punctuation   Concise Writing
Capitalization   Vocabulary
Grammar   Correspondence
Nonverbal Communication

Ethics

This section deals with ethics in the legal assistant's contacts with employers, clients, co-workers and the general public. Unauthorized practice, ethical rules, practice rules and confidentiality are among the topics tested by this section.

Knowledge of the American Bar Association Rules of Professional Conduct and the National Association of Legal Assistants, Inc., Code of Ethics and Professional Responsibility is required by this examination.

Human Relations and Interviewing Techniques

The Human Relations portion encompasses professional and social contacts with the employer, clients and other office visitors, co-workers, including subordinates, and the public outside of the law office. For this reason, the legal assistant should be familiar with: authorized practice, ethical rules, practice rules, delegation of authority, consequences of delegation and confidentiality.

Interviewing Techniques covers basic principles, as agreed upon by most authors on the subject, definitions of terms of basic principles and handling of specialized interviews. Subject areas included in this section of the examination are:

General considerations for the interviewing situation: courtesy, empathy, physical setting, body language

Initial Roadblocks -- lapse of time, prejudice, etc.

Manner of questions

Use of checklists for specific matters

Special handling situations: the elderly, the very young

Both initial and subsequent interviews are included as are both client and witness interviews.

Judgment and Analytical Ability

The sections of this part deal with (1) analyzing and categorizing facts and evidence; (2) the legal assistant's relationship with the lawyer, the legal secretary, the client, the courts and other law firms; (3) the legal assistant's reaction to specific situations; (4) handling telephone situations; and (5) reading comprehension and data interpretation.

Familiarity with the Rules of Professional Conduct of the American Bar Association and the Code of Ethics and Professional Responsibility of the National Association of Legal Assistants, Inc., will also be helpful. Knowledge of logical reasoning and experience as a legal assistant are valuable assets.

Legal Research

It is extremely important for the legal assistant to be able to use the most important "tool" of the legal profession - the law library. The purpose of the Legal Research section of the CLA Certifying Examination is to test your knowledge of the use of state and Federal codes, the statutes, the digests, case reports, various legal encyclopedias, court reports, Shepardizing and research procedure.

The amount of study and practice you will need to pass this section of the examination will depend on your current knowledge and experience with legal research. You can get excellent practice by researching various topics on your own.

Legal Terminology

The sections of this part deal with (1) Latin phrases; (2) legal phrases or terms in general; and (3) utilization and understanding of common legal terms.

The questions involve legal terminology and procedures used in general practice.

Substantive Law

The Substantive Law section of the CLA Certifying examination is divided into nine parts:

(1) General (which includes the American Legal System)
(2) Administrative Law
(3) Bankruptcy
(4) Contract
(5) Business Organizations
(6) Criminal
(7) Litigation
(8) Probate & Estate Planning
(9) Real Estate

Each examinee will be required to take the first part and must select four out of the remaining eight specialty tests.

Those persons who are taking the examination, but have not had formal law courses, would benefit from a study of a current textbook in the area. A great deal of the material covered in this section of the examination is acquired through work experience in the legal field. The Substantive Law mini-tests are designed to test the legal assistant's general knowledge of the fields of law.

STUDY METHODS

Generally, legal assistants study individually for the CLA Certifying Examination. A list of study references for each examination section and sample questions may be found in the Mock Examination and Study Guide available through NALA Headquarters. In addition to providing study references for this examination, this material will aid applicants in developing their own study programs.

Affiliated state and local legal assistant associations of the National Association of Legal Assistants have begun sponsoring study groups or review seminars for those interested in the CLA Certifying Examination. Notices of these programs are included in the NALA bi-monthly publication, FACTS & FINDINGS, and in the membership newsletter when available. Non-members may call NALA Headquarters for this information or contact state or local associations direct.

Formal education courses are recommended, especially in assisting a candidate to prepare for the substantive law section. Should you choose this as a study option be sure to keep in mind that all substantive law sections are based on federal rules, codes, practice and procedure. No state laws, codes or procedures are tested.

TESTING CENTER LOCATIONS

NALA reserves the right to cancel any testing center where less than ten register. In the event a published center is cancelled, all affected applicants will be notified and allowed to transfer to another center. Any applicant desiring to change from one testing center to another must notify NALA Headquarters at least thirty days prior to the examination date.

Applicants receive admission tickets approximately 15 days prior to the examination. The forms show the exact location of the examination center, time schedule, and serve to reconfirm Social Security numbers and the four substantive law areas and/or retake or specialty sections. Exact testing center locations are not publicly announced.

The examinations are administered by members of the NALA Certifying Board or NALA members who have the Certified Legal Assistant designation, as approved by the NALA Certifying Board.

Spring Examination

Generally, the Certified Legal Assistant examination is offered at the locations listed on page 9 based on a minimum registration of ten applications per location.

July Examination

In July, the examination is only administered at the site of the NALA Annual Meeting.

December Examination

Testing sites for the December session are based on the locations of NALA affiliated associations, and only members of NALA affiliated associations are eligible to apply for the December session. Evidence of affiliate association membership is required at the time of filing applications for the December examination.

Grading and Retake Policy

A passing score of 70% is required for each of the examination sections. The substantive law section is graded as a whole. From a total of 500 points, 350 points is passing regardless of the distribution of points among the five parts.

Results are announced by the Certifying Board in writing to all examinees. Results are not available by telephone or by FAX.

Of the seven sections of the CLA Certifying examination, four sections must be successfully completed in order to retake only those sections failed. Applicants in retake status may attend a maximum of five retake sessions within a three year period. Applicants in retake status will be allowed to choose which sections will be retaken during any retake session. Again, an applicant can only attend a retake session five times within the three year period. The examination must be successfully completed within three years or five retake sessions, or credit for all passed sections will be forfeited. If less than four sections are successfully completed, the applicant must reapply for the full examination.

MAINTENANCE OF CERTIFIED LEGAL ASSISTANT DESIGNATION

In recognition of the continuing change in laws and procedures that have a direct impact on the quality of work performed by legal assistants, Certified Legal Assistants are required to maintain their certified status by submitting proof of continuing education. The CLA Certifying designation is for a period of five years and if the Certified Legal Assistant submits proof of attendance in accordance with the requirements as listed on page 23 the certificate is renewed for another five years and the process begins again. Lifetime certification is not available.

ELIGIBILITY REQUIREMENTS

An applicant for the Certified Legal Assistant examination must meet at least one of the three eligibility requirements listed on the Certified Legal Assistant application form beginning on page 11 at the time of filing application.

The Certified Legal Assistant designation may be revoked for any one of the following reasons:

1) Falsification of information on application form.

2) Subsequent conviction of the unauthorized practice of law.

3) Failure to meet continuing legal education requirements as required by the Certifying Board.

4) Divulging the contents of any Examination Questions.

5) Subsequent conviction of a felony.

6) Violation of the NALA Code of Ethics and Professional Responsibility

Individuals currently serving a prison term are ineligible to sit for the CLA examination.

ADMINISTRATIVE RULES AND PROCEDURES -- CLA CERTIFYING EXAMINATION

General:

1. The CLA Certifying examination is administered by members of the NALA Certifying Board for Legal Assistants or others designated by the Board. An administrator forfeits the right to take the Certified Legal Assistant examination offered by NALA.

2. Applications must be received by January 15 for the April examination (June 15 for the July session and October 1 for the December session), and accompanied by a certified check or money order in the amount of $225 for the examination fee. Applications mailed within ten working days after the deadline must be accompanied by a nonrefundable $20 late fee. Applications mailed after the ten working day allowance will not be accepted.

3. Testing centers will be offered throughout the United States in locations selected by the Certifying Board. Additional centers for the Spring examination may be established in areas where ten or more applicants register for testing. NALA reserves the right to cancel any testing center where less than ten (10) applicants register.

4. Applicants will be assigned to the closest available testing center. Any applicant desiring to change from one testing center to another must notify NALA Headquarters at least 30 days prior to the examination date. In the event of cancellation of a published testing center by NALA, affected applicants will be advised of nearest open center and will be entitled to a full refund if distance or other circumstances preclude travel to alternate testing center.

5. If applicant must withdraw due to illness, or if the application is rejected, payment less a $25 processing fee will be refunded, up to ten working days prior to the test date. Requests for withdrawals postmarked within ten working days up to the test date will be subject to a $75 processing fee. Applicants who do not appear at the testing center due to emergency must call either the examination administrator or NALA Headquarters on the day of the examination, and must submit in writing to NALA Headquarters reasons for not appearing within 5 days after the examination in order to be eligible to a partial refund (examination fee less $75 processing charge.) All examination refunds will be issued within a reasonable period _after_ the respective examination date.

6. Successful completion of a minimum of four of the seven sections permits the Certified Legal Assistant applicant to retake only those sections failed ($50 per section). If less than four sections are passed, one must reapply to take the full examination. Applicants in retake status may attend a maximum of five retake sessions within a three year period. Applicants in retake status will be allowed to choose which sections will be retaken during any retake session. Again, an applicant can only attend a retake session five times within the three year period.

The examination must be successfully completed within three years or five retake sessions, or credit for all passed sections will be forfeited. If less than four sections are successfully completed, the full examination must be retaken.

Specific:

1. Administrators will be provided with full instructions approximately 5 days prior to the examination date with prepackaged examinations and a list of registrants.

2. Failure on the part of any applicant to cooperate with the administrator will result in disqualification.

3. All examinations shall be returned promptly to NALA Headquarters and the administrator will be charged with full responsibility to any missing examinations or answer sheets.

4. Time limits will be strictly enforced. No one will be permitted to enter the examination room after testing has begun. Starting the examination early or taking more time than allowed will result in disqualification.

5. No one will be permitted to answer any questions regarding the examination in general, the grading, or any specific items on the examination.

6. No one will be permitted to leave the examination room during testing without advising the administrator and having good reason. Any examinee leaving the room for an unreasonable length of time will be disqualified.

7. After expiration of time allocated for any part of the examination, no candidate will be permitted to go back to that part either for review or for completion.

8. Dictionaries or any other source material will not be permitted in the examination room. Applicants will need only pen or pencil. Scratch paper will be provided. Purses and other personal items must be checked with the administrator.

9. Talking will not be allowed in the examination room during the testing. Similarly, any disruptive behavior is good cause for disqualification.

10. No food or beverages will be permitted in the examination room at any time.

11. Smoking is prohibited in the examination room.

12. The door to the examination room must be clearly marked "Testing -- Do Not Disturb."

13. The administration will be required to check the examination room one hour prior to testing to see that proper seating arrangements have been made, the room is properly lighted and that there is at least one wastebasket and a pencil sharpener.

14. Examinees will be required to show proof of identity during check-in on the first day.

15. Admission tickets will be sent to examinees 15 days prior to examination date. These tickets should be returned to Headquarters in the event the candidate withdraws the application.

16. It is recommended that candidates be assigned seats, properly spaced apart, for the duration of the examination.

17. NALA Certifying Board members are responsible for grading.

18. Examinations will be identified by assigned numbers and social security numbers for grading purposes.

CLA is a certification mark duly registered with the U.S. Patent and Trademark Office (No. 1131999). Any unauthorized use is strictly forbidden.

INDEX

INDEX